Viruses of potatoes and seed-potato production

The terrible famine in Ireland caused by disease epidemics in potatoes in the middle of the last century may no longer be vivid in man's memory. The task of combating such diseases, however, must go on if we are to maintain and increase productivity of this principal food crop. This is an essential part of our efforts to free the world from hunger.

Dr A. H. Boerma
Director-General Food and Agriculture
Organization of the United Nations

Viruses of potatoes and seed-potato production

Edited by J. A. de Bokx

Wageningen
Centre for Agricultural Publishing and Documentation
1972

Editorial Board

ISBN 90 220 0358 2
© Centre for Agricultural Publishing and Documentation, Wageningen, 1972
Cover design: Pudoc, Wageningen
Printed in the Netherlands by A. Verweij, Wageningen

Contributors

A. B. R. Beemster, Institute of Phytopathological Research (IPO), Wageningen
J. A. de Bokx, Institute of Phytopathological Research (IPO), Wageningen
J. Hiddema, General Netherlands Inspection Service for Field Seeds and Seed Potatoes (NAK), Wageningen
D. Hille Ris Lambers, Aphid Research Laboratory, Agricultural Research Council (TNO), Bennekom
H. A. van Hoof, Institute of Phytopathological Research (IPO), Wageningen
D. Z. Maat, Institute of Phytopathological Research (IPO), Wageningen
A. J. Reestman, Research Station for Arable Farming (PA), Wageningen
A. Rozendaal, Department of Phytopathology, Agricultural University, Wageningen
A. Schepers, Research Station for Arable Farming (PA), Wageningen
D. H. M. van Slogteren, Bulb Research Centre (LBO), Lisse
J. P. H. van der Want, Department of Virology, Agricultural University, Wageningen
H. T. Wiersema, Foundation for Agricultural Plant Breeding (SVP), Wageningen
Frederika Quak, Institute of Phytopathological Research (IPO), Wageningen
D. E. van der Zaag, Research Station for Arable Farming (PA), Wageningen

Foreword

Eighty per cent of man's food is cereals. Even so annual production of potatoes, especially in Europe, is still considerable, roughly 220 million tons for the whole world.

Many pests and diseases threaten the crop e.g. Colorado beetle, potato root eelworm, late blight and several virus diseases. Some viruses, such as potato viruses X and S, may multiply in the plant without obvious symptom. Before 1945, potato plants in the United States were almost all infected with potato virus X, whose importance was discounted. Yet careful experiments there showed an average loss in yield of more than 10%.

Some other viruses give even greater losses. Potato leafroll virus and strains of potato virus Y frequently reduce tuber yields by 50–80%. The average loss due to all potato viruses has been estimated at 13%, which amounts to about 30 million tons of valuable food each year. To avoid losses, seed potatoes should be virus-free. As most potato viruses easily spread in the field, virus-free stocks must be maintained carefully for the production of healthy seed potatoes. This is what the General Netherlands Inspection Service for Field Seeds and Seed Potatoes (NAK) is trying to do with help from research institutes. How we try to prevent or even cure these virus diseases in the Netherlands will be explained in this book.

To select and produce healthy seed potatoes, we need information on virus diseases, their early diagnosis, ways of inspection and on the way viruses are spread in the field by man, insects, nematodes and any other vectors. Many methods are now used commercially for the production of virus-free potato stocks. They could not be obtained without close co-operation between research workers and inspectors. Workers in many countries have expressed interest in the way we in the Netherlands obtain and maintain our virus-free seed potatoes. Research institutes and NAK are frequently asked to demonstrate and explain the methods they use.

Research workers, especially from developing countries, often come to our institutes for several months to learn our techniques. Virologists at the Institute of Phytopathological Research (IPO) felt a need for a short compendium to guide their foreign guestworkers. Our discussions with others showed the need for a more comprehensive book collecting the experience of all scientists in the Netherlands concerned with potato virus diseases and with the production of virus-free potato stocks. Such a book should also be useful to the staff of inspection and plant protection services, and to teachers and students at agricultural colleges.

The editors have been very fortunate to find a group of specialists willing and able to write in such an outstanding way. Their work will be of inestimable value to all those interested in the practice and theory of potato production.

Dr J. G. ten Houten
Director Institute of
Phytopathological Research,
Wageningen

Preface

This book outlines the techniques of growing seed potatoes with stress on virus diseases and their control.

Experts have collected information on the growing of seed potatoes and its scientific principles. They all work in the Netherlands and have quoted mainly from experience there. Where necessary, they have indicated differences from other countries. They have not attempted to review all the literature on their topics but mention only books or articles that the reader may turn to for more information. The text sometimes cites authors not listed under Further reading but they can readily be traced in the listed literature.

Certain aspects have been ignored or only touched on: in particular fungal, bacterial and nematodal diseases, some of which are important for production of seed potatoes.

Symptoms of viruses are comprehensively surveyed.

In the literature, potato viruses and diseases appear under many synonyms. To avoid confusion only a few are listed in Chapter 10. An authoritative guide is the Commonwealth Mycological Institute's list of Plant Virus Names (Martyn, 1968). Except for good reason, we have held to names preferred by Martyn. For the reader's convenience a list of abbreviations used in this book is given on page 18. Chapter 10 also includes photographs of some symptoms but cannot begin to illustrate the great variation in symptom expression.

In other spheres too, terminology has sometimes proved difficult. Where possible, we have standardized terminology throughout the book but, particularly in describing resistance, the terminologies of different specialists have proved not completely reconcilable.

The percentages of yield reduction mentioned in this book are based on results of trials where yields have been compared of virus-infected plants and healthy ones. Sometimes the data do not fully agree with observations in practice (Chap. 12).

Diagnostic methods, for instance electron-microscopy (Chap. 6) and serology (Chap. 7), are explained. As most antisera must be prepared with viruses in a purified form, various methods are given for purification (Chap. 5). Such methods are applicable anywhere. Other chapters describe conditions or practices special to the Netherlands: Chapter 3 describes the relation between aphids and the spread of potato viruses in the Netherlands, and the philosophy behind present Dutch practice. Ways of growing potatoes are given in Chapter 16 and rules of field inspection and quality grading in Chapter 17.

Our book is no complete manual, but we hope that it may help in the growing of healthy potatoes elsewhere in the world.

We thank: Agricultural University Fund for a grant;

Pudoc for the attractive presentation of the book, in particular Mr J. C. Rigg and Mr R. J. P. Aalpol for their valuable help with the English and editing, respectively;

Mr K. Boekhorst (Department of Virology, Agricultural University) for preparing the drawings;

Mrs S. J. Nijveldt and Mr P. Piron for typing and retyping the manuscript;

Mr C. F. Scheffel, Mr C. A. Koedam (Institute of Phytopathological Research), Mr G. Eimers (Department of Phytopathology, Agricultural University) and others (named in figure captions) for the photographs.

The Editors

Contents

16

Abbreviations

AMV   = alfalfa mosaic virus
APLV = andean potato latent virus
CMV   = cucumber mosaic virus
PAMV = potato aucuba mosaic virus
PEBV = pea early browning virus
PLRV = potato leafroll virus
PMTV = potato mop-top virus
PSTV = potato spindle tuber virus
PVA   = potato virus A
PVM   = potato virus M
PVS   = potato virus S
PVX   = potato virus X
PVY   = potato virus Y
PVY^C = potato virus Y (stipple streak)
PVY^N = potato virus Y (tobacco veinal necrosis)
PVY^O = potato virus Y (common)
PYDV = potato yellow dwarf virus
TBRV = tomato black ring virus
TMV   = tobacco mosaic virus
TNV   = tobacco necrosis virus
TRV   = tobacco rattle virus

DEP   = dilution end-point
SIDT = stability in desiccated tissue
SIV   = stability in vitro at 20°C
TIP   = thermal inactivation point

18

1 Introduction to plant virology

J. P. H. van der Want

During the Nineteenth Century more and more diseases of man, animals and plants were recognized as infectious, and were ascribed to microbes. Many of these microbes were observed in the infected host by light-microscopy. Some were cultured on artificial media.

Robert Koch formulated criteria that prove whether an organism causes an infectious disease. These 'Koch postulates' are as follows.
1. The organism must be found in or on the affected tissue.
2. The organism must be isolated in pure culture.
3. The organism must evoke the same symptoms when re-introduced into the host species from which it was obtained.
4. The organism must be found again in the artificially infected host.

The Koch postulates are still essential in the study of infectious disease. However another type of infectious agents was discovered and proved difficult to establish as pathogens according to the Koch postulates.

1.1 The discovery of viruses

In the early days, pathologists called any agent of infectious disease 'virus', a Latin word originally meaning a mucous excretion, pus or venom. Pasteur and his team showed that bacteria and other microbes could be retained by passing the liquids through filters of unglazed earthenware. Because of their candle-like form, such filters were called filter candles. The microbes stuck in the wall of the filter candles. The filterable agents that caused disease were first called 'ultra-virus' or 'filterable virus' as they could pass through the extremely fine pores of the filter candles, but the name was gradually abbreviated to 'virus'. Thus 'virus' got a more restricted meaning than it originally had.

In 1892 Ivanowski published experiments in which the agent of a tobacco disease remained in the filtrate. Mayer had earlier called the disease 'tobacco mosaic' because of irregular patches of light and dark green tissue in leaves of affected plants. Mayer had proved the disease to be transmissible by introducing sap from a diseased plant into healthy ones with fine glass capillaries. Although Mayer did not detect any microbes in infected tissue or in sap of diseased tobacco plants, he argued that a bacterium evoked the disease. Ivanowski showed that the agent passed through filter candles. But he thought, like Mayer, that nondescript bacteria were responsible for the infectivity of the filtrate.

Beijerinck performed the same sort of filter experiments. In 1898 he postulated that tobacco mosaic was caused by an infectious agent completely different from pathogenic bacteria and fungi then known. He called the agent *'contagium vivum fluidum'*, i.e. infectious living fluid dispersed in the sap of diseased tobacco plants. Beijerinck concluded that the substance was infective because it could be transmitted from plant to plant, living because it could increase when introduced into the plant, and fluid because it could pass through the pores of the filter candle. He also showed that the infective substance could be precipitated by ethanol, retaining its infectivity, but that it was inactiviated by formaldehyde and boiling. Beijerinck failed to culture it in artificial media.

Likewise for animal diseases, Loeffler & Frosch discovered, also in 1898, that food-and-mouth disease of cattle could be transmitted by bacteria-free filtrates. During World War I, Twort and d'Hérelle independently showed that even bacteria can be infected by such filtrates.

1.2 Virus diseases of potato in history
Many potato diseases are now known to be due to viruses. Horváth (1967) mentions 27 diseases and Martyn (1968) lists 33 types of virus, not counting the many strains within some types but not all are proven viruses. Some may turn out to be mycoplasma-like organisms. Many virus diseases of potato are worldwide but some are local.

There is good evidence that virus diseases started to threaten the potato, soon after it was introduced into Europe. Salaman (1949) states that in the middle of the Eighteenth Century degeneration of potatoes occurred in England. This degeneration was, as we now know, an infectious disease or rather a combination of diseases. Gradually the incidence of these diseases increased as tubers from a diseased crop were used as seed for the next. The most striking symptoms of potato degeneration were curling of the leaves and severe reduction in yield. In certain parts of England, curl increased so much that farmers feared extinction of potatoes as a field crop. Clearly virus diseases were already of economic importance in the early days of potato production. Farmers even then recognized that certain areas were favourable for the production of 'clean' seed potatoes, presumably because of the absence of virus vectors.

Likewise in Germany, France and the Netherlands degeneration of the potato crop prevailed in the Eighteenth and Nineteenth Centuries. The degeneration was ascribed either to a fatigue or deterioration of the crop by continuous vegetative propagation or to unfavourable conditions of climate and soil. However, it was not before the Twentieth Century that research elucidated the true cause of degeneration as the effect of diseases provoked by viruses. Borchardt et al. (1964) have reviewed losses caused by various potato viruses.

1.3 Early research on potato viruses
Because of their economic importance, potato viruses were among the first recog-

nized. Some are now thoroughly studied and an extensive literature exists.

Appel (1906) first described potato leafroll, and thus distinguished it from the complex of 'curl'. Quanjer's group found that potato leafroll, characterized by necrosis of the phloem, was infective, being transmitted by grafting. As no fungus, bacterium or other organism seemed to be responsible for the leafroll, they considered the disease to be viral. The properties of the virus remained long obscure until Peters succeeded in revealing its shape and dimensions by electron-microscopy some years ago.

Oortwijn Botjes studied the spread of PLRV in the field. In greenhouse trials, insects, especially the green peach aphid *Myzus persicae* Sulz. transmitted the virus from diseased to healthy plants. He established that *M. persicae* played a major role in the spread of PLRV.

Orton distinguished other virus diseases involved in potato degeneration by their symptoms. He described streak and mosaic diseases.

An interesting and important discovery by James Johnson (1925) was that sap from apparently healthy potato plants induced virus disease in certain species of plant. It was later understood that virus was actually present in the 'healthy' plants, which tolerated the infection without showing any symptoms. The discovery of such latent virus infections has been of great significance for the production of seed potatoes. Latent infection cannot be ignored as a symptomless variety may be dangerous as a source of infection for a sensitive crop. Latent virus infections of potatoes may be detectable only in other crops: K. M. Smith showed that a strain of PVX producing virtually no symptoms in certain potato varieties is harmful to tomato plants. When infected potato sap was introduced into tomatoes, it caused a condition called 'streak'.

1.4   Properties of viruses and their hosts

Infection.   Before it can multiply, a virus must enter a living cell of a host. Different types of virus can do this in different ways. Purposeful introduction of viruses into organisms is called inoculation. Certain viruses can be introduced by mechanical transmission, e.g. by rubbing virus-containing sap onto the leaf or by a plant infected with a virus touching a healthy plant. Other viruses require a carrier organism called a vector, e.g. aphids. Most viruses can be transmitted by grafting: graft-inoculation.

The term infect itself covers entry and successful multiplication. Infected and infection refer either to this initial process (successful entry) or the resulting state (virus-bearing, virus-containing).

A host is a plant where a certain virus can multiply. Such a plant is susceptible. A plant where the virus cannot multiply is insusceptible or extremely resistant. Resistance can be qualitatively analysed from inoculation tests, e.g. in the field. The potato's behaviour towards viruses illustrates the whole range from complete resistance (immunity) to extreme susceptibility.

In potato production, primary infection of a plant or tuber denotes that the

21

virus entered the plant during the current season. Secondary infection is from a (primarily or secondarily) infected tuber, i.e. initial infection occurred in the previous season or earlier.

Disease. This is the usual but not invariable consequence of infection. If no disease appears, infection is latent and the host is completely tolerant and is a (symptomless) carrier. A virus disturbs metabolic processes in the host cell and consequently the course of processes, such as growth, in the plant may be altered. Such changes may eventually lead to the appearance of symptoms. Study of symptoms, symptomatology, is an essential preliminary for detection and recognition of the disease, i.e. diagnosis. General descriptions of symptoms are contained in Holmes (1964) and Bos (1970). Degree of sensitivity or tolerance of the host can be assessed according to the symptoms. If the host is highly sensitive, symptoms are severe. If the host is so sensitive that host cells die and the virus remains localized, it is hypersensitive. Hypersensitivity gives the plant resistance in the field (field resistance). If the host is more tolerant or less sensitive, symptoms are milder. Symptoms depend partly on external conditions and may be masked by, for instance, drought or lush growth.

A virus causing severe symptoms is virulent and one causing mild symptoms is mild or attenuated. Diagnosis depends usually on either the collection of symptoms at one moment or even on their sequence. The plant may react to the virus at or near the site of entry; the resulting symptoms are called local symptoms. If the virus spreads throughout the plant, systemic symptoms appear, especially on growing parts, which may be far from the site of entry.

Spread. Certain plant viruses need insects, usually leafhoppers or aphids, for their dispersal in the crop. The biological relationship between vector and virus proved to be various. Some viruses even multiply in cells of their insect vector; thus there is no sharp demarcation between viruses of plants and of insects.

Certain viruses can pass in true seed from generation to generation but far less commonly than by vegetative propagation, e.g. potato tubers. Such discoveries established principles for epidemiology of plant viruses. There are at least two groups of vectors involved in the transmission of soilborne viruses: nematodes and zoospores of chytrid fungi. Often vectors are highly specific to particular plants and viruses. Much about the biological relationships of these viruses and their vectors remains to be solved.

Chemistry. Research on the nature of plant viruses was stimulated by Stanley's publication in 1935 of his work on the purification of TMV. He thought that this virus, which he obtained in a crystalline form, consisted of protein only but in 1937 Bawden and Pirie discovered that it contained a small amount of nucleic acid. The viral nucleic acid proved to be the essential part of the virus when in 1957 Gierer and Schramm showed that the nucleic acid from TMV chemically freed from its protein remained infective, though less so than the

22

original complete virus. Each virus is characterised by the form of nucleic acid it possesses, being either ribonucleic acid (RNA) or deoxyribonucleic acid (DNA). It is now generally accepted that either the RNA or the DNA is the virus's genome: it determines the genetic properties of the virus. Genetic properties include shape and dimensions of the virus particles, serological properties of the protein coats, infectivity and virulence and probably also vector relationships.

Cellular organisms contain both RNA and DNA. The RNA or DNA of viruses may each be single-stranded or double-stranded. In viruses of animals and bacteria, all four kinds have been discovered. Most plant viruses seem to contain single-stranded RNA. A few, such as clover wound tumour virus and rice dwarf virus, possess double-stranded RNA. Recent studies by Shepherd's group have presented evidence that cauliflower mosaic virus has double-stranded DNA. Very recently plant viruses (e.g. potato spindle tuber virus) have been found that consist only of nucleic acid.

Viruses need the living cell for multiplication. Multiplication requires the machinery and metabolic functions of the cell. However biochemists have achieved certain steps of the multiplication process in cell-free media. Most research has been on bacteriophages but studies on plant viruses like TMV have been reported.

Virus strains. Like organisms, viruses have variants, generally called strains, which originate by natural changes in the nucleic acid. Strains differ in many ways, e.g. virulence, host range.

New variants of some plant viruses have been produced artificially in the laboratory by treating pure virus strains with mutagens, e.g. nitrous acid.

Thung (1931) and Salaman (1933) independently found that tobacco plants infected with a mild strain of TMV or PVX for as briefly as 5 days were immune to a virulent strain but not to other viruses. This phenomenon is often called cross-protection.

Shape and size. Viruses may be identified only partly by chemical properties. The electron microscope is now indispensable in studying the size and shape of virus particles. Although so important now as a research tool, it has not been introduced in routine diagnosis. The first electron micrographs of viruses were made with purified preparations but more recently methods were developed to examine virus particles without purifying them. The 'dip method', originated by Brandes, has been used with special success to establish the shape and dimensions of many viruses quickly. This method leaves the particles in natural state. Improved methods of fixing, embedding and ultrathin sectioning of plant tissues have allowed virologists to see where virus particles are situated and what structures there are in the infected cell.

Virus particles differ in shape. They may be isometric (almost spherical) or elongated: cylindrical with flat ends (rods), with rounded ends (bacilliform) or with one rounded and one flat end (bullet-shaped). The elongated types may be either straight or curved. Another type is flexuous and thread-like. In recent years,

23

certain types of virus particles have proved to have an enveloping membrane. Particles differ widely in dimensions between viruses but each type is almost constant in shape and size between strains. Nowadays virologists agree that shape and size must be considered in grouping viruses. Noteworthy is that some animal viruses are very similar in form and dimensions to some plant viruses.

1.5 Virus-like disease agents

For many diseases, there is still only circumstantial evidence that they may be caused by viruses. The agents may be transmissible to test plants by grafting, sap or insects. No organisms, such as fungi, bacteria, nematodes or arthropods, have been implicated. Yet neither has any virus been purified, chemically analysed or detected by electron-microscopy. Such negative proof is dangerous. In 1967, the Japanese workers Doi, Teranaka, Yora & Asuyama published electron micrographs of mycoplasma-like organisms in the infected plants. American workers found similar organisms. Descriptions from various countries now suggest that mycoplasma-like organisms are associated with certain yellows diseases.

Mycoplasma is a group of minute organisms (100–1 000 nm) known from the medical field to cause certain diseases in man and animals. Some occur in organisms without evoking symptoms. Others contaminate cell cultures. Certain types of mycoplasma isolated from animals can be cultured on artificial cell-free media. They pass through filter candles. Unlike bacteria and fungi, the cells have no rigid wall but only a thin membrane. In plant diseases, mycoplasma-like organisms still have an uncertain role. Their existence has been established only by electron-microscopy. Diseases evoked by them include aster yellows and clover phyllody. Diagnosis and vector work suggest that they are associated with others such as potato purple top wilt in North America, tomato big bud in Australia, and potato stolbur in Europe.

1.6 Control and cure of virus diseases in potato

The easy spread of virus diseases in certain areas was the first impetus to produce potatoes separately for seed and for food. The growing of potatoes for seed has now become a highly perfected industry in some countries. Stock for seed must be carefully maintained. As aphids spread PLRV, Oortwijn Botjes suggested potato tubers be harvested early to avoid infection when the aphid population built up during the summer. The storage problems arising from this drastic change in seed-potato production were soluble. Schemes for hygiene, for inspection of crops and harvested tubers and for certification were developed in order to reduce the number of infection sources in the crop.

For inspection and certification, rapid tests for potato viruses were essential, especially for latent infections, in which the infected plant escapes attention when inspected only visually. Van Slogteren introduced a routine serological test for viruses to improve the quality of planting stock. Difficulties in the preparation of antiserum against PVA caused de Bruyn Ouboter to discover PVS. Various serological tests are now used in testing potato plants for some viruses.

Virtually all efforts to keep potato crops as free as possible from viruses are based on indirect control, i.e. methods which decrease the infection rate.

But can we cure old valuable cultivars that have become virus-infected? There are indeed a few that have been cured of virus. Kassanis found that tubers from plants with leafroll may be cured by storing them for several weeks at about 37.5°C. Another more general means of freeing potatoes from viruses is meristem culture. Limasset's team found that the virus concentration of tobacco stems infected with TMV decreased towards the apical meristem, which was free from virus. This seems true also of other plant species (e.g. potato) infected with other viruses. Apical meristems excised aseptically from infected sprouts and cultured on artificial media may yield complete virus-free plantlets, which are later transferred to soil. In potato, a few small virus-free tubers may be produced, which should be propagated virus-free and vector-free.

1.7 Further reading

Bawden, F. C., 1964. Plant viruses and virus diseases. 4th ed. Ronald Press Company, New York, 361 p.

Borchardt, G., O. Bode, R. Bartels & W. Holz, 1964. Untersuchungen über die Minderung des Ertrages von Kartoffelpflanzen durch Virusinfektion. NachrBl. dt. PflSchutzdienst, Braunschw. 16: 150–156.

Bos, L., 1965. Virussen en planten. N.V. Uitgeversmaatschappij W. E. J. Tjeenk Willink, Zwolle, 277 p.

Bos, L., 1970. Symptoms of virus diseases in plants. 2nd ed. (revised) Pudoc, Wageningen, 206 p.

Corbett, M. K. & H. D. Sisler (eds), 1964. Plant virology. Univ. Fla Press, Gainesville, 527 p.

Holmes, F. O., 1964. Symptomatology of viral diseases in plants. In: M. K. Corbett & H. D. Sisler (eds), Plant virology. Univ. Fla Press, Gainesville, p. 17–38.

Horváth, J., 1967. Separation and determination of viruses pathogenic to potatoes with special regard to potato virus Y. Acta Phytopath. Acad. Sci. Hung. 2: 319–360.

Johnson, J., 1925. The transmission of viruses from apparently healthy potatoes. Wis. agric. exp. Stn Bull. 63, 12 p.

Klinkowski, M., 1967. Pflanzliche Virologie I. Einführung in die allgemeine Probleme. 2. Aufl. Akademie Verlag, Berlin, 388 p.

Köhler, E., 1964. Allgemeine Viruspathologie der Pflanzen. Paul Parey, Berlin-Hamburg, 178 p.

Matthews, R. E. F., 1970. Plant virology. Acad. Press, New York; London, 778 p.

Salaman, R. N., 1949. Some notes on the history of curl. Tijdschr. PlZiekt. 55: 118–128.

Sommereyns, G., 1967. Les virus des végétaux. Leurs propriétés et leur identification. 2ième éd. J. Duculot S.A., Gembloux, 345 p.

2 Graft and mechanical transmission

J. A. de Bokx

Virus diseases are transmitted in various ways. The route of transmission governs the natural spread. Only when it is known can a disease be produced experimentally in order to trace the spread and to develop control methods.

In nature, viruses spread by contact or transfer in sap, known as mechanical transmission (Section 2.3), by seed or pollen, by vectors such as aphids (Chap. 3), thrips, leafhoppers, fungi (Section 4.2), nematodes (Section 4.3) and dodder (Cuscuta). Vectors, especially aphids, are very important for potato viruses. For experimental work, mechanical transmission is most important, but for viruses that cannot be transmitted mechanically, grafting (Section 2.2) is commonly used. First, however, a warning about hygiene is essential.

2.1 Hygiene

Contamination with viruses occurs in experimental greenhouses and in the open. Even in greenhouses checked regularly by experts, stray infections break out from time to time, perhaps by unintentional introduction of virus vectors (mostly aphids) into the greenhouses or by inadequate hygiene if viruses that are sap-transmissible are propagated in the greenhouse.

To avoid contamination in greenhouses, there are some general rules.

The greenhouse should be insect-free. Check plants regularly for insects (aphids). If any plants are infested, they can be dipped in a 0.2% nicotine solution. As preventive, spray plants with systemic insecticide or fumigate them regularly. Since aphid populations may become resistant to organophosphorus compounds (i.e. systemic insecticides), avoid excessive spraying.

Although spraying with systemic insecticides takes less time, a nicotine solution may be advisable, if the plants are to be used as virus sources in research on insect transmission.

In the open, vectors cannot easily be prevented from spreading virus, except by harvesting before they infect the plants (Chap. 14).

Viruses to be multiplied in greenhouses should be isolated. Some viruses, like PVX and to some extent PVS, are so contagious, that hands or tools merely touching diseased and healthy plants alternately may transmit the virus. Since those viruses are stable in vitro, viruses attached to tools and agricultural machinery may remain long infective.

26

Wash hands with soap and water if infected plants must be touched. *Wash tools and implements* used for virus extraction (pestle, mortar, machine-crushers) thoroughly with trisodium phosphate and soap. Dipping implements for 30 sec in saturated aqueous calcium hydroxide or a 3% trisodium phosphate solution, a mixture of 5% trisodium phosphate and 2.5% soap, 4% trisodium phosphate and 16% soap, or a suspension of bentonite clay prevents them transmitting PVX. Slightly less effective is mercuric chloride (1 : 1 000) or saturated sodium carbonate. Calcium hydroxide is slightly better than trisodium phosphate as a disinfectant for tools contaminated with PVX.

Dipping in 70% or absolute ethanol, flaming and then washing in rapidly flowing water is also effective. Handle plants with clean virus-free hands and tools. Prohibit smoking in greenhouses, since TMV may be transmitted from smoking tobacco to tobacco plants.

Avoid contact between plants by spacing them adequately or by separating them with screens of plastic foil or, even better, screens of wire gauze (Fig. 1). Neither must hands nor equipment, like water hoses, touch the plants.

Fig. 1. Screens of wire gauze used to prevent mechanical transmission in greenhouses.

Steam soil and pots. If the soil is used more than once or even if it is fresh, it may contain infected material, like small potato tubers or virus vectors. Fresh soil may contain soilborne viruses and their vectors. Earthen pots should be steamed, plastic pots must be washed with water and soap or a mixture of trisodium phosphate and soap, and rinsed with water.

Use seed potatoes of suitable size because machinery cannot be disinfected if many tubers have to be cut before planting (Chap. 16). To avoid spread of sap-transmissible viruses, the safest way to grow seed potatoes in the open is to start from healthy tubers. As long as there is no source of virus, adjoining plants cannot infect one another.

2.2 Grafting

Grafting is the attachment of plant parts, usually stems or buds, called the scion, to another plant, called the stock or rootstock, in such a way that tissues fuse and continue to grow. Success depends on intimate contact between the cambia of the stock and scion.

Market-gardeners use grafting, especially of woody plants, to combine the properties of a stock and scion, which may be of different varieties, species or genera, and sometimes even of different families. Tobacco, tomato and potato can be grafted onto one another.

For artificial transmission, grafting was used long before mechanical means and even before viruses were known. Some viruses, such as PLRV, and agents like that of tomato stolbur, cannot be transmitted by sap and therefore grafting is essential for research and in some countries for routine detection. Grafting is useful also for studies on the sensitivity of varieties to different strains of viruses, including sap-transmissible viruses.

Virologists can use grafting at any season. Successful transmission depends on the properties of the virus and on the graft union. A virus like PLRV that is probably restricted to the vascular system can be transmitted only when the vascular tissues have united, whereas a virus present in parenchyma is easier to transmit, depending only on union of cortex or medulla, and highly contagious viruses, like PVX and TMV, need only the mechanical contact between scion and stock. To detect PLRV, the stock is a very sensitive variety like 'Claudia' and the scion is from the plant to be tested. Equally viruses can be transmitted from stock to scion.

Transmission by grafting is reliable only if the virus is systemic. If the virus is irregularly distributed, as is TRV in potato stems and tubers, it often fails.

2.2.1 Methods and materials

Methods of grafting used in horticulture are reviewed by Garner (1967). For transmission between potatoes and other hosts, virologists commonly use crown or side-cleft (or wedge) grafting of stems onto a rootstock and core (or plug) grafting of tubers. Transmission by stem grafting seems more successful than by tuber grafting.

Fig. 2. Side-cleft grafting (A) and crown-cleft grafting (B) of potato onto *Nicotiana glutinosa*.

Crown-cleft grafting. Select a scion of the same diameter as the stock or less. With a disinfected sharp knife or razor blade, cut the scion's base into a wedge (Fig. 2B). For herbaceous plants, the blade must be thin to avoid bruising of delicate tissues; normal razors are usually much too thick to cut well. Lop off the apex of the stock and split the top. Insert the scion in the split so that the cambia are in contact on at least one side. Speed for each operation and disinfection of instruments before and after are essential. Tie the graft with waxed cloth, adhesive tape, raffia, rubber bands or self-sealing crepe rubber. Raffia is widely used, since it is cheap, strong and pliable when wet. Rubber bands, which we use in our laboratory, deteriorate in sunlight and should be covered with tin foil.

If the graft needs support and the stems are hollow, insert a rod of wood into the union. Otherwise insert the graft in a tube. Any tying must be gentle to avoid constriction of succulent tissues. Unlike woody stems, the graft does not usually need sealing with wax or paraffin.

Cut back leaves of the scion and keep the graft in a humid propagating chamber or even in a closed plastic bag to prevent wilting.

Side-cleft grafting. If the top of the stock must be retained intact, side-cleft grafting can be used. The technique differs from crown grafting in the following details. Cut the base of the scion so that one face of the wedge is longer than the other (Fig. 2A). Cut a notch of the same angle, about 20°, in the side of the stock so that a large area of stock and scion are in contact. After the graft has taken, the top of the stock may be lopped off.

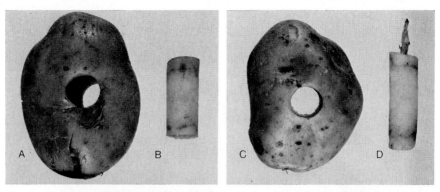

Fig. 3. Core grafting of potato tubers. Virus source (A), plug of virus source (B) to be inserted into healthy tuber (C) and plug with an eye of a healthy tuber, to be planted as a control (D).

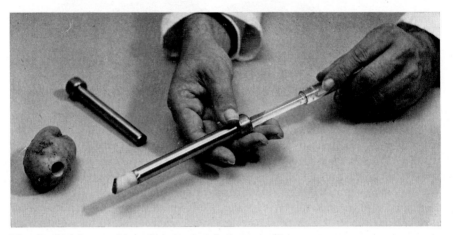

Fig. 4. Cork borer with equipment used for core grafting.

Fig. 5. Equipment for keeping melted paraffin at constant temperature.

30

Core grafting. Infected tuber tissue is implanted in another tuber (Fig. 3). With a sharp disinfected cork borer (Fig. 4), remove a core containing an eye from a healthy tuber. Replace it with a core without an eye from a diseased tuber taken with a slightly bigger borer (e.g. 13 mm diameter against 11 mm). The larger diameter means that some pressure is needed to insert it but ensures close contact. Cover the graft by dipping it in a mixture of paraffin wax of low melting point (42 °C) and bees' wax kept at 85 °C (Fig. 5). Plant all three objects: grafted tuber, diseased tuber and the healthy core. The healthy core acts as a control for the absence of viruses.

2.2.2 Testing varieties for field resistance to PVA, PVX and PVY

Potatoes are sometimes hypersensitive and therefore field-resistant to some viruses transmissible by sap or aphids, especially PVA, PVX and PVY (Section 10.2.2 *Strains*). Hypersensitivity (field resistance) to PVA is confined to certain varieties. Reaction to PVX differs also between strains, so that one variety can be hypersensitive (field-resistant) to one strain but sensitive (susceptible) to another.

Varieties can be tested for hypersensitivity by graft-inoculation. If they are hypersensitive, PVA or certain strains of PVX evoke top necrosis (Fig. 6). Sap inoculation hardly ever evokes top necrosis.

Response of sprouts to PVA seldom kills the plant. If symptoms in the tops are not clear, those in tubers may be decisive. Parallel to severity in the tops (necrosis), they range from a few small internal spots, through widespread necrosis and mal-

Fig. 6. Top necrosis in 'Ambassadeur' after grafting a core infected with PVX into the tuber.

formation, to death of some eyes.

PVX evokes more rapid and widespread necrosis in tops, usually destroying them. Yield of tubers is sometimes very low and necrosis may spread during storage to kill all eyes.

2.2.3 Advantages of inoculation by tuber grafting
1. Tuber grafting is an easy routine.
2. Tubers can be inoculated when field work is impossible in winter and early spring.
3. As long as the plug contains virus, the tuber is almost always infected.
4. Grafted tubers do not require special culture. They can be planted in the open in normal conditions.
5. Symptoms in plants from grafted tubers are usually typical of secondary infection. If the virus is slow to reach foliage, symptoms of primary infection appear first. Sap inoculation (Section 2.3.1) does not always evoke clear symptoms in the season of infection.
6. A hypersensitivity reaction to PVA, PVX and PVY can easily be tested.

2.3 Mechanical transmission
Many viruses are stable in vitro. Expressed plant juices remain infective, so that viruses pass from plant to plant by touch or are transferred on tools, machinery, clothing or animals. Presumably they enter healthy plants through wounds caused during tending of plants. Such viruses are called sap-transmissible. PVX is particularly contagious; PVY less so. Some epidemiological data are available on PSTV, PVS and PVX. Data are lacking on PVA and PVM. PLRV and mycoplasma-like agents (e.g. tomato stolbur) are not sap-transmissible. To produce healthy clones of seed potatoes (Chap. 17) sources of contagion must be removed by regular inspection and laboratory tests (Chap. 7, 8 and 9). Machinery used on ware potatoes should never be used on seed potatoes.

In research and testing, potatoes can be mechanically inoculated with sap-transmissible viruses by rubbing them with virus-containing sap and an abrasive.

2.3.1 Inoculation with sap
Donor plant. For diagnosis, take inoculum from the suspect potatoes or plants. In research on host range or in virus purification, select a herbaceous donor that produces much virus quickly and that can be grown from seed. Systemically infected plants are better than locally infected ones. 'White Burley' tobacco is a good donor for PVA, PVX, PVY, TNV and TRV; Nicotiana glutinosa for PAMV; tomato for PVM. For PVS, only potato has so far proved suitable and must be first checked for stray virus. Capsicum annuum for PVY and Chenopodium spp. for PVS have proved less suitable, perhaps because of inhibitors.

Extraction of inoculum. Leaves usually contain more virus than other parts. Tobacco infected with TRV by nematodes contains virus only in roots for a long time, so that roots should be used rather than leaves.

If only a little inoculum is needed, express sap from leaves with pestle and mortar. For larger amounts, use a mincer and squeeze the macerated tissue through cheesecloth. For routine testing of many samples, use a power-driven crusher (Section 8.2, Fig. 29). Disinfect all equipment before and after use.

Storage of inoculum. For diagnosis or research on host range, use fresh inoculum. Otherwise dry the leaves in a desiccator at 4°C and store at 4°C. Samples with PVX or PVY remain infective for at least 15 years (McKinney et al., 1965); PVM and PVS for at least 12 months. PVA rapidly loses its infectivity.

Sap-transmissible stable viruses are safer maintained in sap stored at −20°C or in dry material than in living hosts.

Application of inoculum. To allow entry of virus, make small wounds by rubbing leaves with an abrasive, nowadays usually carborundum (silicon carbide) of 300–500 mesh, either alone or mixed with inoculum. Apply inoculum with forefinger, a brush, plastic sponge, pad of cotton wool or glass spatula. Instead of sap, crushed infective leaves may be applied directly.

For routine work, pressure spraying has also been used.

2.3.2 Spread by contact or transfer
In epidemiology of contagious viruses, mechanical transmission is significant in spread by contact between plants or by carriage on hands, clothing, implements or animals.

Transmission between potato tubers or sprouts. In a heap of healthy and virus-diseased tubers, virus can be transmitted from diseased to healthy ones, particularly if the tubers are sprouting. Damage to the sprouts or skin of the tubers creates a means of entry for virus. PVX does not seem to be transmitted by handling of tubers.

If tubers are cut before planting, as customary, for instance, in Egypt, Iran, Canada and the United States, the knife or cutting machine may be an excellent means of transmission. PSTV and PVX are transmitted readily by pricking or cutting diseased and healthy tubers or sprouts alternately. The highest percentage transmission is by pricking or cutting from sprout to sprout. Under commercial conditions, bruising on the grader allows transmission of PVX but not of PVY^N. Transmission of PVS has not been tested in this way. In the greenhouse, PVX and PVY^N can be transmitted from tuber to tuber and from sprout to sprout. However the tubers are inoculated under optimum conditions, with a surplus of inoculum and an abrasive.

Transmission between leaves or roots. In greenhouses, PVX is readily transferred, especially when plants carrying PVX are grown close to healthy plants. Routine care, such as watering, stringing and cutting leaves, favours transmission by hands, clothing or equipment touching diseased and healthy plants alternately. A crop can be completely infected in a growing season.

In certain trials, wind was simulated by a ventilator which worked continuously for 2 weeks. Even when the haulms of potato carrying PVX or PVY^N just touched healthy ones, all plants became infected in the greenhouse. In similar trials, 16% of healthy tobacco plants were contamined with PVY^N when they were briefly in contact with infected ones.

Potato plants grown in the open can be infected by virus carried on man, implements, animals or plant material. By walking twice through fields with PVX-bearing plants, 26% of plants may be infected against 3% in untrodden fields. Incidence obviously depends on how often the field is walked on. Walking was more harmful in wet than in dry weather.

PVX adheres to the clothing or boots of men who walk in the field, such as the grower, roguer or inspector. Since PVX remains infective, man can spread it a considerable distance. The rate of transmission of PVX from diseased to healthy plants by contact is not exactly known, since infection in a field might be caused by contact between plants but also by transfer to plants by animals. In Scottish experiments the spread of PVX was observed over a period of 4 years in several crops of 'Majestic', containing about 1% of infected plants. In crops isolated from external sources of infection, the number of infected plants roughly doubled from year to year. Similar results were obtained in Germany. In 'Flava' and 'Ackersegen' crops, the proportion of PVX-infected plants increased from 3.5 and 5% to 8.5 and 13.9%, respectively, in a year.

In French trials, PVS hardly spread in 'Bintje'. PVS-infected plants increased from 3.4% to only 3.9% in a growing season. But according to other reports, PVS may increase from 5% to 20% in a season. The figures are only illustrative and would depend on susceptibility of the variety, virulence of the strain, nutrient status of the crop, spacing between rows and distance between plants.

In Dutch trials, PVY^N was hardly transmitted in the open by contact.

Apparently transmission by contact is more frequent in greenhouses than in the open. Plants in greenhouses are juicy and brittle and probably contain more virus than those outdoors.

In the United States, ridging ploughs and tractor wheels have been shown to transmit PSTV and PVX. The equipment was first driven through some rows of 'Saco' or 'Katahdin' that were all infected with PSTV and PVX, respectively. The contaminated machinery was used in plots with healthy potato plants. Indexing showed that 31% of 'Katahdin' and 65% of 'Green Mountain' was infected with PSTV. PVX was even more effectively transmitted. Virus transmission was positively related to severity of haulm damage. If crops were tilled and ridged before haulms were large, plants were hardly damaged and very little of either virus was transmitted.

Transmission of PVX by root contact has been reported from Germany. A few healthy potato plants were infected by root contact with adjoining diseased plants.

2.4 Further reading

Garner, R. J., 1967. The grafter's handbook. 3rd ed. Faber & Faber, London, 263 p.

Manzer, F. A. & D. Merriam, 1961. Field transmission of the potato spindle tuber virus and virus X by cultivating and hilling equipment. Am. Potato J. 38: 346–352.

McKinney, H. H., G. Silber & L. W. Greeley, 1965. Longevity of some plant viruses stored in chemically dehydrated tissues. Phytopathology 55: 1043–1044.

Murphy, P. A. & R. McKay, 1926. Methods for investigating the virus diseases of the potato, and some results obtained by their use. Scient. Proc. R. Dublin Soc. 18: 169–184.

Todd, J. M., 1958. Spread of potato virus X over a distance. Proc. 3rd Conf. Potato Virus Dis., Lisse-Wageningen 1957, p. 132–143.

3 Aphids: their life cycles and their role as virus vectors

D. Hille Ris Lambers

Aphids transmit virus by inserting the hair-like stylets of their mouthparts into a virus-diseased plant and later into another plant.

In general an aphid cannot or can hardly identify its host at a distance. It has to insert its stylets into the plant. For this probing only the epidermis need be penetrated. If the outcome of probing is satisfactory, the aphid may try to feed and then the particular aphid species must drill to the phloem. Whereas probing takes seconds, reaching the phloem takes half an hour or more. Even on satisfactory hosts, feeding need not ensue from probing and the aphid may move to another plant and probe again.

Viruses differ in their relationship to aphids. Some, like PLRV seem to be picked up only by feeding aphids. An aphid, once infected, remains viruliferous and the virus is called 'persistent'. The virus seems to pass from the intestine to the haemolymph or blood, and thence to the salivary glands, so that the term 'circulative' virus is also used. After ingestion of the virus, many hours elapse before the aphid can infect other plants; this lag is the retention or circulation period. There is evidence that some persistent viruses multiply in their vector.

Non-persistent viruses, like PVY and PVA are acquired by probing, i.e. in seconds. The aphid can immediately infect another plant by probing, but soon loses its infectiviness either by probing healthy plants or in the course of time, usually about an hour. The part of the aphid whence virus is transmitted seems to be at or near the tip of the stylets. Hence the other name stylet-borne viruses. During moulting, the stylets, and therefore the transmissible virus, are lost with the skin. For obscure reasons, deeper probing seems to diminish the chance that an aphid becomes infective.

Clearly a persistent virus can only be transmitted by species of aphid that accept the virus's host as food. For PLRV this limits potential species of vector to nine or ten species, of which only two, *Myzus persicae* Sulzer (in several German papers incorrectly called *Myzodes persicae*), the green peach aphid, and *Myzus ascalonicus* Doncaster, the shallot aphid, seem to be significant vectors.

Because aphids sooner or later try to probe anything, all species of aphid should be suspected of transmitting non-persistent viruses, whether or not they can live on the virus host. So for non-persistent onion yellow dwarf virus, 59 out of 63 aphids listed proved to be vectors, but only one or two of these species could live on onion. There is every reason to assume that a similar situation exists for non-persistent potato viruses. Negative results in the laboratory need not mean that the aphid cannot transmit such a virus in the field: it is well-nigh impossible to make an aphid probe twice within a given time a plant it does not like. But in experiments imitating field conditions I have shown that such an aphid as *Rhopalosiphum padi* L., which feeds only on a few *Prunus* spp. and many Gramineae, is an efficient vector of PVY. In practice all aphids can be assumed to be vectors of non-persistent potato viruses because most specimens of aphid caught in suction traps or in Moericke traps are of species like *Myzus persicae*, *Aphis fabae* Scop., *Aphis nasturtii* Kltb., and *Rhopalosiphum padi*, which are all proved vectors of these viruses.

Laboratory experiments have shown that in almost all aphid vector species, all larvae or nymphs and wingless (apterous) and winged (alate) viviparous females can transmit the virus. Yet many observations in potato fields showed that there was rarely a correlation between numbers of wingless aphids in fields, and spread of virus in those fields. There was, however, a correlation between trapped flying aphids above a field and the amount of virus spread in a field. Thus the wingless larval and adult aphids played a minor role in virus spread. I found in 1937–8 that very frequent eradication of the aphid population with nicotine sprays did not reduce spread of PVY and PLRV in the plots, almost certainly because the probing of passing winged aphids was uninfluenced (Chap. 14). PostWar experiments with PVY and systemic insecticides showed that intensive sprays preventing aphid development did not materially reduce virus spread. The insecticides did not interfere with probing by migrating winged aphids. Therefore in the field, it is the winged aphids that usually transmit virus. But if plants are roughly handled during, for instance, roguing and weeding, virus may be spread considerably by wingless aphids falling off the plants. The difference between wingless aphids and winged aphids in virus spread may be merely a difference in their movement between plants.

For a general review on the subject I refer to the excellent article by Swenson (1968) which lists nearly all the relevant literature. The paper of Leclant (1968) covers about the same field and provides other references.

3.1 Life histories of some relevant aphid species

3.1.1 *Myzus persicae*
How virus is spread in the field depends on aphid biology. Out of doors in the Netherlands, *M. persicae*, the green peach aphid, overwinters almost exclusively as eggs. Satisfactory primary hosts, i.e. host plants on which the aphids successfully overwinter as eggs, are *Prunus persica*, peach and nectarine, *P. serotina*, American bird cherry and *P. tenella*, dwarf almond. Eggs are laid on many other *Prunus* spp., but the emerging larvae do not survive. On adequate hosts the eggs hatch between mid March and early May and the larvae develop into wingless,

mostly pink, females, the fundatrices, with short legs and antennae. These cause a leaf-curl in which the midrib is curved into a spiral, and in these curled leaves the fundatrices produce larvae which again become females, reproducing in the same way. If the population density in these curled leaves is low, all larvae of the 2nd generation develop into wingless females. But often winged females appear by the second generation, i.e. in the first weeks of May in the south of the Netherlands. The third generation matures from the second half of May, and it is usually almost completely winged, as a result of the dense population. By thinning the population, the production of winged specimens can be postponed until at least the 9th generation.

The winged females fly away; remaining wingless females are usually exterminated by predators. Peach aphids are sensitive to colour or rather to light of certain wavelenghts. A newly moulted alate aphid is not repulsed by blue or ultraviolet light and tries to fly straight upwards. After flying or moving by other means for some time, blue or ultraviolet light becomes repulsive. As yellow or green are attractive, the aphids then land and probe. Because flight is slow, of the order of 1 m/sec, wind will usually carry aphids far from their starting point. They are known to have survived flights of nearly 1 500 km, and have been caught over 3 000 m above ground. To take off, they must have a certain environmental temperature as well as light. Take-off has been observed at 15.5°C air temperature but 17°C is more likely to induce flight. Rain and strong wind may prevent or, at moderate wind speeds, postpone take-off. Once in flight, wind speed has no influence.

The first, long, flight is rarely the last, even when the right host is found. Under favourable conditions, such as frequent variation in light intensity from passing clouds, and warmth, alates may take off whenever the sun comes out and land when it clouds over, up to ten times per hour. This restlessness is also reflected in the small groups of larvae on several acceptable host plants each derived from one spring migrant of the peach aphid, rather than the full complement of progeny on one plant. A few days after the initial flight, the flight muscles are resorbed and flight becomes impossible.

Winged *M. persicae* born on a primary host can successfully colonize many kinds of plants, sometimes even vigorously growing shoots of other *Prunus* spp., though this is rare. The normal summer, or secondary, hosts are herbaceous, and potato is one of them. After probing, the migrants may deposit young larvae, which develop into wingless females. When the population has multiplied enough, larvae begin to develop into winged rather than wingless females. So from mid June or later, with rising aphid density, a higher and higher proportion of winged females is produced on potato and other secondary hosts, and they behave like the first migrants from the winter hosts. They colonize other plants of the same or other summer hosts and produce larvae that grow into wingless aphids.

In the autumn the pattern changes. With short days or rather long nights, cold and a sufficiently high density, winged females are produced which do not colonize summer hosts but only a primary host. On its leaves the females deposit pale-greenish larvae that after a moult turn reddish, and develop into brick-red wingless females with thick calves on their hind legs. They are called oviparae and lay eggs that must be fertilized. The winged males develop on the summer hosts and, if they land on primary hosts, they copulate with oviparae, which then lay eggs, initially pale-greenish, on branches, often near buds or on rough parts of the bark. The fertilized eggs soon turn black and overwinter. The return flight to primary hosts begins about mid September and may go on till the end of November, as long as conditions are suitable for flight. Not all aphids leave the secondary hosts. If a suitable food supply remains, wingless females continue to be produced slowly and can survive mild frosts. In exceptionally mild winters, the live aphids can survive in the open. I have observed such colonies a few times on turnips until the beginning of March but they died out. All the evidence suggests that this manner of overwintering of peach aphids in the open is in the Netherlands insignificant. But live aphids commonly overwinter in shelter, in greenhouses, on ornamentals in houses, on stored flower bulbs, and sometimes on stored potatoes or mangolds and produce winged females long before migrants fly from the three *Prunus* spp.

Strains of *M. persicae* occur that have lost the capacity to produce oviparous females. They are common in greenhouses in winter, but can colonize potato in spring and summer. Some of these strains are highly resistant to organophosphorous insecticides.

In summary *M. persicae* has three main periods of long flight during the year.
1. In spring from primary host to secondary host.
2. During dispersal from secondary host to secondary host.
3. In autumn from secondary to primary host.
Certainly in spring flight and dispersal and maybe also in autumn flight, winged aphids after one long flight may take off several times and fly short distances.

3.1.2 Other aphid species
Some other known, and often very numerous, vectors of potato viruses have a similar life cycle but do not overwinter in the Netherlands as live aphids. *Aphis fabae*, black bean aphid, overwinters as eggs on *Euonymus* spp. and has many different secondary hosts, though it does not do well on potato. Its summer flight almost coincides with that of peach aphid. *Aphis nasturtii*, buckthorn potato aphid, formerly known as *Aphis rhamni*, overwinters as eggs on *Rhamnus cathartica* and less successfully on *Frangula alnus* from which it migrates to many secondary hosts including potato, where it can proliferate. In summer only a few migrants are produced, even at high density. *Rhopalosiphum padi*, bird cherry aphid, overwinters as eggs on *Prunus padus*, and on the ornamentals *P. virginiana* and *P. tenella*. It passes the summer on Gramineae, is a well known vector of barley yellow dwarf virus, and transmits PVY. But it cannot live on potato.

Myzus ascalonicus, the shallot aphid, has a very simple life cycle. It cannot produce oviparae and males, and overwinters only as viviparae, killed by severe frost unless sheltered. Though its principal hosts in nature are Caryophyllaceae, it can colonize numerous plants of other families, including potatoes, especially very near the ground. In summer the population dwindles and winged forms become very rare. After mild winters, winged forms may in spring be abundant, and take off about the same time as the spring migrants of *M. persicae*. A second dispersal flight occurs in the autumn. After severe winters, the aphid is usually very rare.

Rhopalosiphoninus latysiphon Davids., bulb and potato aphid, lives under ground or in deep shadow on various plants including potatoes. One report states that it transmits PLRV, but results of experiments by other workers including myself were negative. I could not make it transmit PVY even with thousands of aphids. The aphid is very common on sprouts of stored potatoes. If the seed potatoes infested with aphids are planted on sandy soils, the aphids do not survive. It thrives in heavy clay with enough air pockets, and may then hamper growth. Control in the soil is almost impossible. Males or oviparous females are not produced. Winged forms crawl upwards through the soil, if they can, but they are often trapped in the soil.

Aulacorthum solani Kltb., glasshouse potato aphid, is common on many kinds of plants including potato and is one of the two known species of aphid that can overwinter as eggs on many kinds of plant. Like *M. persicae* it can also overwinter as live aphids. Its saliva is highly toxic. A few aphids may more severely distort top leaves of a potato than many specimens of *M. persicae* can. It hinders recognition of symptoms of some virus diseases and makes a potato crop look as though it is swarming with potato aphids. The aphid begins to produce winged forms even before the potatoes come up. It is numerous on potato only in the low coastal, clayish and peaty parts of the Netherlands. Its role as a virus vector can be neglected.

The life cycle of *Macrosiphum euphorbiae* Thos., the potato aphid, in the Netherlands is not fully understood. In Europe host alternation with *Rosa* spp. as primary host has not been observed. In the Netherlands fertilized eggs are deposited on various herbaceous plants where fundatrices develop. Fundatrices are not uncommon on strawberries. In the second generation, very early in the year, alatae are numerous and they may fly to other herbaceous hosts. On potato very large populations may develop, especially on the upper parts. In the older virus literature, this aphid is generally known as *Macrosiphum solanifolii* Ashmead, a synonym, or as *M. gei* Koch, which is a distinct species. The species can transmit both persistent and non-persistent viruses of potato. It seems to be a poor vector, even though it is more mobile than any other aphid living on potato.

3.2 Climatic influences
Temperature affects an aphid in many ways. The speed of postembryonic development of *M. persicae* in my experiments with sprouted potatoes at constant temperatures, 24 h light and near 100% r.h. is shown in Table 1. Between 10° and 25°C reproduction lasted about 50% longer than development, and on average about 48 larvae were produced, if barren aphids are ignored. From the duration

40

Table 1. Post-embryonic development of winged and wingless *Myzus persicae* in days on sprouted potatoes at different temperatures.

Temperature (°C)	Wingless			Winged		
	number	days	average	number	days	average
10	36	23–29	25.9	7	26–32	28
15	31	14–17	15.2	5	16–19	16.8
20	57	8–13	10.1	10	11–15	12.5
25	64	6– 9	6.9	—	—	—
30	29	7–10	8.5	—	—	—

of the life cycle of first and last born larvae at 25°C, it seems that after 3 months a population from one mother would consist of a mixture of individuals between the 5th and 13th generation. It is easier to use a mean generation time, using the incorrect assumption that halfway through the reproduction period, half the off-spring have been produced. If so, three generations develop, or 50^3 or 125 000 aphids would develop in a month at 27°C, but at 22°C two generations, or $50^2 = 2\ 500$, descendants from one mother. Temperature, therefore, may have an astonishing influence on population size.

Frost, if severe and long enough, kills exposed aphids, but enhances develop-ment of overwintering eggs. A temperature around 5°C considerably prolongs the life of an aphid but interferes with reproduction, while 30°C or more interferes with reproduction and may cause sterility or rapid death. Both cold and heat make aphids lose their foothold more easily when disturbed, and they may fail to climb back onto a plant between 0° and 5°C. Take-off is impeded below 17°C and, like all locomotion of aphids, is stimulated by warmth.

High humidity seems to have no direct influence on aphid growth or reproduc-tion, hardly surprisingly because they normally live in a moist air layer within 1.5 mm of the transpiring leaf. But heavy rain or hail may dislodge many aphids from the plants.

Wind has little influence on sedentary aphids, the more surprisingly since shaking the plant by hand in hot weather may cause many aphids to fall. Hori-zontal and vertical air currents, as already mentioned, considerably affect flight of aphids.

3.3 Aphid population in spring

3.3.1 Winter hosts
Since 1908 it has been known that winged *M. persicae* of the second and third generation developing on primary host plants are structurally different from those developing at any time of the year on secondary hosts. By examining winged forms colonizing potatoes early in the season in the Netherlands for this dif-

ference, I have found that almost all come from primary host plants. Before World War II, peach was the only known primary host in Europe. But just after the War, I found spring colonies with fundatrices on *Prunus serotina*. And still later *P. tenella* was found to be an excellent primary host.

P. tenella and peach are generally more infested in spring than *P. serotina*. Besides, the number of winged forms per fundatrix is lower on *P. serotina* than on peach. Almost all peach trees in the Netherlands have been grown from seed, and so are very variable. Annual surveys have shown that certain trees are always heavier infested than others growing under similar conditions, and some never had more than a few abortive colonies. Peach varieties could probably be bred that would be almost immune to *M. persicae*. Our climate it not suitable for commercial peach production in the open, but in the southern and eastern part of our country many vegetable gardens have a few peach trees in deplorable condition.

In the northern and western provinces, where most seed potatoes are grown, peaches are rare. Some peach varieties that harbour *M. persicae* are grown as ornamentals, but with little success north of the Rhine.

P. serotina as an ornamental used to be rare, but since the early 1930s forestry has used this American tree on a large scale. By 1950 an estimated 30 million *P. serotina* had been planted. Birds eating the fruit have further distributed it, so that it is probably now the most abundant species of tree in the Netherlands. *P. serotina* is almost restricted to the lightest sandy soils. Unlike peach it is quite hardy from the River Rhine northwards to the region where seed potatoes grow. Millions of *P. serotina* grow in the west, along the dunes.

On average *P. serotina* is a poor host of *M. persicae*. However, trees may harbour over 3 000 thriving colonies, far more than I have ever seen on a peach tree. But on many trees not a single colony has been found in 20 years. Trees less than 4 years old are rarely infested in spring. In older trees, primary colonies tend to develop especially on short spurs on the trunk and thick branches, and such spurs are particularly abundant on very old and moribund trees. The leaves of infested short spurs hardly curl but become chlorotic. Primary colonies remain small but larvae may wander to terminal shoots, on which much larger colonies may cause severe leaf-curl. Until then, an infestation on *P. serotina* is very easily overlooked.

P. tenella is too rare to threaten potato crops.

3.3.2 *Estimation of the size of spring population*

So far, only primary hosts in the Netherlands have been considered, but there is evidence that primary hosts abroad, especially peaches, may endanger our seed potatoes. Migrants can travel huge distances on their first flight.

Because less than 10% of all peach aphids in the Netherlands flying in spring come from colonies that overwintered as live aphids, counts on the primary hosts can give a picture of the spring populations.

Logically, overwintering eggs should be counted but this is difficult because several species of aphids deposit eggs on peach, and only the eggs of *Hyalopterus pruni* Geoffr. can be recognized readily. Another possibility was to count the number of oviparous females of *M. persicae* which are easy to recognize. If each female is credited with six eggs, one obtains an estimate of egg numbers. However, the mortality of fertilized eggs inexplicably varies from 4–96% in different years. Oviposition in the autumn is still studied, because if few eggs are laid, few fundatrices can be expected next spring. Mortality of the fundatrix larvae is also unpredictable. So this approach has been abandoned.

Since 1951 only colonies founded by a fundatrix have been counted, as far as possible always on the same, susceptible trees. The fate of the colonies is followed and, as far as possible, time of appearance and number of winged forms determined. Their number cannot be predicted from the number of fundatrices. Predators may wipe out the aphids before winged forms are produced, and predation fluctuates sharply from year to year.

A rough estimate of winged forms can be obtained by putting randomly collected twigs with primary colonies in wide tubes or milk bottles closed with muslin or cotton-wool plugs. The tubes or bottles are put in a heated room out of the sun with their open end towards a window, and the winged forms are for 3 days counted on the muslin or cotton-wool plug. Winged forms can thus be obtained a few days earlier than in nature, giving a valuable forecast. Comparison from one year to another of numbers of winged forms in spring provides good data. Observers have been trained to study peach aphid development on primary hosts in various parts of the country.

Logically, production of winged forms on primary hosts could be checked by trapping. But even with a great many traps (132) other workers and I could never catch more than ten *M. persicae* during spring flight. I then tried sampling potato plants. Searching the plants proved a waste of time, because migrants hide in the folded leaflets. A rapid method which we still use is to beat foliage over a special rimmed board from which workers pick the aphids and send them to our laboratory for identification. Peach aphids are classified into specimens arriving from primary hosts, and specimens arriving from overwintered colonies. The technicians can sample 1 000 plants every few days, but the number may be reduced to 50 or even 20 when aphid density is high. This method, carried out as soon as there are small plants, gives excellent information not only on where *M. persicae* came from, but also about *M. ascalonicus* which cannot be studied on its winter hosts.

Some of the results should be discussed. In view of the distance flown, one would expect that winged forms would land almost randomly over an area of say, 30 000 ha stretching at least 15 km from any winter host. However one field in flat shelterless country may inexplicably hold up to 25 times as many landed migrants as a similar field 15 km away.

Even at the beginning of beat-sampling, we find occasional larvae and even wingless adults of *Aulacorthum solani*, *Macrosiphum euphorbiae* Thos., and very rarely *M. persicae*. If wingless adults are then found, the migrants that produced them must have arrived almost a fortnight before. The finding of migrants so early can be expected for *A. solani* and *M. euphorbiae*, but for *M. persicae* they must have come either from peach trees growing several hundred kilometres to the south, or from overwintering live colonies in sheltered places.

The number of winged *M. persicae* found per 1 000 small plants varied from 0 to 2 000 in different counts. Once, on 2 May 1959, 2 000 were found per 1 000 plants, when winged forms had not yet appeared on primary hosts in the Netherlands. These beat-sampled migrants all proved to have originated from primary winter hosts, so that aphids from abroad certainly seem a threat to potatoes in the Netherlands. Early counting on potato is essential for the study of migrants.

3.4 Aphid population in summer

The spring migrants of *M. persicae* found colonies on potato, and these colonies consist only of wingless females. They produce more wingless females, but as the population increases in density, more of the larvae tend to develop into winged females. Although recent research on other aphid species has shown that the quality of the food may also play a role in wing development, the main stimulus seems to be close contact between mother aphids, or between their newborn offspring. The important parameter of population density is number of aphids on a certain area of leaf rather than number of aphids on a certain area of land. It is necessary to discriminate between these two interpretations of population density because the distribution of aphids on a potato plant is not random. There is a marked preference for top and bottom leaves, and on older plants most peach aphids are near the ground. Nymphs of winged forms with ready-formed wing pads appear first low on the plant. Just before moulting, they leave the colony and crawl upwards, giving a false impression that they were first produced near the top of the plant.

3.4.1 Estimation of the size of summer population

The aphid population on potato plants has since 1937 been estimated by beating plants over a plywood board 40 × 50 cm, divided into squares 10 × 10 cm. Much of the population is dislodged by beating; the aphids can easily be identified; small numbers can be counted; large numbers estimated by counting aphids in a few squares. Numbers found on the board were up to 42 000 per plant. Beating also dislodges most of the larval and adult aphid-predators from the plant, and they can be counted too. The data obtained evidently relate to population density per unit ground area. Counts on 100 leaves (three leaves per plant), as practised in England, was done only when the population was not to be disturbed. The disadvantage of this technique is that it gives no indication of population per plant: as plants grow, they get more leaves but all the time only three leaves per plant are examined; varieties differing in leaf production cannot be compared for, for instance, suitability as aphid host plants.

Beating also yields some winged aphids, but understandably does not indicate their density. They may just have taken off. The incredible variation on a certain day in numbers found by beating gave me the first clue to the rapid landing of

Fig. 7. Suction trap to sample aphids.

winged *M. persicae* under passing cloud. The Russians count nymphs with wing pads as a forecast of the production of winged forms during the next few days.

The summer aphid swarm is large enough to be studied by trapping.

A very similar pink to brown aphid, *M. certus* Wlk, is common in the Netherlands. The alates are almost identical with those of *M. persicae*.

M. certus could not be induced to live on potato and therefore could not be a vector of PLRV, but research in Canada showed that, like many other non-potato aphids, it can transmit PVY. Trapping results soon showed the need to distinguish alates of this aphid from those of *M. persicae*.

Alates can be trapped in various ways.

1. Suction traps sample aphids per unit volume of air. The current types are expensive but a greater objection is that they need a source of electric power rarely available where one wants to sample in the open (Fig. 7).

2. Sticky traps catch aphids drifting against them, or attracted by their colour. The glue is messy and has to be dissolved away from the aphids.

Fig. 8. Moericke water-trap to sample aphids.

3. Very elegant for vector studies are the water-traps invented by Moericke[1], a shallow pan painted yellow inside and filled with an aphicide (Fig. 8).

These traps are selective, attracting almost entirely insects with a preference for yellow or for water. Among these insects are many vectors of potato viruses but, unfortunately, relative to other species, very few *Rhopalosiphum padi*, which is a vector of PVY. This kind of trap indicates the landing of migrants, which is just the information needed in studies on spread of viruses by aphids.

The traps used in the Netherlands are made of sheet metal, with a bottom of 49.5 × 32.5 cm, sides of 8 cm at an angle of 65°. In one corner of the bottom is a bunged outlet 19 mm in diameter, 4 cm long with a rim at the bottom; a piece of muslin can be held against the bottom of the outlet by a metal clasp. Inside the pans the bottom and the lower 2 cm of the sides are painted with Hansa yellow varnish, while the rest of the sides and the outside are painted dark-gray. The traps are placed in potato fields in pairs at least 5 m apart, and at least 5 m in from the edge of the field on stilts or a platform so that the bottom of the trap is 60 cm above the soil. Plants underneath the trap or plants that might touch the stilts are removed to prevent aphids crawling into the traps. The traps are filled with water beyond the yellow on the sides, and some aphicide is added. First we used nicotine sulphate but it corroded the varnish; later we used a household detergent, which reduced repainting to once a year. The traps are emptied daily before 08.30 h. A cut piece of muslin is fixed to the outlet and pulled down to form a small bag, a bucket is placed under the outlet and the bung is removed. The aphids, sometimes with the help of rinsing, collect on the muslin, the bung is replaced and the bucket emptied into the trap. The muslin is gently rolled up and inserted in a very thick-walled glass tube holding household

1. The impact cannot be overestimated of research at Bonn by Moericke on the behaviour of *M. persicae*. The yellow trap which he invented must have saved Dutch seed-potato growers many millions of guilders if one reckons that one day's difference in lifting of seed potatoes may rise the value of the harvest by 1.5–3.5 million guilders (30 000 ha; 600 kg tubers per ha each day).

spirits. After the tube has been closed with a bung, it is inserted in a wooden block with 2–6 holes each with a number corresponding to a number painted on a trap. Trap operators have printed gummed labels for mailing the wooden blocks. The material hardly wears despite 10–18 years of use. From experiments with six traps per field, we found that two traps per field provide sufficiently reliable information. Catches can be identified with a ×6 hand-lens, without clearing. After training, about 3 000 winged aphids an hour can be identified and classified into *M. persicae* and other aphids. If catches become excessively large, parts of each catch can be analysed. Observant people without any entomological or biological experience can be trained in a three-day course to identify trapped aphids, and the common potato aphids. The regional certifying laboratories (Chap. 17) then send one or more of their technicians for training and afterwards catches are sent first to these laboratories. After they have been sorted and counted the aphids are returned to their tube, separated into *M. persicae* and other aphids or into *M. persicae, M. ascalonicus, Aulacorthum solani* and other aphids by cotton plugs between each category. At the central laboratory every aphid is checked and the '*M. persicae*' sorted into true *M. persicae* and *M. certus*. Wrongly identified aphids are sent back to the technicians. Since interest in trapping is great, 250 traps are now set. The number of trained technicians has grown each year. The check for *M. certus* by an experienced and gifted technician remains indispensable.

The Dutch regional certifying organizations mail a preliminary aphid bulletin to each other every day, and the next day a corrected set of figures for the country is distributed by mail, or sometimes by telephone, to the directors concerned. The procedure has continued for 20 years with little modification.

3.4.2 Natural enemies

In the Netherlands aphid counts in potato fields were begun in 1936 by examining whole plants in situ, but in 1937 beating onto a board was tried. In the same year studies were begun on insect enemies of aphids living in potato fields. The intention was to find the influence of climatic conditions on the development and reproduction of aphids, and on the most numerous and effective aphid enemies. Aphids and aphid parasites were reared on sprouted potatoes pinned to a beer coaster (beer mat) covered by a bell jar to maintain humidity, predators singly in Petri dishes 2.5–3.5 cm diameter and covered by pieces of glass held in position by rubber bands. The predators were reared from eggs and every day they were offered a surfeit of counted adult wingless *M. persicae*. Surviving aphids were counted and thrown away. Every series was done at 5°, 10°, 15°, 20°, 25° and 30°C. Simultaneously predators were beaten out in the field, and many larvae of predators reared to maturity. After 3 years of this work, it was realized that a detailed quantitative analysis of what happened to aphids in a potato field was hopeless. Not only was there competition between the numerous species of common predators, but they also attacked one another, and were cannibalistic. Adult *Chrysopa abbreviata* Curtis and *C. phyllochroma* Wesmael ate their own eggs as well as aphids, *Chrysopa* larvae immediately after descending from the egg stalk ate one another, and when larger, also small syrphid larvae, and larvae and pupae of coccinellids, especially when the latter were moulting. But even worse: the more numerous the predator larvae became, the more they suffered from parasites. In an average potato field about 50 species of coccinellids, parasites of coccinellids, syrphids, parasites and probably hyperparasites of syrphids, chrysopids and parasites of chrysopids, cecidomyids, anthocorids, aphid parasites and hyperparasites had an impact on three or four species of aphids. The reaction of various predators and the aphid parasites to warmth or cold differed greatly, e.g. the aphid parasite simply became inactive at 10°C but not the aphids. But at 30°C the aphids became restless and hardly multiplied, whereas the parasites were most active. During cool rainy weather, adult syrphids did not mate or fly, their larvae started to wander over the plants, but the aphids seemed unaffected. However interesting this analysis, it had to be abandoned.

Predators hardly ever lay eggs unless the crop is infested with aphids and always, in my observation, lay their eggs fairly close to aphids. Syrphids fly predominantly upwind towards the field with aphids. Flight direction in coccinellids could not be determined. Chrysopid adults were never observed flying by day, except if disturbed, when they were usually carried downwind. In nearly all fields studied, the count of predator larvae increased with the count of aphids, up to a certain moment at which the aphid population went down before the population of predator larvae. The higher the population peak, the faster the population declined.

There were two possible reasons for the collapse of the aphid population: the alates fly away after the population has reached its peak; or the combined activities of aphid enemies overtake reproduction by the aphids. At any rate it was clear that during the collapse of the aphid population, predators wiped out what was left after the alates had flown away. After the aphid population was gone, there were still many predator larvae searching for prey, and the last predators alive were usually chrysopid larvae, because they search very actively for prey and can stand considerable starvation. Apparently mortality among alates is very large. Over a large area departures should equal arrivals, but evidently predators hunt out the arrivals.

In the Netherlands syrphids are the most numerous predators in potato fields during aphid years. Coccinellids follow. Other predators are very much less numerous, but chrysopid larvae are significant because they reduce the population to its lowest level. Parasites on aphids were insignificant, both as shown by the field count of mummies and by counting emergence from lots of 1 000 adult or near adult apterous *M. persicae* placed in a tube with a piece of potato plant. The highest proportion of mummies obtained by the latter method amounted to 4% in aphids from potato fields.

Several predators have gone into diapause at the time of the collapse of the aphid population. Others, including many coccinellids, wander about as adults and retire into hibernation before reproducing again. Many multivoltine predators are

48

hampered by increasing parasitism. Hence pressure on the aphid population falls off and aphids build up once more. This becomes noticeable at the end of August and with very little interference by aphid enemies, an autumn peak as high as the summer one may result. Once more, many alates are produced but they hardly colonize potatoes and other secondary host plants. Long nights and cold induce production of alates that prefer leaves of the primary hosts, on which they deposit larvae that will grow up to egg-laying females. The detailed behaviour of these migrants has not been studied. After their initial long flight, they may make short flights, during which they probe potato plants. But if so, breakdown of their flight muscles may prevent them reaching their destiny. Evidence from virus spread also suggests that the autumn migrants differ in behaviour from spring and summer migrants.

3.4.3 Variations in the summer flights

Yellow Moericke traps have given much information about the summer flights. Invariably flights are recorded earlier in the south than in the north of the country, more clearly so in some years than others. The difference varies from a few days to 2 weeks. The total catch of *Myzus* spp. is usually larger in the south than in the north, but not always. The opposite may occur. In years with many aphids, the total catch of summer alates may be about 3 000 times that in years with few alates. Certain areas almost every year have inexplicably much lower catches of alates than any other area. In years with many aphids summer migrations end abruptly, in correspondence to the low level to which the aphid population falls, but in years with few aphids small catches of migrants continue a long time after the peak. During flight periods, low catches may occur as a result of bad weather (wind, rain, cold). In demonstration fields on experimental farms, many more alates are trapped than in surrounding fields and this is not reflected in the virus spread. Large catches of alates may be trapped in areas where the aphid population in the field is extremely small.

M. certus tends to fly earlier than *M. persicae*, though their flight periods may overlap. It can fly in large enough numbers to cause great alarm, if it is not recognized. Catches may consist of 4% *M. persicae* and 96% of *M. certus*. Certain areas are known for the abundance of *M. certus* both on weeds and in traps but, in some years (e.g. 1968), *M. certus* may be numerous in traps in most parts of the country. Almost always catches of it from traps in the north are much greater than in the south.

The peaks of winged *Aphis fabae* mostly coincide with those of *M. persicae* in summer.

A year with very large summer flights of *M. persicae* is followed by a year with very small flights. Presumably most predators from a year with a high aphid population survive into the next year to keep down the aphids. A year with very few aphids is not necessarily followed by a year with many aphids. There is no simple correlation in one year between the size of the autumn migration and the size of the summer flight but there is a correlation between the spring migration and summer flight, both in time and in size.

Still unknown is how many of the alates caught in a Moericke trap in a field were born in that same field. We know that many alates may be trapped in a field that, like the area around it, was almost free from wingless aphids. The problem could be solved by using ^{32}P fertilizer on a field, and testing alates trapped in that field, but there are too many risks from the use of radioactive isotopes in such experiments.

3.5 Introduction and spread of virus in a field

Aphids may spread viruses in a field in two ways. The aphid may arrive in a field without virus but pick it up from a diseased plant there and infect one or more healthy plants with virus: virus spread within the field. Or the aphid may arrive infective with virus and infect healthy plants with virus: virus introduction or spread into the field. The two components of virus spread can be separated when tubers harvested from each plant in a field are numbered and later replanted in the pattern in which they grew. Spread into a completely healthy field shows at replanting as randomly distributed infected plants; spread within a field shows up as one or more diseased plants near a plant that was already secondarily infected in the original field (see Chap. 14).

During spring migration, aphids, developed on their winter hosts, arrive free of virus. As they have had their initial long flight before landing, they may pick up virus while probing or feeding in the field, but will not carry the virus far during subsequent short flights, so that most spread will be within the field, perhaps into an adjacent field.

In summer, aphids born on plants not containing one of the potato viruses are like spring migrants, and may cause spread within another field. Some aphids of the summer flight will have developed on virus-diseased potato plants and they may be viruliferous when they begin their initial long flight. These aphids are therefore responsible for distant spread of virus and will cause spread into a field far away. The picture looks simple, but there are some complications.

An aphid born on a plant infected with PLRV will at some time during its development ingest virus and retain it for life or most of its life inside its body. At take-off it will be infective and, when feeding after its long flight, it may introduce virus into healthy plants. The distance over which the virus can be transported will equal the duration of the first flight multiplied by the average wind velocity during flight. So PLRV can be spread over very long distances. The same does not hold for non-persistent viruses. An aphid picking up such virus from the plant on which it developed will lose its infectiveness at moulting, since the stylets, which carry such virus, are shed with the skin. So also an alate just after its final moult will not carry a non-persistent virus and, unless it probes before first take-off, it will not be infective at the end of its first flight. Hardly any migrants probe between their final moult and take-off. However some alates from other species of plants with non-persistent viruses have proved to take off with virus, perhaps because adverse conditions delayed take-off and made them

50

probe into the plant on which they developed. Presumably potato aphids may also do this and start their initial flight carrying non-persistent virus. Even so, there will be a limit to the distance they carry that virus. As we saw earlier, non-persistent virus at the stylet tips becomes non-infective in an hour or so. So the virus cannot be carried further than that number of hours multiplied by the value (in km/h) of average wind velocity during that time. This means that non-persistent virus is unlikely to be transported more than about 40 km at a wind velocity of 20 km/h and that some of the aphids starting with non-persistent virus from the plant on which they developed will land without infective virus. The estimated speed of 40 km per year, with which PVY^N spread across the Netherlands, agrees with these assumptions.

The mechanism of transmission of persistent and non-persistent virus leads to a great difference in the rapidity of their spread within a field. Acquisition of PLRV, circulation period in the aphid, and injection into a healthy plant take much of the time during which an aphid can fly. Only one or two species of aphid can transmit the virus. But a virus like PVY^N can be picked up by probes of a minute or less, and can be passed to a healthy plant immediately. As mentioned, migrants may land and probe up to ten times per hour. Because there are several vector species, the number of aphid specimens active in virus spread is much greater than for PLRV. Whereas an aphid infective with PLRV can infect many plants, an aphid carrying a non-persistent virus can infect only very few, often only one plant, because its stylets are wiped clean of virus during probing.

Spread of virus by wingless aphids will normally be within a field. In trials where nicotine was sprayed every third or fourth day, both from above and from below, the standing population was killed but virus spread within the field was not reduced. Presumably traffic of passing and probing alates was not appreciably reduced, though wingless aphids were killed. Thus spread in unsprayed plots would also be by alates. Yet experiments in the laboratory commonly use wingless aphids for virus transmission. Wingless aphids can walk quite far over the ground, up to 8 m, as was found in Swedish experiments with radioactive aphids in beet fields. Evidently wingless aphids do not often walk from plant to plant in undisturbed potato fields. But when aphids are shaken from virus-diseased plants by roguing too late or by walking across fields with many aphids, wingless aphids may spread virus alarmingly. The path of a man carrying plants from the field may then be marked by primary virus infections.

Virus spread within a field depends on the number of virus sources, the number of healthy plants, and how often the vector moves from plant to plant in that field. A field may be smothered with aphids and may produce hordes of alates but, because of their initial long flight, they will rather spread the virus outside the field and into and within another field. It is, therefore, no surprise that aphid counts on plants in fields do not correlate with virus spread in the same fields. The migrants coming from elsewhere, with or without virus, are responsible for most of the spread. These are only found by trapping. Heavy spread of virus has been observed in fields with very few aphids developing on the plants, but the traps in those fields indicated high activity of migrants, which had flown an estimated 100–150 km.

Leafroll seems to favour reproduction of *Myzus* spp., perhaps because of the composition of the food. But as the plants remain small, the population becomes crowded on a small total leaf surface, and alates are produced earlier and in greater numbers than on equal-aged healthy plants. This enhances the spread of PLRV from such plants into other fields.

The information obtained by trapping migrants looks impressive but it is not really sufficient. It gives the number of landings of vectors but not how many of them are viruliferous. This will vary with the local or total number of virus sources, but also with the efficiency as a vector of the prevalent aphid clones. Certainly different clones of *M. persicae* differ widely in efficiency as vectors of various virus diseases, and crosses of such clones in Sweden have shown that the ability of a clone to transmit virus may be different from that of the parents of the fundatrix whence the clone began. Annually a number of aphid genes recombine on the primary host plants, and the outcome in efficiency of a mixed population of vector species of the same size may be different from one year to another. Clearly it is very difficult to predict how much a virus will spread, even though we can determine how many aphids flew. The suitability of host plants as sources and recipients for virus varies also with age (Chap. 11).

3.6 Use of aphid data in virus control

In spring, aphids spread virus almost entirely within the field. The number of virus sources is of supreme importance and can be decreased by roguing. But if spring flight is very early, virus may spread before diseased plants show symptoms. Control must then be with systemic aphicides, which stop spread of PLRV but not of non-persistent viruses. For such early spraying alarm should be raised, preferably before aphids reach potato fields. South of the Rhine, advice is given each year to treat seed potatoes just after they come up and again 2 weeks later. This advice is countermanded if counts on primary hosts suggest no imminent danger. This strange policy ensures that everybody is prepared to act and that enough chemicals are available. North of the Rhine, chemical control is advised only when aphids might become really dangerous.

Roguing may be risky when symptoms take a long time to show, for then aphids may have developed and be shaken from the plants that are pulled up. If late roguing is unavoidable, a non-residual aphicide should be applied some days before roguing. Spraying could be limited to recognizably diseased plants.

In summer, virus spreads also from outside the field and cannot be stopped by aphicides. The oldest method of control, in use since at least 1810, is early lifting. Since aphid trapping began, early lifting has been based on trap catches of *M. persicae* and other aphids. The present policy is that the highest grades of seed potatoes should be lifted 8–10 days after traps in the area have caught about two alates of *M. persicae* per day. Lower-grade seed can be harvested later and the further course of aphid flight can be considered. The interval of 8–10 days between a 'critical' aphid flight and lifting is based on the time the virus takes to reach tubers after being introduced into the top of the haulms.

The greatest difficulty in this aphid policy is from *M. certus*, as mentioned before. Lifting a day too early reduces yield by 500–1 000 kg per ha. *M. certus* usually begins to fly before *M. persicae*, sometimes a fortnight earlier. Some traps contained 25 times as much *M. certus* as *M. persicae*. Clearly failure to distinguish *M. certus* from *M. persicae* would in some years cause disastrous losses in yield. Usually this false peach aphid is caught in traps in the north and north-west of the Netherlands, particularly in the polders of Lake Yssel, but hardly at all elsewhere. But in 1968 it occurred abundantly in most traps. So far the complication of *M. certus* has been recognized only in the Netherlands. However the aphid occurs in other seed-producing areas, like Scotland, Maine (USA), eastern Canada, and East Germany, in all of which trapping has been practised.

Other aphids than *M. persicae* transmit non-persistent viruses of which PVY^N is the most important. Unfortunately we do not know much about differences between virus vectors in efficiency. For other aphid species, we do not know whether they are vectors at all. Fortunately most aphids trapped are *Aphis fabae*, which is known as a vector of PVY^N and which flies in summer almost simultaneously with *M. persicae*. Hence, until more is known, advice on lifting dates is being based on the flight of all aphids other than *M. persicae*. If there are large flights of these other species, lifting may be advised before catches of *M. persicae* reach two aphids per trap.

Evidently no serious errors have been made with the lifting policy. In practice seed health does not differ much from the grade allotted during field inspection. Lower grades may perhaps in some years have been lifted earlier than necessary, but now that the dates for successively lower grades are also fixed on the latest evidence from catches, it is unlikely that seed is being lifted much too early. Only in 1959 did the whole operation fail, because massive aphid flights began at a time when, partly through drought, tubers had hardly started to form. The few people that asked and got advice by telephone, and acted on it, managed to get a meagre harvest of small, healthy, and exceedingly valuable, seed potatoes.

It is interesting to examine what happens in two consecutive years, e.g. 1959 and 1960. The weather during the aphid season was exceptionally sunny and dry in 1959.

On 2 May, before aphid flight from Dutch primary winter hosts began, 2 000 migrants of *M. persicae* were found per 1 000 potato plants. All came from primary hosts, evidently abroad. Such numbers have never again been found in spring, and the date was at least 3 weeks earlier than that on which the number has reached 50 per 1 000 plants in any other year. The number of aphid predators was low and the colonies founded on potato flourished with the favourable weather. The drought caused the potato plants to grow very poorly. Hence the initially large population reached a high density per unit leaf area, ideal conditions for production of alates. Flight conditions were excellent and traps began to register them in the first week of June, at least a fortnight earlier than usual. The daily catch rose rapidly till, on 20 June, figures easily exceeded 100 *M. persicae* per trap, locally exceeding 1 000 per trap a few days later. After 20 days, flights suddenly decreased sharply, and in the last week of July hardly any aphids were caught. Not until the end of August did the aphids recover, and once more, favoured by uninterrupted sunny weather, an enormous population built up. Catches at the end of September and the beginning of October were at least as high as during the summer. In the south of the country, so many aphids were in flight that the press began to write about traffic being hindered by the mist of aphids. However comparatively few eggs were laid because leaves of many primary hosts had withered or fallen because of the drought. In 1959 all factors had enhanced the production of alates and their activity.

In 1960, fundatrices on the primary hosts were locally dense and produced many migrants in the second generation. This was again reflected in exceptionally early catches of *M. persicae* in traps in the first week of June 1960. Since predators produced in the summer of 1959 were numerous, the average per trap did not exceed 30 *Myzus* in any district. However aphid flight expectedly lasted much longer than in 1959.

Virus spread in 1959 was enormous. In the first week of May, the whole country was advised to spray seed potatoes with systemic aphicides, and this may have reduced the effect of the large early spring flight of *M. persicae*. Fortunately PVY[N] was no great problem early that year. The very early enormous summer flight of aphids made timely lifting impracticable and the crop was left in till after the flight. Early roguing in fields that had not been sprayed may have done more harm than good; symptoms were not observed until late, because of drought, when plants were already heavily infested. Just before lifting, as many diseased plants as could be recognized were removed. The autumn flight played no role. At that time there was no second crop.

In 1960, many diseased plants turned up in the fields. Spraying was still advised. But virus hardly spread because predators kept the aphids down; very early lifting was advised. In 1961 PLRV was back to normal but PVY[N], for other reasons, remained a problem.

Early in the 1950s it proved possible to grow a second crop of seed potatoes after the first. This looked promising and trials were planted in various parts of the country. Aphid catches showed that during growth of the second crop, flights of *M. persicae* were as large as or larger than in summer. Yet virus spread was usually unexpectedly low, though some heavy infections occurred. Continued aphid research gave a clue. If the potatoes came up before the summer flight was over, the crop was ruined. Autumn flights took place when the crop was at least 6 weeks old, and caused no significant spread of virus. So the policy was to plant tubers late enough for summer flight to be just over when the potatoes came up.

Summer flight ends abruptly when it is large but continues over a long period when it is small. The trials soon showed that in areas with small and therefore long summer flights, there was normally considerable spread of virus in an autumn crop. The time a larger summer flight would be over is predictable so that planting dates could be advised that allowed 4 days from when flights ended until when the plants came up. Small errors of judgment have probably been camouflaged because a virus infection just after a plant comes up causes symptoms that are hardly distinguishable from those of secondarily infected plants. Roguing is easy. The method was abandoned not because of the virus, but because a new physiological race of potato blight attacked 'Spartaan', which earlier could be grown in the autumn because it was resistant to blight.

Few areas in Europe seem suitable for growing seed potatoes. Even in a small country like the Netherlands, seed potatoes are concentrated in areas with the highest average wind speeds, with a cool wet climate. Such areas are least suitable for winged aphids. It has long been known that even in areas where aphid-borne viruses are no great problem, as in Scotland and Ireland, fields to the lee of farm buildings or other windbreaks are much more infected by virus than other fields. This point is now important in view of current propaganda on the benefits of windbreaks to agricultural productivity. Crops attacked by aphid-borne viruses should be protected against windbreaks.

3.7 Prospects of biological control of vectors
If all primary host plants of *M. persicae* were eradicated in Western Europe, early colonization of potatoes by this aphid would in the Netherlands be reduced by 90–98%, and allow later lifting. It has been advocated that peaches in the Netherlands be eradicated of sprayed. But *Prunus serotina* would also have to be eliminated as an aphid source. Anyway in spring, surrounding countries might provide more migrating *M. persicae* than produced within the country.

Predators take a heavy toll of aphids and it would be nice if we could utilize them to control aphids, as happens naturally in the year after a population explosion of aphids. Predators native to the Netherlands are normally kept in check by their parasites and by aphid numbers. Perhaps a foreign predator could be introduced with several generations per year and not susceptible to the parasites of their indigenous relatives. In 1949–50 colleagues in Maine (USA) kindly sent us some coccinellids from potato fields. They were large univoltine species that laid no eggs and they failed to overwinter.

One category of aphid parasites looks more promising: aphicidal fungi. In some years, they reduce many aphid species to a level otherwise possible only with the most efficient chemical aphicides. This can happen at any time from June to August, sometimes simultaneously over enormous areas. Populations of 1 000 aphids per plant may be wiped out within a few days. There has been some research abroad but information, briefly summarized by Hagen & van den Bosch (1968), is insufficient and unsatisfactory. Several authors assert that the population density must be high before fungi operate, and that the impact of the fungi comes too late. But I have seen small populations almost wiped out at the same time as dense populations elsewhere. Presumably spore density of the fungi, not density of the aphid population on the leaf surface, governs success. That parasitic fungi behave as self-propagating insecticides makes research necessary. Weather probably influences the incidence of fungal attacks on aphids but suitable weather conditions are likely to recur regularly.

3.8 Further reading

Hagen, K. S. & R. van den Bosch, 1968. Impact of pathogens, parasites and predators on aphids. A. Rev. Ent. 13: 325–384.

Kennedy, J. S., M. F. Day & V. F. Eastop, 1962. A conspectus of aphids as vectors of plant viruses. Commonwealth Inst. Entomol., London, 114 p.

Leclant, F., 1968. Connaissances actuelles sur les pucerons dans leur relations avec les maladies à virus des plantes. Annls Épiphyt. 19 (3): 455–482.

Swenson, K. S., 1968. Role of aphids in the ecology of plant viruses. A. Rev. Phytopath. 6: 351–374.

4 Soilborne viruses

H. A. van Hoof

For a long time certain plant viruses have been known with a special role as soil pathogens. Since a susceptible crop always became virus-diseased when grown on certain fields or parts thereof, a correlation was suspected between the disease and the soil. The viruses were called 'soilborne' long before the mode of transmission was known.

Only recently Hewitt et al. (1958) found that grapevine fanleaf virus in California was transmitted by the dagger nematode *Xiphinema index* Thorne et Allen. Shortly afterwards nematodes were discovered to be vectors of many soilborne viruses. All nematodal vectors found so far are ectoparasites. They feed on plant roots through a stylet which is inserted into the host tissue. The nematodes themselves do not penetrate the roots.

The next step in research on soilborne viruses was taken when it was found that zoospores of the chytrid fungus *Olpidium brassicae* (Woron.) Dang. may transmit several of them, including TNV (Teakle & Hiruki, 1964).

So far transmission by fungi of soilborne potato viruses seems to be of minor interest in the Netherlands, because the viruses TNV and PMTV do not often attack potatoes. For PVX mechanical transmission is economically more important than transmission by zoospores.

For some soilborne viruses, however, vectors have still not been found.

The most typical property of the soilborne virus is not that infection starts at the roots but that the virus is usually restricted to the root system for a long time. After infection of the roots, virus is often untraceable in leaves throughout the plant's life. Besides, when virus can be demonstrated in aerial parts these often do not show typical virus symptoms but stay symptomless.

Soilborne viruses are primarily viruses of the weed vegetation, which as a rule also remain symptomless. Exceptionally they cause symptoms on cultivated crops.

The nematode-transmitted soilborne viruses are often borne on a high proportion of seeds, and sometimes also on pollen.

For a general review of soilborne viruses, see Cadman (1963) and for soilborne viruses of potato, Todd (1965).

4.1 Classification
Soilborne viruses can be divided into two groups: those that remain infective

after drying soil at room temperature and those that lose infectivity during drying.

Viruses of the first group (Section 4.2) are transmitted by zoospores of chytrid fungi.

Viruses of the second group are transmitted by ectoparasitic nematodes (Section 4.3). They can be subdivided according to shape of the virus particles.

Polyhedral viruses are transmitted by dagger and needle nematodes, *Xiphinema* and *Longidorus* spp., respectively. They are often indicated as Nepoviruses, i.e. nematode-transmitted and polyhedral (Section 4.3.1). They are also called ringspot viruses because they cause characteristic ringspots when inoculated into tobacco. Serological tests are essential to identify them. Of the ten Nepoviruses only TBRV causes symptoms in potato.

The rod-shaped viruses are grouped under the name of Netuviruses, i.e. nematode-transmitted and tubular (Section 4.3.2). Their vectors are the stubby root nematodes of the genus *Trichodorus*. Viruses belonging to this group are PEBV and TRV. Only TRV is found in potatoes, in which it may cause necrosis and deformation of tubers, stem and leaves.

4.2 Fungus-transmitted viruses

4.2.1 *Tobacco necrosis virus*
This virus is found in Europe, North and South America. It is transmitted by zoospores of *Olpidium brassicae*. Usually only the root system of the host is infected but occasionally hosts are infected systemically. Noordam (1957) isolated TNV from necrotic spots of potatoes with ABC disease, which derives its name from three types of symptoms in the tubers.

A. Black-brown blisters on the tuber skin 3–10 mm in diameter, later passing into symptoms of Type B.

Fig. 9. Symptoms of ABC disease on 'Eersteling' tubers. Symptoms of Type A (A) and symptoms of Type C (B).

B. Superficial, black-brown, round, sometimes horseshoe-shaped sunken patches, which during storage may become very deep. Tissue beneath the discoloured patches is black-brown, dry and sharply marked off from healthy tissue (Fig. 9).
C. Light-brown patches with parallel or starshaped cracks, thus looking like scab lesions. This attack is very superficial.

Symptoms A and B are rarely, if ever, present at harvest. They develop during storage. They are common in certain years in 'Eersteling', an early ware potato, grown in certain areas. Mechanical inoculation with TNV of potato tubers abraded with carborundum did not cause formation of typical spots.

4.2.2 Potato mop-top virus
Symptoms resembling spraing and stem mottle (Section 4.3.2) are found in potatoes in Ireland and Great Britain. 'Arran Pilot' often shows these symptoms. But so far TRV has never been isolated from this variety. Only rarely was it possible to isolate an unknown virus from leaves of diseased potato plants with the test plant *Chenopodium amaranticolor* (Loughnane & McKay, 1967). In Ulster and Great Britain Calvert (1966) and Calvert & Harrison (1966) were more successful in isolating PMTV from potato haulm and tuber. In contrast to TRV, PMTV occurs in medium to heavy loam and in peat soil. In these soils *Trichodorus* does not occur. No infection could be found in weeds, clovers, grasses or cereals from infested fields. The fungus *Spongospora subterranea* (Wallr.) Lagerh. is thought to be the vector of this virus (Jones & Harrison, 1969). The presence of PMTV in the Netherlands was stated in 1968.

4.2.3 Potato virus X
Nienhaus & Stille (1965) found that the zoospores of *Synchytrium endobioticum* (Schilb.) Percival can transmit PVX. This virus was never considered to be a soilborne virus because it has other more effective modes of transmission. The zoospores of *S. endobioticum* are only vectors when the fungus has completed its development on a potato tuber infected with PVX, unlike zoospores of *Olpidium brassicae,* which become infected after addition of a virus suspension to their medium.

4.3 Nematode-transmitted viruses

4.3.1 Tomato black ring virus (Nepovirus)
Köhler described a disease of potato in Germany under the name pseudo-aucuba (1955) and Bukettkrankheit (bouquet). The virus causing these disorders belongs to the group of ringspot viruses. For pseudo-aucuba the large yellow spots on the leaves are the most characteristic symptom. It is difficult to distinguish the symptoms from those of PAMV. But for this discoloration of the leaves the development of the plant is normal. For bouquet disease the deformation and stagnation in development of one or more stems or part of one stem is typical. Often the main veins on the undersurface of the leaf are locally necrotic.

Originally Köhler thought both disorders were caused by the American tobacco ringspot virus. But Harrison (1958) found by serology and cross-protection tests that the virus causing bouquet disease was identical with the beet ringspot strain of TBRV, that he had isolated from potatoes in Scotland. The virus occurs in sandy soils and is far from common. Different strains occur. Harrison et al. (1961) found that the Scottish strain was transmitted by *Longidorus elongatus* (de Man). The English strain, however, was transmitted by *Longidorus attenuatus* Hooper. I found that even different populations of the same vector species differ in transmission of the same isolate of TBRV. Some populations transmit the virus and others not. Several weeds act as hosts for the virus. During a winter fallow, *L. elongatus* loses its infectivity within some months. In the spring, however, the nematodes can become viruliferous again after feeding on infected plants. Young weed seedlings originating from infected seeds may act as virus reservoirs.

In the Netherlands, except for the southernmost part of the Province of Limburg, *Xiphinema* and *Longidorus* spp. are not as widespread as *Trichodorus* spp. which transmit TRV. Nepoviruses are therefore not as often encountered as Netuviruses. In the south of Dutch Limburg, *Xiphinema* and *Longidorus* spp. are much more frequent, whereas *Trichodorus* spp. are rare. There the soils are from weathered limestone soil or loess; most other Dutch soil types are fluvial. Soil type is therefore decisive in the occurrence of certain soilborne viruses.

4.3.2 Tobacco rattle virus (Netuvirus)
At the turn of the century tobacco at Druten, a former centre of tobacco growing in the Netherlands, was affected by what the farmers called rattle disease. Symptoms were necrosis and later the drying of the lower leaves which rattled in the wind. When the cause of the disease was found to be a virus it was named tobacco rattle virus. In Germany the name Tabak Mauche or Mauke is used. TRV is found in diverse weeds, which are usually symptomless (Schmelzer, 1957). Seeds transmit the disease but not as often as for Nepoviruses. Besides weeds TRV infects cultivated plants. Symptoms are often typical. TRV is widespread in Europe, North and South America and Asia (Japan). Strains of TRV vary in serological properties and in particle size. These differences are found also between TRV isolates from the same country, and may be so distinct that they could be better described as different viruses belonging to the TRV group. The specificity of nematodes as vectors for different strains of TRV is much greater than of *Longidorus elongatus* for strains of TBRV. A population of *Trichodorus pachydermus* Seinhorst from one area transmits the local TRV isolate but a population from elsewhere rarely can.

TRV strains cause two symptoms in the potato plant. Necrosis in the tubers is known as spraing (a Scottish word of Norse origin for bright streak or stripe), kringerigheid (Dutch) or Pfropfenbildung (German). Mottling in leaves and stems is known as stengelbont (Dutch) or stem mottle.

In regions with certain isolates of TRV, spraing is more prominent. In tubers from such potatoes stem mottle symptoms are rarely observed. In regions where

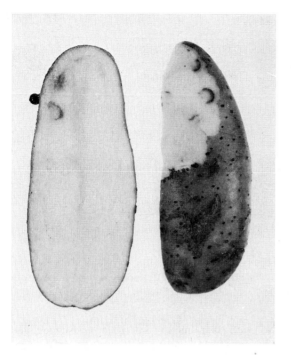

Fig. 10. Spraing symptoms developed after abrasive inoculation of freshly harvested 'Eersteling' tubers with TRV.

other TRV strains occur, the tuber necrosis is light and often not visible. Many progeny of these tubers, however, often have stem mottle symptoms. The spraing strains of TRV remain more confined in the plant because of the severe necrosis in the tuber in contrast to the stem mottle isolates.

Tuber necrosis results directly from the tuber tissue's reaction to inoculation with TRV. The same symptoms can be produced by abrasive inoculation of newly harvested potatoes with TRV (Fig. 10).

To assess the susceptibility of potato varieties to spraing mechanical inoculation is not reliable enough. Also indexing potato varieties for spraing resistance by planting them on infected fields does not yield reliable results. The results are rarely identical because different strains of TRV occur in different fields. TRV is easily isolated from tubers of some varieties with spraing symptoms (e.g. from tubers of 'Voran'). But isolation from others may be difficult ('Ambassadeur', 'Sirtema'). It seems to depend on the variety. After harvesting the difficulty of isolating TRV from the tubers increases rapidly. Normally stem mottle symptoms can be observed the year after infection in plants with secondary infection. Only if many viruliferous nematodes are present at the soil surface so that young shoots become infected directly by the nematodes and the virus does not have to be transmitted from roots or tubers, does stem mottle occur in the year of infection. The proportion of plants with stem mottle from infected tubers can vary greatly but is usually high. Probably the symptoms depend on origin of the TRV

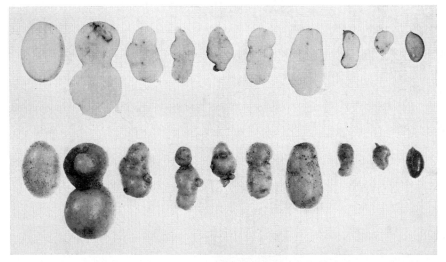

Fig. 11. Stem mottle symptoms in 'Eersteling' tubers after inoculation of foliage with an isolate of TRV stem mottle.

isolate. Tubers formed on plants with stem mottle are often mis-shapen and internally necrotic (Fig. 11). Isolating TRV from leaves of plants with stem mottle is usually difficult, but not always and sometimes may even be easy. To isolate TRV from a certain field it is much easier to start not with the infected potato grown on this field but with the soil itself by growing bait plants. A bait plant is a suitable indicator for presence of soilborne viruses. Nematodes feed on the bait plant and transmit the viruses which can be readily isolated from roots. *Solanum nigrum, Stellaria media* or *Nicotiana tabacum* plants are suitable bait plants for TRV. After some weeks the root of the bait is macerated and tested for TRV by inoculation of full-grown tobacco leaves. Lesions appear within 5 days (Fig. 12). This method showed that TRV rarely infects a field regularly but forms patches as for all soilborne viruses. The specificity of different populations of TRV vectors has already been mentioned.

One viruliferous nematode can infect several test plants in succession, if transferred from plant to plant. Alle nine *Trichodorus* spp. of the Netherlands can transmit TRV but some species are rare. *T. pachydermus* is most widespread, followed by *T. similis* Seinhorst, *T. viruliferus* Hooper, *T. primitivus* (de Man) and *T. teres* Hooper. Less frequent are *T. cylindricus* Hooper and *T. sparsus* Szczygiel. In the Netherlands *T. anemonus* Loof is found only in one place and *T. nanus* Allen is probably a poor vector. In the United States, *T. allius* Jensen, *T. christiei* Allen and *T. porosus* Allen are vectors of TRV. The stubby root nematodes are usually restricted to open soils: sandy soils, light clay soils or sandy peat soils. Of the stubby root nematodes *T. pachydermus* is most common in sandy soils and *T. primitivus* occurs in more clayey soils. Whereas most nematodes

Fig. 12. 'White Burley' tobacco leaf showing local lesions 5 days after inoculation with TRV.

are most numerous in the top soil (0–20 cm) and their numbers decrease sharply with depth, *Trichodorus* spp. prefer a depth of 20–40 or even 40–60 cm. If the watertable is low, *Trichodorus* may even occur more than 1 m down.

4.4 Control

The depth at which *Trichodorus* spp. live in the soil makes effective control by chemicals very complicated.

It would be difficult to kill all nematodes and the residual population could quickly regenerate. Anyway chemical control would be too expensive for a potato crop. Growing varieties resistant to spraing or stem mottle is a much more sophisticated method of controlling soilborne viruses in potatoes (Chap. 15).

How far crop rotation will assist is not yet clear.

4.5 Further reading

Cadman, C. H., 1963. Biology of soil-borne viruses. A. Rev. Phytopath. 1: 143–172.
Calvert, E. L., 1966. Potato mop-top virus. Proc. 3rd trienn. Conf. Eur. Ass. Potato Res. Zürich, p. 225.
Calvert, E. L. & B. D. Harrison, 1966. Potato mop-top: a soil-borne virus. Pl. Path. 15: 134–139.
Harrison, B. D., 1958. Relationship between beet ringspot, potato bouquet and tomato black ring viruses. J. gen. Microbiol. 18: 450–460.
Harrison, B. D., W. P. Mowat & C. E. Taylor, 1961. Transmission of a strain of tomato black ring virus by Longidorus elongatus (Nematoda). Virology 14: 480–485.
Hewitt, W. B., D. J. Raski & A. C. Goheen, 1958. Nematode vector of soil-borne fanleaf virus of grapevines. Phytopathology 48: 586–595.
Jones, R. A. C. & B. D. Harrison, 1969. The behaviour of potato mop-top virus in soil and evidence for its transmission by Spongospora subterranea (Wallr.) Lagerh. Ann. appl. Biol. 63: 1–17.
Köhler, E., 1955. Über weniger bekannte Kartoffelvirosen. Proc. 2nd Conf. Potato Virus Dis., Lisse-Wageningen 1954, p. 148–152.

Loughnane, J. B. & J. McKay, 1967. Observations on 'spraing' of potatoes in the Republic of Ireland. Scient. Proc. R. Dublin Soc. series B, 2: 57–63.

Nienhaus, F. & B. Stille, 1965. Uebertragung des Kartoffel-X-Virus durch Zoosporen von Synchytrium endobioticum. Phytopath. Z. 54: 335–337.

Noordam, D., 1957. Tabaksnecrosevirus in samenhang met een oppervlakkige aantasting van aardappelknollen. Tijdschr. PlZiekt. 63: 237–241.

Schmelzer, K., 1957. Untersuchungen über den Wirtspflanzenkreis des Tabakmauche-Virus. Phytopath. Z. 33: 281–314.

Teakle, D. S. & C. Hiruki, 1964. Vector specificity in Olpidium. Virology 24: 539–544.

Todd, J. M., 1965. Soil-borne virus diseases of potato. Scott. Pl. Breeding Stn Rec. p. 209–235.

5 Virus purification

D. Z. Maat

To allow study of the properties of a virus, such as chemical composition, molecular weight, antigenic specificity and sometimes also size and shape of virus particles, it must be sufficiently pure.

Potato viruses have been purified especially for the preparation of antisera for diagnosis or identification. The quality of antisera depends on concentration and purity of the virus preparation injected into animals to induce antibody formation.

Before purification infected plants must be macerated to provide a mixture of normal (= non-viral) cell constituents and virus. Each step of purification should increase the ratio of virus particles to normal cell material by removing as much normal plant constituents as possible, in every step of the procedure. Procedures are based on physical and physico-chemical differences between virus particles and other substances. As these differences vary between viruses and between hosts and according to conditions, it is not surprising that there is no universal method for all viruses. A worker must elaborate his own procedures by checking each step. The method used in a certain case depends on the nature of the virus, the host used for its propagation, and the properties to be investigated. Also the equipment available may influence the choice.

This chapter will review factors influencing virus multiplication for purification, and ways of treating the virus-containing material to purify the virus. A list with some indications about methods that have been used in the purification of most of the potato viruses is also given. Finally an example is given of a method that proved useful in partial purification of several viruses, including PVS, PVX, PVY and TRV.

The intention is to show how an antigen may be prepared for serological studies and antiserum production. No special attention will be paid to the isolation of different virus components. This chapter is not comprehensive and the suggested further reading should help in the development of multipurpose methods.

5.1 Propagating virus

Before propagating a virus for purification, make sure that the isolate in the host plant is not contaminated with other unwanted viruses.

The ratio of virus to normal plant constituents should be as high as possible in the starting material for successful purification.

To find the best way of propagating virus, its concentration must be checked with a local-lesion host (Chap. 8) or with a specific antiserum (Chap. 7). These and other methods are described by Bawden (1964). The virus concentration must be checked at each step of purification. Important factors in virus propagation are the following.

Production host. Obviously the host plant in which the highest concentration of virus is reached will be preferred. But other factors, such as ease of culture, rate of growth, total yield, the occurrence of virus inhibitors or proteins difficult to separate from the virus, and the ease of working up the material, help to decide final choice of production host. For instance, rather than the potato plant itself, one often uses tobacco for PVA, PVX, PVY, TRV and some others, and tomato for PVM and PVX.

Environmental conditions under which the plants are grown, such as temperature, light, and nutrient conditions. Potato viruses such as PVS, PVX, PVY, and TRV can be propagated successfully in a greenhouse at about 20°C. In the Netherlands (52°N, oceanic climate), during the season of high light intensity (April–August), the greenhouse should be shaded with whitewash or cheesecloth, whereas in winter during daytime extra light is given by fluorescent tubes, just enough to secure good plant growth. Supply of the major nutrient elements (N, P, K) to the plants before inoculation may raise concentrations of virus.

Age of the plants at the time of inoculation. In general only young actively growing plants should be used.

Time of harvesting of the infected material. After reaching a peak, virus concentration may drop rapidly. In different parts of the plants, highest concentrations may be found at different times. Viruses inducing visible symptoms in a host usually reach maximum concentration in a certain tissue about the time when symptoms are developing. When symptoms are necrotic, never wait until necrosis is widespread or hardly any virus will be extracted, if at all.

Parts of plant used. Instead of the whole plant with inoculated and systemically infected leaves, it may be advantageous to take only the inoculated leaves. More virus has been obtained from inoculated leaves of rather large plants of *Nicotiana tabacum* with PVY[N], and from *Nicotiana rustica* with TRV harvested at optimum time, than when much smaller plants were inoculated and the whole plant harvested at a later stage after the virus has become systemic. PVS in potato plants with secondary infection was found to have the highest concentration in the leaves just below the tip of a shoot. Several viruses also have higher concentrations in the mesophyll than in the main veins or petioles, and therefore these are sometimes removed before leaves are macerated.

Virus concentration in the inoculum. The inoculum for inoculation of the production host should be taken from plants that have a high concentration of virus.

5.2 Storing virus-infected plant material
If virus-containing plant material cannot be used immediately, it can be stored

for some time. For this purpose the material must be externally dry. Two common ways of storage are:

In a refrigerator or cold room at 0°–4°C, for periods up to 1 week. At this temperature, physiological activity is largely reduced and the material practically retains its original properties. The material is loosely packed in a plastic bag to avoid deterioration.

In a deep-freeze at −20°C, for up to several months. Gradual changes go on in the material, some advantageous (e.g. coagulation of chloroplasts). But part of the virus may be lost.

Anyhow the material should be chilled before macerating to inhibit the activity of harmful oxidizing enzymes in the extracted juice.

5.3 Macerating infected tissue and extracting juice

Several methods are available for these purposes. Important is that the material be ground very fine, the temperature be kept low (Section 5.2) and foaming be avoided as much as possible.

Fresh material may be ground with pestle and mortar with or without buffer and silver sand. Often blenders are used with buffer or water. Several other motor-driven or hand machines may be used.

Frozen material may, before thawing, be ground with pestle and mortar or in a meat grinder, or after thawing be macerated with a blender.

Sap is obtained from the macerate by pressing through cheesecloth or muslin or filtering through glass wool or filter paper.

5.4 Use of buffers in maceration and virus purification

During maceration, a buffer is usually added. It raises the yield of virus from the macerate. It also stabilizes the virus during maceration and purification and helps to avoid undesired aggregation or precipitation. Different viruses, or even strains of one virus, may require buffers different in buffer ions or in concentration and pH values. Phosphate, borate and citrate buffers are among those used. Buffer concentrations may be from 0.001–0.5 M, the highest concentrations generally being used only during maceration, the lowest as a medium for the partially purified virus suspensions. Buffer pH values are almost all between 6 and 9, usually 7–8.

For data on the preparation of buffers, see Kolthoff (1953). Suitable buffers can also be made with a pH meter.

Phosphate buffers have been used very often but some workers prefer borate buffers in the purification of certain viruses. Citrate buffers have been recommended to prevent aggregation of PVX particles.

Sometimes detergents (e.g. Igepon T 73) and chelating agents, such as sodium ethylenediaminetetra-acetate (EDTA), have also been used to inhibit aggregation.

To the buffers used in maceration, reducing agents or enzyme inhibitors such as $NaHSO_3$, ascorbic acid, thioglycollic acid, cysteine hydrochloride, sodium diethyl-dithiocarbamate, KCN or combinations of these (in concentrations of 0.01 M) may be added (Hampton & Fulton, 1959; 1961). These substances diminish oxidation of the sap components, yield clearer virus preparations and decrease losses of virus during purification.

Buffers that stabilize viruses in crude sap may less effectively stabilize the highly purified virus. Sometimes additives such as particular ions (e.g. Mg^{2+}), sucrose, egg albumen, or reducing agents have been found helpful.

5.5 Clarification of crude sap

After obtaining a crude extract from the infected material, the first step is usually to remove as many other plant constituents as possible, leaving the virus dispersed and unchanged. The extract may be clarified in various ways.

1. Centrifugation at low speed, e.g. 10–30 min at 3 000–10 000 g. Particles much larger than virus including large fragments of cells and chloroplasts settle out.
2. Heating of sap for 5–10 min at 50°–60°C. This denatures and coagulates several components of sap. The method can be used only for viruses with a rather high thermal inactivation point (e.g. PVX).
3. Freezing and thawing. The effect is similar to that of heating (Section 5.2).
4. Mixing the sap with organic solvents such as:
a. chloroform (1 part to 1–7 parts of sap)
b. diethyl ether, carbon tetrachloride, or both successively or in a mixture of equal volumes of the two, 1 part to 1–4 parts of sap
c. a mixture of equal parts of chloroform and n-butanol, 2 volumes of the mixture with 1 volume of sap
d. n-butanol, e.g. 8.5% by volume
e. ethanol.

Solvents mentioned under a, b or c may also be added to leaf material before it is macerated with a buffer. They mix with the sap and form an emulsion. Stir while adding slowly butanol and ethanol to sap.

5. Addition of adsorbents, such as charcoal, bentonite, calcium phosphate gel.
6. Acidification. The usefulness of this procedure depends on the virus's isoelectric point and stability at low pH.
7. Addition of ammonium sulphate, if the normal plant proteins precipitate out with lower concentrations of salt than the virus.

Treatments 2–7 are followed by low-speed centrifugation to remove the organic solvents or denatured plant material, or the adsorbents. Especially with organic solvents or acidification, the mixture may be incubated to increase denaturation of normal plant proteins.

Material of low molecular weight (e.g. undesired salts) may be removed by dialysis against water or buffer.

5.6 Further purification of clarified extracts

After finding a suitable clarification method (or combination of methods) by tests for virus activity, virus must usually be further separated from normal plant proteins, and often has to be concentrated. Methods are based on different properties of the virus.

1. Sedimentation of virus by ultracentrifugation, e.g. 1–3 h at 80 000 g. When time and speed are correctly chosen, it is possible to sediment the virus completely, whereas other plant proteins of much lower molecular weight are only partly sedimented.

2. Precipitation of virus with ammonium sulphate. While the ammonium sulphate is added as solid or as a saturated solution (76 g $(NH_4)_2SO_4$ in 100 ml water at 20°C), the mixture is stirred. Most viruses precipitate at ammonium sulphate concentrations between 30–50% of saturation.

3. Precipitation of virus with cold acetone, 40–70% by volume.

4. Precipitation of virus at its isoelectric point.

5. Precipitation of virus with polyethylene glycol (e.g. 4–8%), sometimes in combination with NaCl (e.g. up to 4%). Isometric viruses may need higher concentrations of polyethylene glycol than elongated viruses.

Methods 2–5, are followed by low-speed centrifugation. Sediments obtained by methods 1–5 are resuspended in a suitable buffer or distilled water, after which these are centrifuged again at low speed to remove insoluble material. Precipitation and sedimentation may be repeated as required to obtain purer preparations. Residues of ammonium sulphate or acid can be removed from the suspension by dialysis.

6. Precipitation of normal plant proteins with antisera (Gold, 1961).

7. Separation of virus and normal plant proteins by density-gradient centrifugation (Brakke, 1960; 1967). Partially purified preparations are ultracentrifuged in tubes in swing-out rotors, on top of a column of a sucrose solution whose density increases from the top to the bottom, or with a solution of a heavy salt (e.g. CsCl), whose density gradient develops during centrifugation so that normal plant constituents and virus separate. More recently, special zonal rotors became available (Anderson & Cline, 1967); they separate virus much better than swing-out rotors.

8. Separation of virus and normal plant proteins with molecular sieves (Steere, 1964; Ackers & Steere, 1967). Virus-containing suspensions are passed through columns of a granular gel. Depending on the pore size of the gel, particles of different size may move at different rates. Agar, agarose, sephadex and others may be used as gel.

9. Separation by electrophoresis, such as free electrophoresis, hanging curtain electrophoresis, gel electrophoresis, pH-gradient electrophoresis and density-gradient zone electrophoresis. Especially the last (van Regenmortel, 1964; Polson & Russell, 1967) has been used for final purification of several viruses, including PVX and PVY.

10. Purification by chromatography. Venekamp et al. (1966, p. 118) used cellulose columns and solutions containing polyethylene glycol as solvents. They were especially successful in the purification of PVX. Their method is based on the distribution of macromolecular particles in aqueous high-polymer two-phase systems.

To concentrate the virus, methods 1–5 are especially useful. Concentration is achieved by resuspending the sediments obtained in a smaller volume of buffer than the original sap volume. Dialysis against polyethylene glycol may also serve this purpose.

A test is necessary not only for the particular virus but also for normal plant proteins residual in the purified preparation. Unfortunately the formation of antibodies in an animal may be induced by concentrations of normal plant proteins not detectable by one of the test methods such as electrophoresis, electron-microscopy, analytical and density-gradient centrifugation, and even serology. Yet, if a good antiserum against normal plant proteins is available, the serological test is one of the most sensitive, in particular the agar double-diffusion test (Section 7.2.4).

The purified virus suspension may have to be stored. Buffers suitable during purification may not stabilize purified suspensions. Bacterial contamination may occur. Several viruses can be preserved in the refrigerator by adding a few drops of chloroform or in a deep-freeze by adding glycerol (10–50% by volume).

5.7 Purification of viruses occurring in potato

Potato virus X. This virus is one of the most stable and infectious potato viruses. It occurs in high concentrations in many of its hosts and purification gives little problem. Propagation hosts include *Nicotiana tabacum, N. rustica* and tomato. Although citrate buffers have been recommended to avoid aggregation during purification, phosphate and other buffers are also efficient. The preparation can be clarified by one of the following procedures: low-speed centrifugation alone or in combination with heating, freezing, mixing with chloroform or diethyl ether and carbon tetrachloride or adsorption of normal plant material onto charcoal. It can be further purified by ultracentrifugation (1 h at 80 000 g), precipitation with ammonium sulphate (a third of saturation), precipitation at the isoelectric point (pH 4.5), density-gradient centrifugation, sephadex-gel filtration, and density-gradient zone electrophoresis. Another technique successfully applied in the purification of this virus is the chromatographic one described by Venekamp et al. (1966, p. 118) and using cellulose columns, and polyethylene glycol and NaCl-containing solutions as solvents.

Potato virus Y. *Nicotiana tabacum* is commonly used as a production host. It has been reported that the best results for PVY[N] were obtained by using only inoculated leaves. Several buffers, and even water, with or without reducing agents have been used for maceration. The sap may be clarified by low-speed centrifugation and the chloroform or diethyl ether and carbon tetrachloride procedures. For further purification, ultracentrifugation, ammonium sulphate precipitation, density-gradient centrifugation, and density-gradient zone electrophoresis have been used.

Potato virus S. Potato is the production host. Sap has been clarified by low-speed centrifugation and the chloroform or diethyl ether and carbon tetrachloride procedure. Ultracentrifugation, ammonium sulphate precipitation, and density-gradient centrifugation are used for further purification.

Potato virus M. Potato and tomato are good production hosts. Freezing and diethyl ether and carbon tetrachloride procedures, followed by low-speed centrifugation have been used for clarification. Further purification as for PVS.

Tobacco rattle virus. *Nicotiana tabacum,* and especially *N. rustica* are suitable production hosts. Several clarification procedures are useful: low-speed centrifugation, alone or with freezing, chloroform or diethyl ether and carbon tetrachloride or chloroform and butanol. The preparation is further purified by ultracentrifugation, which may be followed by density-gradient centrifugation. Chromatography can also be used for purification with cellulose columns and solutions containing polyethylene glycol as solvents.

Potato virus A. Only a few reports are known on the purification of this virus. After production on *Nicotiana tabacum,* the virus was clarified with chloroform, low-speed centrifugation, and further purified by ammonium sulphate precipitation.

Potato aucuba mosaic virus. The production host is *Nicotiana tabacum.* The preparation is clarified with butanol, low-speed centrifugation and further purified by ultracentrifugation.
Potato spindle tuber virus. Potato and tomato have been used for propagation.

Organic solvents and freezing have been used for clarification of sap containing the virus. Concentrating was with ethanol.

Tobacco necrosis virus. *Nicotiana tabacum* and *Phaseolus vulgaris* may be useful production hosts. Several clarification procedures may be used, among others low-speed centrifugation, freezing, precipitation of normal plant proteins at pH 4.5 and clarification with chloroform and butanol. Ultracentrifugation and ammonium sulphate precipitation are used for further purification.

Tomato black ring virus. *Nicotiana tabacum, N. rustica* and petunia may serve as hosts for propagation. Freezing, chloroform or diethyl ether and carbon tetrachloride have been used for clarification, and ultracentrifugation, ammonium sulphate precipitation, acetone precipitation and density-gradient centrifugation for further purification.

Potato yellow dwarf virus. For the purification of this virus, which is rather unstable especially in a purified form, special buffers are recommended. Mg^{2+} has been found efficient in stabilizing it. It may be propagated on *Nicotiana rustica* and clarified by e.g., low-speed centrifugation, treatments with chloroform,

71

or butanol, or ethanol (21%), and ammonium sulphate. The virus is readily sedimented by centrifuging for 40 min at 20 000 g. Furthermore density-gradient centrifugation and zone electrophoresis proved useful for further purification.

Tomato spotted wilt virus. *Nicotiana rustica*, *N. glutinosa*, and tomato are good production hosts. The virus may precipitate out during low-speed centrifugation especially in strong buffers (0.1 M). A 0.01 M concentration of Na_2SO_3 was found to stabilize the virus, and is therefore used alone or in combination with buffer in the purification of this virus, which is mainly by centrifugation.

Alfalfa mosaic virus. *Nicotiana tabacum* is commonly used as production host but also *N. rustica*. Sap containing this virus may be clarified by low-speed centrifugation, freezing, chloroform and chloroform and butanol. Further purification is by ultracentrifugation and density-gradient centrifugation.

Cucumber mosaic virus. Tobacco is a good production host. Among the many different isolates that have been made of this virus are several that need special purification methods. Buffers effective for one isolate proved less satisfactory for others. Borate or phosphate buffers have been used for butanol clarification and citrate buffers for chloroform. Also diethyl ether and precipitation of normal plant proteins at pH 4.6 have been used. Further purification is by ultracentrifugation which may then be followed by density-gradient centrifugation or density-gradient zone electrophoresis.

5.8 Example of a purification
Some methods have proved useful for purification of several viruses. The diethyl ether and carbon tetrachloride method is especially used for clarifying preparations of potato viruses. The preparation is then alternately sedimented in the ultracentrifuge, resuspended and centrifuged at low speed. (This combination is called differential centrifugation or alternate high-speed and low-speed centrifugation.) If no ultracentrifuge is available, some viruses can be precipitated with ammonium sulphate.

The following method was used successfully in the partial purification of PVS, PVX, PVY and TBRV (of which potato bouquet virus is a strain), TRV and several others. Production hosts were *Nicotiana tabacum* 'White Burley' and, especially for TRV and TBRV, *N. rustica*, and for PVS, potato.

Purification procedure. If possible keep everything chilled. Otherwise cool the material beforehand. Macerate 100 g of tobacco leaf in a Waring Blendor together with:

100 ml² buffer (e.g. McIlvaine's phosphate citric acid buffer; 0.18 M; pH 7; containing 0.1% thioglycollic acid)

---

2. If potato leaves are used, double the volume of buffer and organic solvents.

72

25 ml diethyl ether
25 ml carbon tetrachloride.
Centrifuge the homogenate for 20 min at 3 800 g.
Take supernatant (water phase) and centrifuge it for 1 h[3] at 80 000 g.
Resuspend sediment in 25 ml buffer (e.g. phosphate citric acid 0.05 M; pH 7).
Stand for at least 1 h.
Centrifuge for 20 min at 3 800 g.
Take supernatant and centrifuge it for 90 min[3] at 80 000 g.
Resuspend sediment in 5 ml (or less) buffer.
Stand overnight in refrigerator.
Centrifuge for 10 min at 3 800 g.
Use supernatant or, if necessary, further purify, for instance by more ultracentrifugation, density-gradient centrifugation or zone electrophoresis.

Of the viruses mentioned, PVS, PVX, PVY and TBRV have been precipitated successfully with ammonium sulphate. This may be done as follows.
Add 1 vol of saturated ammonium sulphate to 2 vol of clarified sap, while stirring[4].
Stand for 30 min.
Centrifuge 10 min at 11 500 g.
Resuspend the sediment in buffer, water or saline (0.85% NaCl).
Dialyse 2 h against running tap water, and then overnight against buffer or saline.
Centrifuge for 10 min at 3 800 g.
Use supernatant directly or for further purification.

As with ultracentrifugation, the ammonium sulphate precipitation may be repeated several times. If so, the preparation is usually dialysed only after the last precipitation. Afterwards, one or more of the other methods may be used to obtain purer preparations.

5.9 Further reading

Ackers, G. K. & R. L. Steere, 1967. Molecular sieve methods. In: K. Maramorosch & H. Koprowski (eds), Methods in virology II. Acad. Press, New York; London, p. 325–365.
Anderson, N. G. & G. B. Cline, 1967. New centrifugal methods for virus isolation. In: K. Maramorosch & H. Koprowski (eds), Methods in virology II. Acad. Press, New York; London, p. 137–178.
Bawden, F. C., 1964. Plant viruses and virus diseases. 4th ed. Ronald Press Company, New York, p. 148–169.

3. For PVS, PVX, PVY and TRV. Viruses with smaller particles, (e.g. TBRV) need centrifuging for longer or at higher speed.
4. PVS can be precipitated from sap clarified with diethyl ether and carbon tetrachloride by adding 2 vol of saturated ammonium sulphate (at room temperature) to 5 vol of sap. In this way much less of the normal plant proteins are precipitated, whereas the virus precipitates completely.

Brakke, M. K., 1960. Density-gradient centrifugation and its application to plant viruses. Adv. Virus Res. 7: 193–224.

Brakke, M. K., 1967. Density-gradient centrifugation. In: K. Maramorosch & H. Koprowski (eds), Methods in virology II. Acad. Press, New York; London, p. 93–118.

Gold, A. H., 1961. Antihost serum improves plant virus purification. Phytopathology 51: 561–565.

Hampton, R. E. & R. W. Fulton, 1959. Factors responsible for the instability of some labile plant viruses. Phytopathology 49: 540.

Hampton, R. E. & R. W. Fulton, 1961. The relation of polyphenol oxidase to instability in vitro of prune dwarf and sour cherry necrotic ringspot viruses. Virology 13: 44–52.

Kolthoff, I. M., 1953. Acid-base indicators. MacMillan Company, New York, p. 239–276.

Polson, A. & B. Russell, 1967. Electrophoresis of viruses. In: K. Maramorosch & H. Koprowski (eds), Methods in virology II. Acad. Press, New York; London, p. 391–426.

Regenmortel, M. H. V. van, 1964. Purification of plant viruses by zone electrophoresis. Virology 23: 495–502.

Steere, R. L., 1959. The purification of plant viruses. Adv. Virus Res. 6: 1–73.

Steere, R. L., 1964. Purification. In: M. K. Corbett & H. D. Sisler (eds), Plant virology. Univ. Fla Press, Gainesville, p. 211–234.

Venekamp, J. H., W. H. M. Mosch & J. P. W. Noordink, 1966. Chromatographic purification of plant viruses. In: A. B. R. Beemster & Jeanne Dijkstra (eds), Viruses of plants. North-Holland Publishing Company, Amsterdam, p. 108–124.

6 Electron-microscopy

J. A. de Bokx

The human eye cannot observe particles smaller than 0.1 mm. The invention of the light microscope in the Seventeenth Century allowed man to intrude into the world of microbes.

The magnifying power of this instrument is limited by its resolution (minimum distance between two points that can be detected distinctly and separately) as can be calculated from Abbe's formula:

$$d = \frac{0.61}{A} \lambda$$

where

d = resolution
λ = wavelength of the light employed
A = numerical aperture of the objective lens.

This formula shows that the resolution is strongly limited by the wavelength (λ) of the light used and may be set at roughly half the wavelength. Hence through the light microscope, particles can be observed as small as 200 nm (Table 2). However even the relatively long thread-like particles of PVY (size 750 × 15 nm), the small isometric particles of PLRV (diam. 23 nm), are too small to be detected by light microscope.

Table 2. Units of length recommended by SI (Système internationale) using subunits of the metre in divisions of 1000.

	SI system	Other systems
10^0 m	1 metre (m)	
10^{-3} m	1 millimetre (mm)	
10^{-6} m	1 micrometre (μm)	1 micron (μ)
10^{-9} m	1 nanometre (nm)	1 millimicron (mμ)
		10 Ångström units (Å)
10^{-12} m	1 picometre (pm)	1 micromicron ($\mu\mu$)
10^{-15} m	1 femtometre (fm)	
10^{-18} m	1 attometre (am)	

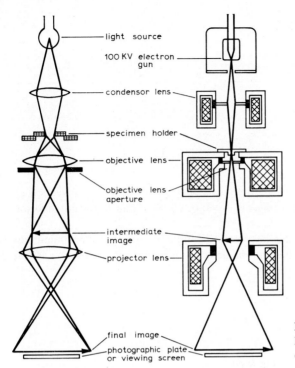

light source

100 KV electron gun

condensor lens

specimen holder

objective lens

objective lens aperture

intermediate image

projector lens

final image

photographic plate or viewing screen

Fig. 13. The principles of a light microscope (left) and an electron microscope (right).

When de Broglie (1926) and Busch (1927) found that streams of electrons have a very short wavelength and that electrons can be focused, the electron microscope became feasible. Thus the light microscope and electron microscope work on the same principle (Fig. 13).

In 1932 Knoll & Ruska succeeded in developing an electron microscope with a resolution of 50 nm and a maximum magnification of 10 000. Technical refinement has now increased the resolution to about 0.5 nm. Figure 14 depicts some modern electron microscopes used by biologists.

The electron microscope can make a valuable contribution to the identification of viruses. Efforts are also being made to introduce the electron microscope in practical diagnosis.

6.1 Use of the electron microscope

Electron beams are scattered in air and so must be projected through a vacuum. The image of the specimen is not directly visible but is projected onto a fluorescent screen or onto a photographic plate.

As the penetrativity of electrons is very low, preparations must be very thin (10–100 nm). They must be able to withstand the effects of vacuum and of electrons. The specimen can easily be altered with electron bombardment. The biological material must be stabilized.

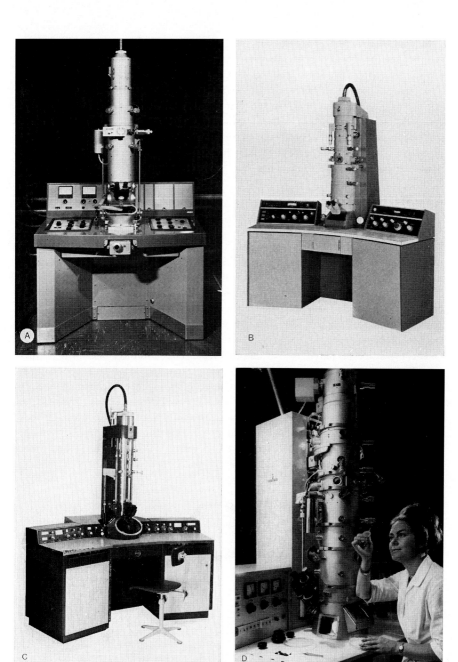

Fig. 14. Various types of modern electron microscopes of high resolution. AEI Electronics EM 80 (A), Japan Electron Optics Lab. (Jeol.) JEM 100B (B), Philips EM 300 (C) and Siemens Elmiskop 101 (D).

In a thin specimen or in partially purified suspensions of virus, virus particles can be readily observed. However if large amounts of plant constituents are mounted too, the virus can rarely be seen.

A second use of the electron microscope is for study of ultrathin sections. After fixing and embedding infected plant material, thin sections (30–50 nm) are cut with an ultramicrotome. The sections are stained with a positive electron stain and mounted on a grid for observation in the electron microcope. The position of the virus in the cells of their hosts can thus be examined. This method is not yet developed for routine use.

6.2   Making virus preparations

6.2.1   Support grids and films
Due to the low penetrativity of electrons, objects for observation in the electron microscope must be mounted on very thin films (about 20 nm). Those films are mounted on grids, which are discs containing a number of apertures (Fig. 15).

Various types of grids are now available in the standard 3-mm size. They can be supplied by Veco Company, the Netherlands or Smethurst, England. Generally grids are made of copper, but they are also supplied in gold, platinum, stainless steel or nickel.

The films are prepared by various methods. Two common ones will be mentioned.

Formvar on glass.   A fresh standard microscope slide is cleaned with a soft cloth. The slide is dipped into a 0.5% solution of Formvar (polyvinylformaldehyde) in ethylene dichloride and mechanically pulled out with a constant speed of 0.5 cm per sec (Fig. 16). This technique yields films of uniform thickness. After the film has been cut loose from the edges of the slide, it is floated onto a water surface by lowering the slide slowly into a dish with distilled water at a

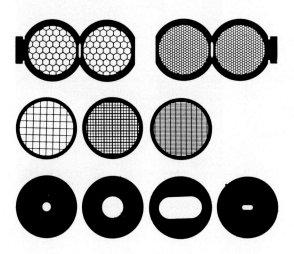

Fig. 15. Types of grids supplied by Veco Company, the Netherlands.

Fig. 16. Apparatus for preparing Formvar films on glass. (Designed by the Technical and Physical Engineering Research Service, Wageningen.)

shallow angle. With forceps the grids are placed on the floating film. With stainless steel wire gauze, the film containing the grids is picked off the water surface.

Collodion on water. A drop of 2% Collodion solution in amyl acetate is allowed to fall onto the surface of clean distilled water. After the solvent has evaporated, grids are placed on the film that has formed. The film is picked off the water with stainless steel gauze.

The Collodion method is very easy but the Formvar films are stronger.

Films must be completely structureless. Otherwise structures in the film may be mistaken for those of the specimen. Plastic films (Formvar and Collodion) are sometimes reinforced with carbon. Films may also be prepared from pure carbon which is used for high-resolution work.

6.2.2 *Shadow-casting and staining*

As important as a thin specimen is contrast between specimen and background. Normally the contrast in a biological preparation is very slight because differences in electron scattering are slight. Contrast can be enhanced by shadow-casting or staining with heavy metals.

In shadow-casting, a thin layer of electron-dense material such as palladium, uranium or platinum is evaporated obliquely onto the dried specimen in a vacuum before mounting the film.

The virus particles are only covered in metal on the side facing the metal source. The other side of the particle and an adjoining bit of the film remain clear. Thus those parts will let electrons pass, whereas the metal-covered areas will scatter them. The resulting shadows clearly show the outline of the particles. This method is effective only if few non-viral constituents are present on the film.

Another way of contrasting virus particles is staining, either positive or negative. According to Hall (1964), positive stains are those which combine chemically with the virus particles and negative stains act by 'embedding' a particle in a heavy unreactive compound. In negative staining the film is covered with heavy metal ions, which scatter the electrons of the beam more than the clear virus particles. Common positive stains are lead salts, osmium tetroxide and uranyl compounds. A negative stain is phosphotungstic acid in water adjusted by adding droplets of 1 N KOH to pH 5.5–7.0.

As a negative stain, phosphotungstic acid adjusted to about neutrality is now used widely in plant virology. However a drawback is that phosphotungstic acid may disintegrate virus particles after some time. The specimen must therefore be examined soon after preparation.

6.2.3 Depositing viruses on the film

Droplet method. Virus particles can be deposited directly on a film very easily. A droplet of a partially purified virus suspension can be put onto the film-coated grid with a Pasteur pipette. The droplet is allowed to stand for one or two

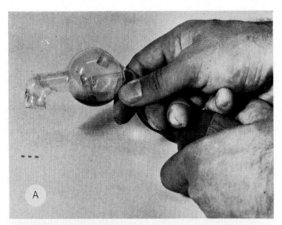

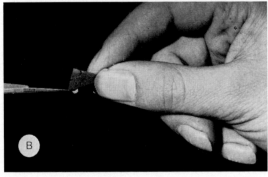

Fig. 17. Depositing the viruses on the grid. Glass nebulizer (A) and dip method (B).

minutes; then it is slowly removed with a piece of filter paper. By removing the droplet carefully, sufficient virus particles attach to the film. A difficulty of the droplet method is that with a high concentration of virus the suspension dries into large aggregates, which cause problems in interpretation and measurement of the particles. The preparation must therefore be suitably diluted before putting it on the film.

Spraying method. Various methods have been developed to spray virus suspensions onto a film. They are used especially if only minute amounts of virus suspension are available. Crude virus-containing sap can successfully be manipulated too. The glass nebulizer (Fig. 17A) is a device which is often used for spraying.

Exudate method. Other methods of depositing viruses on the film (e.g. exudate and dip method) avoid the problem of virus aggregation on the film. By water pressure virus-containing leaves are forced to exude droplets, which are put onto a film-coated grid. A clean specimen can so be prepared; normal cell constituents are not present in excess.

Dip method. The dip method is simpler than the exudate method (Fig. 17B). A cut surface of virus-containing leaves or sprouts from potato tubers are dipped for some seconds into a droplet of double-distilled water on a film-coated grid. After several minutes the virus particles in the droplet have attached to the film and excess water is removed with a wedge of filter paper. After it has dried, the specimen is shadow-cast before examination with the electron microscope. Clean preparations can be obtained. For some reason, the virus particles leave the fresh wounds of leaves and sprouts much faster than normal cell constituents. Dipping of cut leaves for too long should be avoided, as many chloroplasts then settle on the grid.

After the specimen has dried out, it is ready for shadow-casting or staining with a heavy metal (Section 6.2.2).

6.3 Size, measurement and counts of virus particles

6.3.1 Size of particles

Particles of some viruses are elongated and others isometric. Elongated viruses can be subdivided as follows.
1. Tobacco rattle virus group: particle size 130–210 nm × 25 nm
2. Tobacco mosaic virus group: particle size 300 nm × 18 nm
3. Potato virus X group: particle size 480–580 nm × 13 nm
4. Potato virus S group: particle size from 620–700 nm × 15 nm
5. Potato virus Y group: particle size from 720–770 nm × 15 nm
6. Beet yellows virus group: particle size 1250 nm × 10 nm.

PLRV, APLV, TBRV and TNV are isometric. AMV has bacilliform particles of at least four distinct lengths; the particles of PYDV are complex bacilliform or bullet-shaped (Gibbs, 1969); and PSTV has the properties of a free nucleic acid. Thus most potato viruses are elongated and relatively long.

The length of the particles can be estimated from electron micrographs by allowing for magnification.

The magnification, however, is seldom accurately known. Usually it is set according to the current flowing in the lens coils without allowing for the magnetic condition of the lens, so that it cannot be calibrated better than about 5%. The magnification given by the manufacturers may fluctuate by 10%.

The variation between mounts in distance from the objective may yield an uncertainty in magnification of another 5%. Shrinkage of the photographic paper, used for preparing enlargements of the pictures, may further increase the unreliability.

For many purposes such uncertainty can be tolerated. However, for measurement of virus particles the magnification should be calibrated more accurately against a standard (Section 6.3.2). The virus particles can be measured as follows. From the micrographs, prints are made at a magnification of 40 000 by using a standard photographed at the same magnification and time as the virus preparations. The virus particles are measured on the prints with a ruler and sorted into 1-mm ranges of length, which is equivalent to 25 nm. At least a hundred particles should be measured (Brandes, 1964). A histogram is drawn of the length groups. From the length groups (five to eight) around the peak, the arithmetic mean can be calculated. This average is called normal length. The (normal) length of most rod-shaped viruses is known.

6.3.2 Standards for calibrating magnification

Latex spheres or virus particles. A suspension of latex spheres of known diameter (260 nm) or of TMV particles (length 300 nm) are mixed with the preparation to be examined on the grid. From the size of the polystyrene latex particles or TMV particles, the size of the unknown virus can be calculated in any enlargement of the electron micrograph.

However to estimate the average length of TMV, at least a hundred particles should be measured, since TMV particles vary in length, as also do polystyrene latex spheres. Moreover the size of the spheres on the grids depends on drying of the specimen and on the intensity of the electron beam.

Lattice spacing of crystals. In electron microscopes of high resolution various crystal-lattice spacings have been used as size standards. Negatively stained catalase crystals have readily visible lattice spacings. However the crystals dissolve rapidly on mixing with the material under study. With glutaraldehyde fixation, the catalase crystals are more stable and are suitable as a calibration standard in the magnfication range 10 000 to 150 000 (Wrigley, 1968).

Replica of diffraction grating. Gratings of very fine line spacings (54 864 per inch) are now used for calibration. The specimen and the replica are photographed at the same magnification directly after each other. From the known distance between the lines of the replica on the enlarged micrograph, the magnification can be calculated. However an uncertainty of about 5% remains by variation in the specimen-to-objective distance.

82

6.3.3 Virus particle counts

A good method of counting has been developed by Backus & Williams (1950). Equal volumes of virus suspension and a known latex suspension are mixed and sprayed onto grids. Patterns containing virus particles and latex spheres are formed on the grids corresponding with the droplets sprayed onto the grids. In each droplet virus and latex particles are counted. The ratio between the types of particles in the droplets equals their ratio in the suspensions and the concentration of the latex suspension is known, so that the concentration of the virus suspension can be calculated.

6.4 Use in diagnosis

The electron microscope gives much information on size, shape and structure of the virus particles. By the techniques described, the virus particles can be made visible (Fig. 18) and their size estimated. The size of the particles is characteristic for the type of virus (Section 6.3) and is used for its identification. By the dip method (Section 6.2.3), virus particles could be deposited on the grid rapidly but shadow-casting of the preparations always made it too complicated for a routine test.

Combination of the dip method with negative staining of the specimens greatly simplifies electron-microscopy. There are various modifications of this method, e.g. a cut surface of virus-containing leaves or stripped epidermal layers are dipped in a droplet of 2% potassium phosphotungstate solution of pH 6.5 on a Formvar film-coated copper grid for 4 sec. Two minutes after dipping, the excess fluid is soaked up with filter paper and the specimen is ready for examination with the electron microscope. Instead of cut virus-containing leaves, sap or diluted sap of those leaves can be mixed with equal parts of phosphotungstate stain. Or a piece of virus-containing material is brought into a droplet of phosphotungstate and chopped with a razor blade. A Pasteur pipette leaves behind the debris and the liquid is deposited on the grid.

As shown in Figure 19, electron-microscopy with the dip method and negative staining is more sensitive than serology for the detection of PVM and PVS. It is a little less sensitive than or as sensitive as the local-lesion host 'A6' for detection of various isolates of PVY. However isometric viruses cannot be detected easily; PLRV, probably due to its low concentration in the plant, cannot be detected at all by common procedures of electron-microscopy.

As well as for detection of viruses in living plant material, the electron microscope can be used to check samples of virus suspensions during purification. Step by step, the virus preparation can be checked quickly for the presence of virus particles. It gives immediate information, unlike test plants or serology.

In conclusion, the electron microscope is highly suitable for identification of plant viruses.

Although the electron microscope is more sensitive than serology for the detection of PVM and PVS and nearly equal to that of test plants for indexing PVY, it is not yet widely used for routine indexing of those viruses. This is due to the

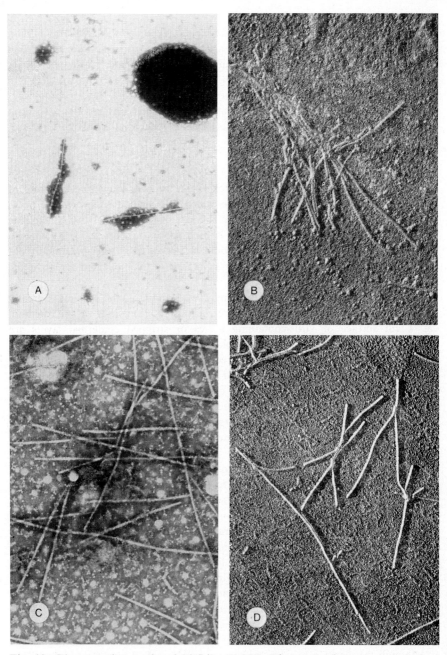

Fig. 18. Electron micrographs of PVS ($\times$ 40 000). Dip preparation negatively stained with phosphotungstate (A), dip preparation shadow-cast (B), purified preparation negatively stained (C) and purified preparation shadow-cast (D).

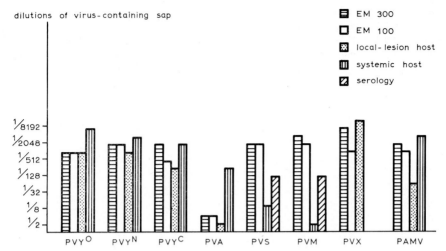

Fig. 19. Sensitivity of electron-microscopy with the dip method and negative staining against that of serology and reaction of test plants on indexing of various potato viruses in sap dilutions. EM 300: Philips electron microscope EM 300. EM 100: Philips electron microscope EM 100. Local-lesion host PAMV, PVA and PVY: detached 'A6' leaves. Local-lesion host PVX: *Gomphrena globosa*. Systemic host PAMV, PVA and PVY: *Nicotiana tabacum* 'White Burley'. Systemic host PVM and PVS: *Nicotiana debneyi*.

fact that the procedure is still too time-consuming with electron microscopes which contain specimen holders with one grid.

However new types of electron microscopes (Associated Electrical Industries International/E 801 and Siemens Elmiskop 51) have specimen holders that accommodate six to fifteen specimens at one loading and should allow quicker handling. Applications of the electron microscope in diagnosis of viruses are likely to increase in the future.

6.5 Further reading

Backus, R. C. & R. C. Williams, 1950. The use of spraying methods and of volatile suspending media in the preparation of specimens for electron microscopy. J. appl. Phys. 21: 11–15.

Brandes, J., 1964. Identifizierung von gestreckten pflanzenpathogenen Viren auf morphologischer Grundlage. Mitt. biol. BundAnst. Ld- u. Forstw. 110: 5–130.

Brandes, J., 1967. Electron microscopy of plant viruses bibliography 1939–1965. Mitt. biol. BundAnst. Ld- u. Forstw. 112: 1–91.

Gibbs, A., 1969. Plant virus classification. Adv. Virus Res. 14: 263–328.

Hall, C. E., 1964. Electron microscopy. Principles and application to virus research. In: M. K. Corbett & H. D. Sisler (eds), Plant virology. Univ. Fla Press, Gainesville, p. 253–266.

Hitchborn, J. H. & G. J. Hills, 1965. The use of negative staining in the electron microscopic examination of plant viruses in crude extracts. Virology 27: 528–540.

Juniper, B. E., G. C. Cox, A. J. Gilchrist & P. R. Williams, 1970. Techniques for plant electron microscopy. Blackwell, Oxford; Edinburgh, 108 p.

Kay, D., 1961. Techniques for electron microscopy. Blackwell, Oxford, 331 p.

Wrigley, N. G., 1968. The lattice spacing of crystalline catalase as an internal standard of length in electron microscopy. J. Ultrastruct. Res. 24: 454–464.

7 Serology

D. H. M. van Slogteren

Serological methods are based on reactions between antigens and antibodies. When injected into the body of an animal, antigens cause the formation of specific antibodies, which are proteins of the γ-globulin type. Antibodies are part of the defence system of the body against pathogens but they form also when antigens are artificially introduced. In vitro, outside the animal body, antibodies can react by flocculating with their corresponding antigens and can therefore be used as highly specific reagents. After formation in special cells in the body, antibodies pass into the blood, being present in blood serum, the fluid left after standing blood has clotted. Blood serum containing specific antibodies is called antiserum.

A prerequisite of antigens is a sufficiently large molecule. Macromolecules such as nucleoproteins, including many plant viruses, are good antigens. The antigenicity of plant viruses is determined by 'antigenic determinants', chemical groupings on the protein coating which envelopes the nucleic acid.

Both antigens and antibodies carry polar groups that make them completely soluble in water. The flocculation that takes place when antigen and antibody combine can be explained by mutual binding of their polar groups. As this process blocks the polarities, the antigen-antibody complex becomes insoluble and precipitates.

7.1 Production of antisera
To make antisera against plant viruses, as a rule rabbits are used. When much antiserum is needed (e.g. for indexing programmes of seed potatoes), horses and sheep have sometimes been used.

7.1.1 Preparation of antigen suspensions for injection
Virus suspensions should have been sufficiently purified to avoid adverse response of the animals to toxins in plant sap. As a rule partially purified virus suspensions contain antigens from the host plant, host antigens, that are shared by all plant species. Consequently antisera resulting from injection of such suspensions contain antibodies against host antigens as well as antibodies against the virus. The host-specific antibodies may give rise to misleading positive reactions when plants are tested serologically for presence of virus. Fortunately many plant viruses produce antibodies better than host antigens do, so that antisera generally show

higher titres against the virus than against host antigens. For most practical purposes, antisera are 'absorbed' with sap from virus-free plants (Section 7.1.5) to precipitate host-specific antibodies before using the antisera in tests for virus. For special purposes, antisera entirely free from host-specific antibodies can be obtained by injecting highly purified virus suspensions into animals.

Before injection, virus preparations should be made isotonic by adding NaCl to make a 0.85% solution.

7.1.2   Immunization procedures

Rabbits 9 to 24 months old are preferred. As not all rabbits are equally good producers of antibody, at least three should be injected with each type of antigen. Antigen may be injected by different routes: intravenously, subcutaneously, intramuscularly or intraperitoneally.

Intravenous injection may in rabbits be into the external marginal vein of the ear, which runs parallel to the hind edge and about 4 mm from it along the upper surface. Figure 20 shows the position of this vein, the antigen suspension being injected with a 2-ml or 5-ml syringe and a 25-gauge hypodermic needle. The needle should be inserted in the direction of flow in the vein which is towards the base of the ear, the initial injection being made near the tip and later injections progressively nearer the base, to avoid scar tissue. As blood samples are usually taken from the ear as well, one ear should be used for injections, the other for sampling. If a vein does not obtrude enough for the needle to be inserted after rubbing it with cotton wool dipped in 70% ethanol, a little xylene may be applied but must be washed off afterwards with ethanol to avoid irritation.

Experience is needed to insert the needle properly. The ear is held in the left hand, the thumb supporting the needle at the point of entry during the injection. The needle is placed, bevel upwards, at an angle of less than 45° to the upper surface of the ear. Once inserted in the vein, it is brought horizontal with the surface of the ear. Moving the tip a little further, the plunger of the syringe can be pushed gently down without any resistance being felt and as the liquid slowly enters, the vein visibly dilates. Any resistance to flow indicates that the needle is not in the vein. If so, further pressure would force the injection fluid into the perivascular tissue and spoil the ear for later injections.

Many different schemes for intravenous injections have been used. When only a little antigen is available, this should be injected in several small doses rather than the total amount in one dose. If an animal that has been treated with a primary course of injections later receives a secondary injection, called a booster, its antibody production often increases considerably. Results should be satisfactory if from 8 to 16 injections are distributed over a period of 2 to 4 weeks. The total dose injected may range from less than 10 mg up to 200 mg of virus per rabbit. As a rule graded successive doses, increasing from 0.5 ml up to a maximum of 8 ml, are injected. Rozendaal & van Slogteren (1958) prepared antisera against PVM by injecting partially purified virus suspensions concentrated about nine times by giving eight intravenous injections over a period of 11 days. They in-

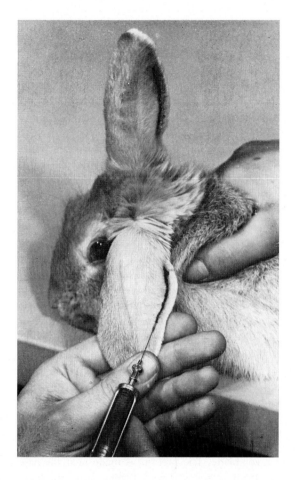

Fig. 20. Intravenous injection into the external marginal vein of the ear of a rabbit. The vein is outlined in Indian ink. (From van der Veken et al., 1962.)

jected 2, 4, 6, 8, 8, 8, 8 and 8 ml on successive days except for one-day gaps after the first, fourth and sixth injection. The resulting antisera taken 10 days after the last injection showed precipitin titres of 1 : 2 560.

Subcutaneous and intraperitoneal injections are seldom used for preparing anti-sera against plant viruses. Subcutaneous injections are sometimes used in desen-sitizing procedures to prevent anaphylactic shock if there has been a lapse of 3 days or more between intravenous injections.

Intramuscular injections with virus antigens emulsified in Freund's adjuvant oil have been used increasingly in recent years. With small doses of antigen, the antibody response is better than with intravenous injections. It takes about twice as long for antibodies to reach maximum concentration in 6 weeks against 3 weeks for intravenous injection. But antibodies often remain longer at the same level if the virus is stable. Various authors have found that antibodies remain constant and high for 3 months in rabbits injected intramuscularly with PVS in adjuvant. This method of immunization requires smaller doses of antigen (1–10 mg). Both the incomplete and the complete form of Freund's adjuvant oil, the latter containing killed mycobacteria, are commercially available. No difference between the two forms has been found in their efficacy to stimulate production of antibodies against plant viruses. Before injection of the antigen preparation, it must be thoroughly emulsified into the adjuvant oil, e.g. by alternatively sucking up and ejecting the mixture with a syringe with a short 18-gauge needle. One or two millilitres emulsion is injected intramuscularly into each hind leg of a rabbit.

Combinations of different routes of injection have been used to obtain a still greater antibody response. It has not been established which injection scheme or combination of injection routes is best. Comparisons are difficult because exact data on the amounts of injected virus are scarce and because individual animals vary in response to different antigens.

7.1.3   Taking blood from rabbits

Before taking blood, the rabbits should be starved for at least 12 hours to decrease lipid in the blood. If the antibody titre of a small sample, taken on the 6th day after the last injection of a course of intravenous injections is sufficiently high, a large amount of blood can be drawn 2 or 3 days later. If the titre is still too low for the purpose, the injection scheme must be resumed. After intramuscular injection with adjuvant, the rise in titre of samples taken after 4, 5 or 6 weeks indicates when larger amounts should be taken. About 40 ml blood can be taken from the external marginal vein of the ear (Fig. 20).

During the operation the rabbit can be secured in a special box or must be held by an assistant. To promote blood flow, the ear is rubbed with 70% ethanol before bleeding. It may be helpful to clamp the vein with a clothes-peg padded with cotton wool, placed between the base of the ear and the place to be punc-tured. After the area has been shaved and washed with 70% ethanol, a small cut is made in the vein with a sharp razor blade. The first cut is made near the base of the ear, later samples are taken from cuts successively further from the base. While drawing blood, the ear is held vein downwards over a glass tube to receive the blood. When enough has been taken, the clamp is moved to the other side of the bleeding area and bleeding is stopped by firmly pressing a wad of cotton wool over the puncture, whereupon the wound can be sealed with some Collodion dissolved in ethanol and ether. Rabbits may be bled of about 40 ml blood on each of 3 successive days. They can be bled once more a week later. A further series may be taken 4 weeks later after another course of injections.

7.1.4   Separation of serum

The collected blood is left for several hours at room temperature to clot, after which the clot is loosened from the wall of the tube with a glass rod. The tube is then kept at about 3°C for about 24 h for the clot to contract. Serum can be periodically decanted off or removed with a pipette. The final aliquots may require centrifuging to remove red blood cells.

7.1.5 Absorption of antisera

As mentioned in Section 7.1.1, antisera prepared by injection with partially puri-fied virus suspensions may contain host-specific antibodies as well as virus anti-bodies. The unwanted antibodies can be removed by adding their antigens; this procedure is called 'absorption'. According to the titre of host-specific antibodies, antisera against elongated potato viruses are usually absorbed with 4 to 9 volumes of sap from virus-free potato leaves. The mixture is incubated at 37°C for 2 h. It is then kept at about 5°C for at least 8 h (or overnight) and cleared by slow centrifuging, e.g. 10 min at 6 000 r.p.m. (3 800 g). The resulting supernatant (absorbed antiserum) can be used to test plants for the particular virus or it can be freeze-dried for later use.

Absorption with plant sap to some extent dilutes antiserum and introduces foreign substances which for special purposes (e.g. in some gel-diffusion tech-niques) may be undesirable. If so, absorption can be made with smaller amounts of purified concentrated preparations of plant proteins.

7.1.6 Storage of antisera

Serum can be stored frozen at $-15°$ to $-25°C$ in small glass bottles. As too frequent thawing and refreezing is destructive, serum should be stored in moderate amounts, i.e. the average weekly consumption. The full content of a bottle must be thawed and thoroughly mixed before taking out the desired amount. As sera are not sterile, merthiolate or sodium azide should be added to final concentra-tions of 1 : 10 000 and 1 : 5 000, respectively.

Antisera may also be efficiently preserved by freeze-drying in ampoules that can be sealed. Freeze-dried serum keeps for a long time when warm and is there-fore specially convenient for transport. For permanent storage, freeze-dried sera are best kept below freezing point.

7.2 Use of serology for identifying plant viruses

Different types of serological reactions can be distinguished. Only two will be mentioned. In the precipitin reaction (Section 7.2.1–2), the bond between the two reactants, antigen and antibody, causes a visible precipitate of antigen-antibody complex to form.

In the agglutination reaction (Section 7.2.3), small particles (e.g. blood corpus-cles, chloroplasts or other particulate materials, either attached to antigen or anti-body) take part in the flocculation. In virus-infected potato plants, chloroplasts carry virus antigens on their surface. When crude sap of such plants is mixed with antiserum to the virus, large aggregates of chloroplasts form, visible to the naked eye.

Agglutination methods have recently been developed, in which antibodies are linked artificially to particles of latex, bentonite or barium sulphate. The particles flocculate if the corresponding antigen is added to the system (Bercks, 1967). However this method has not yet been introduced for routine detection of potato viruses.

7.2.1 Precipitin tests in tubes

Either cleared plant sap of suspensions of purified virus can be tested. Equal amounts (e.g. 0.5 or 1.0 ml) of virus suspension and of an appropriate dilution of antiserum are mixed in glass tubes about 7 mm in diameter. Different dilutions of each reagent should be tried to avoid failure to precipitate through excess of either antigen or antibody. For cleared sap, the temperature should not exceed 37°C, the tubes being placed in a temperature-controlled waterbath. If the fluid columns in the tubes are half-immersed in the water, precipitation is accelerated by convection currents. Readings are made at intervals, the interval between the mixing of antigen and antibody and the appearance of the precipitate being briefest in the tube where the ratio of the concentrations of the reagents is optimum.

7.2.2 Precipitin tests in droplets

Various precipitin tests in droplets have become common practice, because they economize on antisera and because their results have proved as accurate as for the tube tests. Their sensitivity is increased by taking readings under the microscope with dark-field illumination at magnification $\times 60$ to $\times 100$. This allows the detection of minor precipitates, which are of particular interest in quantitative studies of dilution end-point.

The precipitin test on slides is described by Wetter (1965) as follows: on a microscope slide, aliquots of 0.03 to 0.05 ml of antiserum and of a clear sample of the antigen are pipetted side by side and the droplets are mixed with a glass rod. The slide is then incubated at 25°C at high humidity for 20 to 50 min (incubation time depending on the virus). The precipitate is then observed under the microscope with dark-field illumination at a magnification of $\times 80$ to $\times 100$.

The micro-precipitin test under paraffin oil, introduced in 1955, has the advantage that evaporation of the mixed droplets is avoided completely. Reactions can therefore be initiated with antiserum droplets of about 0.007 ml and incubation can be extended to periods of 3 h or longer at any desired temperature. The test is carried out in a Petri dish whose inner glass surface has been coated with polyvinylformaldehyde (Formvar). An equally suitable polyvinyl compound is available under the name Mowital B 30 H. The glass is coated by pouring a 1% solution of either polyvinyl compound in chloroform into a dry Petri dish, emptying it immediately into the next dish to be coated, and so on. The thin film which remains is left to dry for about 8 h. A Pasteur pipette with a finely drawn out point is used to place small droplets of the antiserum in rows on the bottom of the dish and droplets of clear plant sap or of virus suspension are added. About 150 microtests can be made with 1 ml dilute antiserum. By placing the Petri dish on paper with squares of 8 × 8 mm (Fig. 21), the droplets can be put in straight rows. The hydrophobic property of the polyvinyl coating keeps the mixed droplets from spreading over the glass surface when paraffin oil is poured over them. Oozing of the droplets through small holes in the coating may occur if the chloroform solvent has not been quite water-free but can be prevented by

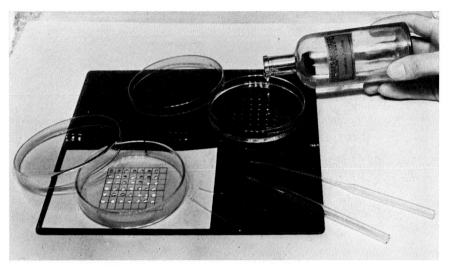
Fig. 21. Aids and appliances for serological microtests under paraffin oil.

silicone-coating the glass before applying the polyvinyl coating. The reactions can be observed at ×80 with a dark-field microscope. From 36 to 64 tests can be made in one Petri dish. Comparisons are eased if dilutions of antiserum and normal serum run in alternate rows.

7.2.3 Agglutination tests

These tests are based on serological reactions on the surface of larger particles and on the resulting clumping or agglutination of those particles. Thus particles sensitized with antigen are clumped by addition of antibody, those sensitized with antibody by addition of antigen.

The agglutination test depends on chloroplasts on whose surface viruses have been adsorbed. In the slide agglutination test, five drops of diluted antiserum are mixed on a glass slide with two drops of crude sap from the plant to be tested. This test has been used for screening seed-potato stocks for PVX and PVS. The typical aggregation of the chloroplasts can be observed with a hand-lens or microscope at a magnification ×40 to × 60 with direct illumination.

The slide agglutination test has been modified into a micro-agglutination test under paraffin oil, a technique now used in the Netherlands for indexing potato plants for PVX, PVS and PVM. The microtest requires only about a thirtieth of the amount of antiserum needed for the slide test. A tiny bit of crude sap, pressed from leaves of the potato plant, is mingled with a rounded glass rod through a droplet of about 0.007 ml diluted antiserum pipetted onto the bottom of a poly-vinyl-coated Petri dish. For the same purpose, special dishes made entirely of polythene, not requiring additional coating have been used in recent years. As the volume of sap should be about a quarter of that of the antiserum, a convenient

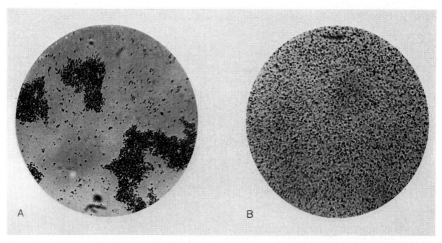

Fig. 22. Agglutination tests. Positive reaction, antiserum against PVX mixed with sap from potato leaves infected with PVX (A) and negative reaction, antiserum against PVX mixed with sap from virus-free potato leaves (B).

procedure is to dip the rounded end of a thin glass rod once or twice in the sap and thoroughly stir it in the antiserum droplet. Although very little sap is needed, it is important that the leaves are completely pressed as more virus is expelled from the crushed plant cells at the second pressing than at the first. As soon as about 36 to 49 reactions have been laid out in a dish, the mixed droplets are slowly covered with paraffin oil. Particularly in agglutination tests, paraffin should be poured in slowly. Dishes should be incubated at 20°–25°C and the reaction can be observed every half hour. Sap with PVX agglutinates rapidly. Chloroplasts flocculate visibly in about 15 min. PVM and PVS require at least half an hour. Often a mixed antiserum against PVM, PVS and PVX is used, so the reaction needs checking after at least half an hour and not more than 2 h. Tap the dish slightly to enhance the visibility of the floating aggregates, especially in test for PVM and PVS, since aggregates may be minute. The flocculation of PVX is readily visible. Figure 22 shows a positive and a negative agglutination reaction as seen through the microscope.

7.2.4 Gel-diffusion tests
In this type of serological test, antigens and antibodies are made to diffuse towards each other in a layer of agar gel. Agar layers about 2 mm thick are poured into a plastic Petri dish or onto microscope slides. Wells 2 to 5 mm diameter can be punched out from the agar layer with a small cork borer. The cylinders of agar thus loosened can be sucked out with a pipette. For this technique, clear pectin-free agar is now commercially available. The concentrations of agar most commonly used range from 0.8 to 1.0%. Serological reactions show up as lines of

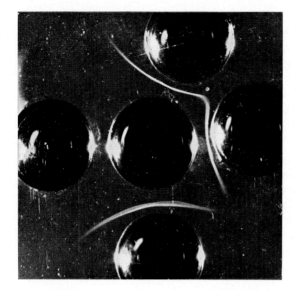

Fig. 23. Gel diffusion in agar. Antiserum against **PVX** has been pipetted into the centre well, sap from PVX-infected tobacco into both the bottom and the top-right wells. The left well contains a preparation from virus-free tobacco. Precipitates are visible as lines between the centre well and those containing PVX antigens, slightly curving around the side wells. As the top and right well were made closer to each other, their precipitation lines fuse.

precipitation in the gel between the wells containing antigen and antibody. Where the line of precipitate forms depends on the diffusion coefficients of the reagents and on the ratio of their concentrations in the agar medium. In the line the ratio is nearest to its optimum, a sharp line indicating that the conditions of the optimum ratio are fulfilled whereas a more diffuse line or band indicates that one of the reagents is in excess.

Two or more wells can be arranged around a central well with antiserum. Fusion of the lines formed when two antigens diffuse from adjacent wells towards a third well containing antibody indicates that the two antigens are serologically related.

For further details on the interpretation of different line patterns and on the theoretical background of agar double-diffusion (Ouchterlony) tests, see van der Veken et al. (1962) and van Regenmortel (1966).

The gel-diffusion test is most suitable for isometric viruses and rod-shaped viruses with lengths up to about 600 nm. Less satisfactory results with flexible elongated viruses may be attributed to a low diffusion coefficient and to their tendency to form aggregates. Ball et al. (1964) obtained sharp precipitation lines with purified preparations of PVX but only when aggregation was minimized by making the preparations in citrate phosphate buffer of pH 8.0. I have observed precipitation lines with PVX in crude sap of infected plants (Fig. 23). More recently elongated plant viruses have been degraded by different procedures into fragments suitable for serological analysis by gel-diffusion methods (Purcifull & Shepherd, 1964).

The single radial-diffusion technique has now become interesting to plant virologists. Antiserum at the proper dilution is mixed with liquid agar and poured into Petri dishes. The antigen is placed in wells cut in the gel and diffuses radially into the gel. Around the wells, rings of precipitate form. The test works with PVM, PVS and PVX. The procedure depends on degradation of the virus into serologically active fragments (Shepard et al., 1971).

7.2.5 Serological relationships between plant viruses
Antisera have been prepared against all potato viruses except PLRV. Serological test (Sections 7.2.1–4) provide a useful criterion for establishing whether two virus isolates are related.

To demonstrate that two viruses are serologically unrelated, good antisera must be prepared against each of them. It must be shown that each isolate reacts with its own antiserum (homologous reaction) but gives no reaction with the other antiserum (heterologous reaction). There are examples of virus strains which are always present in plant sap at too low a concentration to react serologically in vitro but still produce a fair amount of specific antibody, if injected into the rabbit at the same low concentration. Hence reciprocal testing is necessary since two virus isolates may be related serologically but one of them may be at too low a concentration.

The titre of an antiserum influences its specificity, the amount of antibody responsible for cross-reactions being increased by the number and frequency of injections. Thus in studying close serological relationships between strains of PVX, antisera obtained after a single injection with a relatively low titre of about 1 : 512 are preferable. But to establish distant serological relationships, e.g. between PVM and PVS, high-titred antisera should be used, produced over long periods by repetitive injection.

With due precautions, serological tests also give some estimate of the relationship between virus strains. For this purpose the cross-absorption test must be used. Absorb antiserum against isolate A (Section 7.1.5) with a preparation of isolate B. Likewise absorb antiserum against isolate B with isolate A. After ensuring that all antibodies against the respective heterologous antigens have been removed, both antisera are then tested with their homologous antigens. If the two virus isolates are related but distinct, reactions will occur between the absorbed antisera and their homologous antigens after absorption. For further information about how to measure the amounts of antibodies reacting with homologous and heterologous antigens, in the cross-absorption test, see Matthews (1957) and van der Veken et al. (1962), respectively.

7.3 Factors influencing precipitin reactions

7.3.1 Purity
For precipitin tests reactions should be carried out with clear virus suspensions free from particulate materials. Sap of infected plants cleared by slow centrifuging, for instance 10 min at about 5 600 g or 30 min at about 1 000 g or purified virus preparations should be used.

7.3.2 Concentration

For a visible reaction, each reagent must exceed a certain concentration. The titre of an antiserum indicates the final dilution still producing a visible reaction with a given dilution of antigen. The final dilution of an antigen reacting with a given dilution of antiserum is the dilution end-point of the antigen. Titres of antisera and dilution end-points of antigen suspensions are a measure of the ratio of antibody and antigen, allowing comparison of these amounts in different solutions. Thus an antiserum with a titre of 1 : 4 000 for a given dilution of antigen contains ten times as much antibody as an antiserum with a titre of 1 : 400 for the same antigen dilution. An antigen solution with a dilution end-point of 1 : 64 is eight times stronger than that with a dilution end-point of 1 : 8.

Plant viruses can be regarded as polyvalent antigens, possessing numerous reactive sites capable of binding antibody molecules. Antibodies are assumed to be bivalent, each combining with two antigen molecules, e.g. virus molecules. According to Marrack's lattice theory (see van der Veken et al., 1962), specific precipitates consist of multivalent antigen particles linked together by bivalent antibodies, whereby a lattice is formed increasing in size over a range of proportions of the reagents. If one of the reagents is too much in excess, the other reactant will be completely locked in small aggregates, which cannot combine into a lattice. These small aggregates will remain soluble, no visible precipitate being formed as is illustrated in Figure 24. Thus, whether an aggregation or lattice is visible or not in precipitin reactions does not depend on the concentration of either antigen or antibody but on the ratio of the concentrations.

7.3.3 Zone phenomenon

If increasing amounts of antigen are added to a constant amount of antiserum, the amounts of precipitate formed can be plotted in a curve as shown in Figure 25.

This curve distinguishes three zones.

1. The zone of antibody excess which contains precipitate and free antibody.
2. The zone of equivalence in which all antigen and antibody are combined in the precipitate, no free molecules of either reagent remaining in solution.
3. The zone of antigen excess which contains precipitate and free antigen.

No precipitate is formed if there is an extreme excess of antigen and, in some systems, with an extreme excess of antibody. In Figure 25 the time needed for precipitation is indicated by the dotted line. The equivalence zone with an optimum ratio of concentrations of antigen and antibody is characterized by most rapid precipitation. When different dilutions of antigen are mixed with one dilution of antiserum, the dilution of the antigen giving rise to the most rapid precipitation indicates the α optimum which is constant for a given batch of antiserum. If an antiserum at a dilution 1 : 10 precipitates most rapidly with antigen diluted 1 : 100, the same antiserum diluted 1 : 20 will do so with antigen diluted 1 : 200. A practical consequence of the zone phenomenon is that, at least at the beginning of a testing programme, precipitin tests must be carried out with various concentrations of antigen and antibody in order to find out which ratio of the

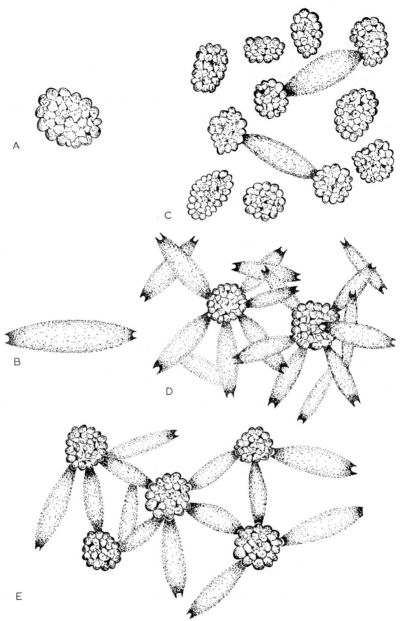

Fig. 24. Diagram of the combination of the polyvalent antigen (A) and bivalent anti-body (B) molecules to form soluble complexes or an insoluble lattice. At antigen excess (C) and antibody excess (D) soluble invisible complexes are formed. Antigen and anti-body in optimum proportions (E) for formation of a visible insoluble lattice. (After Cushing and Campbell, 1957; with permission of McGraw-Hill Book Company.)

total amount of precipitate   time for precipitation

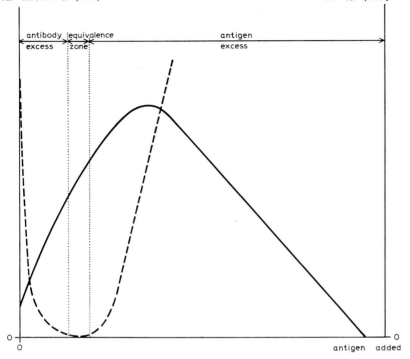

Fig. 25. Scheme of the relationships between time for precipitation, total amount of precipitate and equivalence zone. – – – –: time for precipitation; ————: amount of precipitate. (After Matthews, 1957; with permission of Cambridge University Press.)

concentrations is near to the equivalence zone. As the curve shows, the maximum amount of precipitate is not formed in the equivalence zone but in the region of antigen excess. This holds for some virus antigens, e.g. TMV. For other viruses, the point of maximum precipitation is near the equivalence zone.

7.3.4 Presence of salt, pH and temperature
As electrolytes must be present in the medium for serological reactions, a 0.85% NaCl solution is usually used for making up the dilutions of both antigen and antiserum.

In testing plant extracts, the pH should be between 6.5 and 7.5 as plant sap may contain substances which, especially at low pH, could cause spontaneous flocculation (Section 7.3.5).

For indexing viruses in cleared sap, incubation temperatures are usually between 30° and 37°C. The warmer the solution, the more rapidly it precipitates. With stable viruses in purified preparations, incubation temperatures up to 50°C are sometimes used.

7.3.5 Spontaneous flocculation

Various substances in plant extracts may cause spontaneous or non-specific precipitation, thus obscuring specific precipitates in serological reactions. Attempts to find the causal contaminants are often impeded by the haphazardness of spontaneous flocculation. Formation of non-specific precipitates depends on factors such as the species of the plant, its age and growth conditions. Addition of adequate buffer solutions during extraction of plant species, whose sap has a pH below 5.5 may prevent spontaneous flocculation. The adverse effect of the formation of brown pigments by oxidative enzymes (e.g. in testing mature potato plants) can be prevented by including 0.5% Na_2SO_3 and 1.5% Na_2HPO_4 in the extractive medium. Spontaneous flocculation often increases at high temperatures, used to speed up serological reactions. When plant sap is incubated at 37°C for 30 min before centrifuging, non-specific precipitates form and can be removed by centrifuging.

7.3.6 Control tests

To be aware of non-specific or spontaneous reactions, in each test series, the necessary controls should be included: a mixture of the sap to be tested with normal serum (similarly diluted as the antiserum); a mixture of antiserum and sap of a virus-free sample of the plant species tested for the presence of virus. Positive reactions in the tests with antiserum are reliable only if the controls do not flocculate.

7.4 Conclusions

In conclusion, the serological techniques are ideal for the detection of PVM, PVS and PVX. The best results are obtained if the juice of infected foliage is examined. Although, according to published data, potato viruses can be detected by serological methods in the sap of infected sprouts and tubers, it is not yet routine because of the time it takes to clear the sap. For the same reason the General Netherlands Inspection Service (NAK) prefers the agglutination test to the precipitin test for the detection of potato viruses (Chap. 17).

7.5 Further reading

Ball, Ellen M., 1964. Serology: techniques used in plant virus research. In: M. K. Corbett & H. D. Sisler (eds), Plant virology. Univ. Fla Press, Gainesville, p. 235–252.

Bercks, R., 1967. Methodische Untersuchungen über den serologischen Nachweis pflanzenpathogener Viren mit dem Bentonit-Flockungstest, dem Latex-Test und dem Bariumsulfat-Test. Phytopath. Z. 58: 1–17.

Cushing, J. E. & D. H. Campbell, 1957. Principles of immunology. McGraw-Hill, New York, 344 p.

Matthews, R. E. F., 1957. Plant virus serology. Cambridge Univ. Press, Cambridge, 128 p.

Purcifull, D. E. & R. J. Shepherd, 1964. Preparation of the protein fragments of several rod-shaped plant viruses and their use in agar-gel diffusion tests. Phytopathology 54: 1102–1108.

Regenmortel, M. H. V. van, 1966, Plant virus serology. Adv. Virus Res. 12: 207–271.

Rozendaal, A. & D. H. M. van Slogteren, 1958. A potato virus identified with potato virus M and its relationship with potato virus S. Proc. 3rd Conf. Potato Virus Dis., Lisse-Wageningen 1957, p. 20–36.

Shepard, J. F., J. W. Jutila, J. E. Catlin, F. S. Newman & W. H. Hawkins, 1971. Immunodiffusion assay for potato virus M infection. Phytopathology 61: 873–874.

Slogteren, D. H. M. van, 1969. Analytical serology of plant viruses. In: J. B. G. Kwapinski (ed.), Interscience publishers, New York, p. 353–409.

Slogteren, E. van & D. H. M. van Slogteren, 1957. Serological identification of plant viruses and serological diagnosis of virus diseases of plants. A. Rev. Microbiol. 11: 149–164.

Veken, J. A. van der, D. H. M. van Slogteren & J. P. H. van der Want, 1962. Immunological methods. In: H. F. Linskens & M. V. Tracey (eds), Modern methods of plant analysis 5. Springer Verlag, Berlin, p. 422–463.

Wetter, C., 1965. Serology in virus disease diagnosis. A. Rev. Phytopath. 3: 19–42.

8   Test plants

J. A. de Bokx

Many potato varieties react to virus infection with clear symptoms, e.g. the mosaic of PVY^O and rolling of PLRV (Sections 10.2.2 and 10.2.6). The deviations are sometimes characteristic of a certain virus.

Looking for symptoms has been and still is the oldest, cheapest and easiest way of indexing a potato crop.

The seed-potato grower scrutinizes his crop for diseased plants and rogues them. The inspector classifies the crop according to the number of plants with symptoms. However sometimes, because of weather conditions, not all plants show symptoms. Other means, such as serology (Chap. 7) and test plants, must then be used to detect virus.

8.1   Types of test plant
Particularly for diagnosing sap-transmissible viruses, lesions on specially selected hosts (test plants or indicator plants) are often used.

Two types of test plants are common: those that develop systemic symptoms after inoculation and those that develop local lesions. Local lesions often consist of necrotic or chlorotic spots or rings.

8.1.1   Systemic hosts
Systemic symptoms only appear after the virus has spread to uninoculated parts of the plants. They are often less pronounced than local lesions. *Nicotiana tabacum* develops systemic symptoms after inoculation with various potato viruses, such as PVA, PVX and PVY. Differences between strains of viruses on this test plant cannot always be observed, except between PVY^N and PVY^O. The first produces characteristic symptoms on the leaves of tobacco: necrosis of the veins and midrib, the second mosaic only.

8.1.2   Local-lesion hosts
If an inoculated test plant reacts with local lesions, there are often no systemic symptoms. Exceptional are the reactions of the clone 'A6' (*Solanum demissum* × *Solanum tuberosum* 'Aquila') and *Physalis floridana* Rydb. after inoculation with PVY^O. Both local and systemic necrosis develop after inoculation of those test plants. However detached leaves from various local-lesion hosts can be used for

102

Fig. 26. Local lesions on *Gomphrena globosa* 12 days after inoculation with PVX.

Fig. 27. Local lesions on 'A6' 5 days after inoculation with PVA (A), PVX (B) and
PVY^N (C).

inoculation. Detached leaves have the advantage that many samples can easily be
tested routinely. Detached leaves are used for detection of potato viruses and for
other viruses.

Many test plants are not specific in their reaction. *Gomphrena globosa* L.,
local-lesion host for PVX (Fig. 26), also develops local lesions after inoculation
with some strains of PVM, TBRV and with papaw mild mosaic virus. *Chenopodium amaranticolor* Coste et Reyn is a local-lesion host for PVY^O, CMV and pea
enation mosaic virus. *Tetragonia expansa* Murr. develops local lesions after inoculation with PVY^O and PAMV, and also after inoculation with anemone brown
ring virus, anemone mosaic strain of turnip mosaic virus, beet ringspot strain of

103

Table 3. Test plants developing local lesions after inoculation with various potato viruses.

	AMV	PAMV	PMTV	PVA	PVM	PVS	PVX	PVY	TMV	TRV
Capsicum annuum		+					+			
Cassia occidentalis							+			
Chenopodium album				+	+					
Chenopodium amaranticolor			(+)	+	(+)			(+)		
Chenopodium quinoa				+	(+)					
Cyamopsis tetragonolobus				(+)	(+)					
Datura metel				+						
Datura stramonium							(+)			
Gomphrena globosa	+	(+)			(+)	(+)	+			
Lycium barbarum								+		
Lycium chinense								+		
Lycium rhombifolium								+		
Nicandra physaloides				(+)						
Nicotiana glutinosa									+	
Nicotiana tabacum										+
Phaseolus vulgaris	+	(+)			(+)					
Physalis floridana				(+)				+		
Pisum sativum		+								
Solanum demissum 'A6'		+		+			(+)	+		
Solanum rostratum					+	+				
Vigna sinensis					+	+				

(+) = development of local lesions haphazard

TBRV, cabbage black ringspot strain of turnip mosaic virus, carnation mottle virus, AMV, tobacco severe etch strain of tobacco etch virus and bean yellow mosaic virus. *Chenopodium quinoa* Willd. develops local lesions after inoculation with PVS, bean yellow mosaic, clover yellow vein or apple chlorotic leafspot viruses.

The potato clone 'A6' develops local lesions after inoculation with many strains of PVA, PVY, including PVY^C, PVY^N and PVY^O, and some severe strains of PVX (Fig. 27).

Although local-lesion hosts are often not specific, they are most suitable for detection of a virus in a crop. Unfortunately test plants are not known for all potato viruses. Reliable ones for PVM and PVS are not available yet (Table 3).

It is also feasible to use test plants for identifying viruses exclusively transmitted by aphids. Thus the test plant *Physalis floridana* is used for PLRV transmitted by *Myzus persicae*. Fifteen to twenty days after viruliferous aphids have fed on them, plants develop interveinal yellowing and stunted growth. In view of the minor practical importance of this method, only those used for sap-transmitted viruses will be mentioned here.

8.2 Methods of inoculation

Before inoculation with sap, the test leaves are dusted with an abrasive. The abrasive causes extremely small wounds without the epidermal cells being injured so severely that they die. The small wounds allow the virus to enter the living epidermal cells of the plant.

Since sand was used as an abrasive for virus inoculation in the early thirties, much research has been done on inoculation. Usually carborundum powder (360–500 mesh) is used as an abrasive but also Celite (diatomaceous earth) can be used. A moderate dusting of abrasive can be applied to the test leaves with an insufflator (Fig. 28); a surplus of abrasive reduces the number of local lesions.

The inoculum (virus-containing sap) can be put onto the test leaves in different ways: with a cheesecloth pad, thumb or forefinger, glass spatula, plastic sponge or a brush. For routine inoculation of many plants, a spraygun can be used to advantage (Chap. 15).

Sap can be extracted from infectious plants with pestle and mortar or, if many plants must be tested, with a handpress or by a power-driven crusher (Fig. 29).

Rubbing the surface of infectious foliage, abraded with sandpaper, onto test leaves, called dry inoculation, is often adequate for infection (Fig. 28). Dry inoculation of 'A6' leaves with foliage containing PVA or PVY yields more lesions than inoculation by finger, glass spatula or plastic sponge. Cut potato tubers or squashed sprouts from potato tubers can be used as inoculum too.

The Rindite method (Section 17.3.4) is used for breaking dormancy when sprouts have to be tested. When the sprouts have reached a length of 1.5–2 cm, about 4 weeks after treatment, crush them and bring them against 'A6' leaves.

Fig. 28. Dry inoculation. Test leaves dusted with carborundum powder from an insufflator. Infectious foliage is rubbed and crushed on sandpaper and used for inoculation.

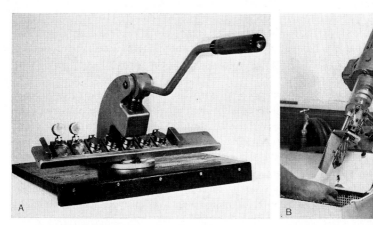

Fig. 29. Handpress (A) and power-driven crusher (B) suitable for extracting sap from leaves and sprouts.

Do not detach the sprouts from the tubers.

However sometimes after dry inoculation with cut tubers from plants with secondary infection, local lesions unaccountably do not develop on test leaves. Squashed sprouts from tubers infected with PVA or PVY used as inoculum yield as many local lesions on 'A6' leaves as after inoculation with crude sap.

The method is not much used, because little time is saved compared with the growing of plantlets from tubers (Section 17.3.4).

Various factors influence infection. The virus concentration may be too low, because of the developmental stage of plant or tuber. The sap may contain a compound that inhibits infection. Addition of buffers (often phosphate buffers) or nicotine sulphate may overcome the effect of such an inhibitor.

The infectivity of the virus in sap may be decreased by enzymic or oxidative reactions on exposure to the air. Addition of sodium sulphite (0.2%) or glycollic acid (0.1%) can reduce this effect (Chap. 5). Rinsing the test leaves after inoculation may sometimes increase and sometimes decrease the number of local lesions. Rinsing inoculated 'A6' leaves does not have any effect. Although rinsing cleans the abrasive off test leaves, droplets of water may transmit virus from one test leaf to another.

8.3   Factors in the susceptibility of test leaves

8.3.1   Variation within and between plants
On leaves from the top of 'A6' plants, there are few local lesions after inoculation with PVY. Leaves from the base also produce few lesions, although those lesions appear some days earlier than those on the top leaves. The lesions at the top are always smaller in diameter than at the base. Leaves midway up the stem have most lesions. Susceptibility depends also on the plant's stage of development. It is

high when the plants are about 4 weeks old, decreases during flowering and increases thereafter. The increase, however, is due only to the high susceptibility of leaves on young shoots, forming after flowering.

In 'A6' plants, age of the tubers can affect susceptibility of the test leaves. Leaves grown from physiologically young tubers are more susceptible to virus infection than those grown from old ones. 'A6' tubers should therefore be stored at low temperatures until planting.

Leaves of *Physalis floridana* and *Chenopodium quinoa*, test plants for PVY, act in a similar way. Leaves from old *C. quinoa* plants, 50 days, and very young plants, 15–20 days after transplanting, yielded few lesions, whereas leaves of plants, 30 days after transplanting, produced 3–4 times as many. Lesions on young plants were more intense coloured and better delimited than those on older plants.

Age and position of test leaves on the plant seem to be only partly responsible for the variation in the lesion counts. The capacity of a local-lesion host to produce lesions may differ considerably from plant to plant or even, as with the test plant 'A6' and PVY, from leaf to leaf. The number of local lesions also depends on the man who inoculates the test plant. A high pressure during inoculation yields more lesions than a low pressure.

8.3.2 Fertilizers
The effect of fertilizers on the susceptibility of test plants to virus infection has been investigated for several combinations of host and virus, such as *Nicotiana glutinosa* and tomato aucuba mosaic strain of TMV; *Chenopodium amaranticolor* and CMV; 'A6' or *Solanum demissum* 'Y' (SdY) and PVY.

In general, test plants with high N rates have more local lesions than those with low rates, but plants with balanced nutrition grow best and produce leaves with a high susceptibility for longest.

8.3.3 Light before inoculation
Illumination influences susceptibility both by its duration in the 24-h cycle and by its intensity.

Leaves of 'A6' plants grown under long-day conditions (16 h light a day) produced 4–20 times as many local lesions as leaves grown on plants lit only for 9 h a day. However leaves of *Solanum demissum* 'Y' subjected to those conditions did not differ at all in reaction to inoculation with PVY^N.

Plants kept in darkness before inoculation are usually very sensitive to infection by viruses. Leaves of *Physalis floridana* plants that were kept in the dark for 24 h before inoculation were more susceptible to PVY than leaves of plants exposed to light.

Light intensity affects the susceptibility of 'A6' leaves. Shaded before inoculation with PVY^N, they yield more local lesions than unshaded leaves. Very intense light can be unfavourable. Intense light may have been the reason for virus-like lesions induced spontaneously on the leaves of *Gomphrena globosa* grown in greenhouses.

107

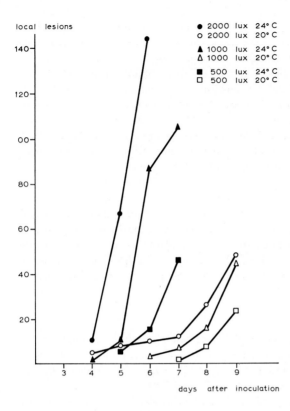

local lesions

●	2000	lux	24° C
○	2000	lux	20° C
▲	1000	lux	24° C
△	1000	lux	20° C
■	500	lux	24° C
□	500	lux	20° C

days   after   inoculation

Fig. 30. Effect of illumination on number of local lesions on 'A6' leaves after inoculation with PVY[N] at 20° and 24°C.

8.3.4   Light after inoculation

An illumination of 2 000 lx gives more infection than 1 000 and 500 lx, if 'A6' leaves inoculated with PVY[N] are kept at 24° or 20°C (Fig. 30). Five days after inoculation, the 'A6' leaves show local lesions. 'A6' leaves kept in dimmer light (1 000 or 500 lx) show local lesions 2–4 days later.

The cycle of illumination in the 24 h affects the incubation period. 'A6' leaves inoculated with PVY[N] and lit for 8 h a day produce an average of 3 lesions whereas illumination yields an average of 18 lesions 5 days after inoculation.

Without illumination inoculated 'A6' leaves do not produce lesions. On *Gomphrena globosa* inoculated with PVX or red clover vein mosaic virus, darkness reduces the numbers of local lesions.

8.3.5   Temperature

Temperature before inoculation had no effect on the susceptibility of plants grown in a greenhouse at a constant temperature of 20°C or with a temperature fluctuating between 15° and 25°C. However the susceptibility of *Physalis floridana* to PVY increased if the plants were kept at 4°–10°C for a short time. The optimum temperature for development of local lesions on leaves of *Chenopodium*

108

quinoa after inoculation with PVY is 22°C, whereas detached 'A6' leaves inoculated with PVY^N produce most local lesions if leaves are stored at 24°C. However 'A6' inoculated with PVA produces most lesions after incubation at about 20°C. Obviously each virus requires a special temperature in each host to produce most lesions.

The temperature during incubation affects the time when local lesions appear and their size. With warmth, local lesions, if they appear at all, develop more quickly and have a larger average diameter than with cold. This phenomenon is general.

8.3.6 Virus concentration

In 1929, when Holmes laid the basis for local-lesion assay of plant viruses, he observed that the number of local lesions TMV induced on *Nicotiana glutinosa* was proportional to the concentration of the inoculum. However with various dilutions of virus preparation, this rule proved valid only within certain limits of virus concentration. If the concentration is extremely low or high, no clear correlation between concentration and number of local lesions can be observed.

For statistical analysis of the results, inoculation schemes must be used in assay. Each inoculum has to be applied an equal number of times to leaves from each position on the plant.

Opposite halves of each leaf produce an almost equal number of lesions after inoculation: hence the 'half-leaf method', which permits less complicated inoculation schemes. Also opposite leaves or opposite leaflets of a compound leaf may be used to compare different inocula. Further information on statistical analysis of virus assay can be found in Kleczkowski (1955).

8.4 Routine application of 'A6' leaf test

Grow 'A6' in an aphid-free greenhouse. The plants need a fertile soil and bright illumination. In winter supplement the illumination with mercury lamps. About 4–6 weeks after planting pick suitable leaves. Leaves of moderate age react best. As the plants mature, they become less susceptible.

Place the detached leaves on wet filter paper, dust them with carborundum powder. Pass the potato leaves to be tested through a crusher. Two inoculation methods are suitable. With a small plastic sponge rub the expressed sap into the test leaf.

Or: fold the leaves to be tested and rub them onto sandpaper and then onto the 'A6' leaf. Rub each leaf to be tested onto a clean piece of sandpaper.

Rinse residual carborundum powder off the 'A6' leaves with water. Place the inoculated leaves in suitably sized boxes of plastic (e.g. $20 \times 34 \times 4$ cm) or of zinc (e.g. $61 \times 32 \times 5$ cm). The plastic boxes are put in plastic bags, the zinc boxes covered with glass plates to maintain humidity and to prevent leaves from wilting. In tests for PVY keep the boxes for 7 days at 24°C and about 1 000 lx. In tests for PVA keep at about 18°C for 5 days. In combined tests for PVA and PVY keep at about 20°C for 9 days.

8.5 General remarks

Test plants inoculated mechanically are in general use for virus diagnosis. This reliable method is based on the infectivity of the viruses. Test plants are usually more reliable but tests take longer than serology for indexing viruses. However suitable test plants are not yet available for all viruses.

The search for test plants is laborious, because they must fulfil so many requirements. They should be easy to raise at all seasons, should remain susceptible to a virus over a long period of their growth, should be easy to inoculate and should give a uniform response under a wide range of environmental conditions.

8.6 Further reading

Arenz, B. & M. Vulic, 1961. Über die Erfassung von Y- und A-Virus durch direkte Knollenabreibung auf 'A6'. Bayer. landw. Jb. 38: 454–466.

Bokx, J. A. de, 1964. Onderzoekingen over het aantonen van aardappel-Y^N-virus met behulp van toetsplanten (With a summary: Detection of potato virus Y^N by means of test plants). Doctoral thesis Wageningen, 84 p. (also: Meded. Inst. Plziektenk. Onderz. Wageningen, 342).

Bokx, J. A. de, 1970. Reactions of various plant species to inoculation with potato virus S. Neth. J. Pl. Path. 76: 70–78.

Hollings, M., 1959. Host range studies with fifty-two plant viruses. Ann. appl. Biol. 47: 98–108.

Hollings, M., 1966. Local-lesion and other test plants. In: A. B. R. Beemster & J. Dijkstra (eds), Viruses of plants. North-Holland Publishing Company, Amsterdam, p. 230–241.

Kleczkowski, A., 1955. The statistical analysis of plant virus assays: a transformation to include lesion numbers with small means. J. gen. Microbiol. 13: 91–98.

Roberts, D. A., 1964. Local-lesion assay of plant viruses. In: M. K. Corbett & H. D. Sisler (eds), Plant virology. Univ. Fla Press, Gainesville, p. 194–210.

9 Histological, cytological and biochemical methods

J. A. de Bokx

Viruses disturb the metabolism of plants, often in characteristic ways. Besides the symptoms visible to the naked eye that are used in field inspection, the biochemical disturbances in cells cause abnormalities visible in tissues and even single cells. Literature on symptoms and their use in diagnosis has been reviewed by Bode (1962) and Bos (1970). Except for excessive formation of callose, research has provided no practical basis for diagnosis of potato viruses by these means. Cytological deviations (Section 9.3) have been widely studied but have no practical use yet. Biochemical disturbances are only of theoretical interest.

9.1 Phloem necrosis
Quanjer (1931) discovered that PLRV causes phloem necrosis in potato stems. Phloem necrosis becomes visible also in mature tubers. In stems, its visibility can be enhanced with stains, either phloroglucinol and HCl, or Diamant fuchsin and HCl. Although these stains have been recommended by various workers for detection of PLRV, they are not commonly used.

9.2 Callose formation
Callose is a normal constituent on sieve plates of many species. Young healthy sieve plates contain only small plugs. Larger amounts are formed to seal sieve tubes that have ceased to function sometimes temporarily for the winter or in response to wounding. Winter callose can be rapidly dissolved away in spring; wound callose can likewise be dissolved. Callose increases as the plant ages.

Excessive formation of callose, sometimes completely filled tubes, is a response to some virus diseases, e.g. PLRV in potato and beet yellows in sugar beet. For practical diagnosis of PLRV in seed potatoes, detection of excessive callose in stems and tubers has been introduced in the Netherlands, Austria, Bavaria and Switzerland. Although Igel and Lange claimed the test could detect other viruses in potato it has succeeded only for tomato stolbur. Attempts with PVY have been unsuccessful.

9.2.1 The Igel Lange test
Stains. Callose stains are aniline blue, resorcin blue and rosolic acid. The best is a 1% aqueous solution of resorcin blue, which turns callose deep-blue. Dissolve

Fig. 31. Slicing a potato tuber for the Igel Lange test with a double knife (A) or with a mounted razor blade (B).

10 g pure white resorcin (metadioxybenzol) in 1 000 ml distilled water and add 12 ml 25% ammonia. Keep the mixture in an open container at room temperature for 10–14 days until the smell of ammonia disappears. The dye is then greenish-blue. Preparations stored for a year or two may turn dark blue. They still stain callose but slightly stain xylem and starch too.

To detect callose in stems. Stain longitudinal slices 2 mm thick from fresh potato stems for 10 min in resorcin blue and examine them at a magnification of ×25. The chlorophyll in the stem obscures the staining of sieve tubes. Results for tubers are more decisive.

To detect callose in tubers. Cut longitudinal slices 2–3 mm thick and 3–4 mm wide from the heel of potato with a double knife or razor blade (Fig. 31). Stain for 10 min and examine under magnification (Fig. 32). Since old sieve tubes whether diseased or not often contain a lot of callose, young ones from near the cambium should be examined by preference (Fig. 33). The extreme heel almost always contains callose and should be overlooked! Starch does not interfere with the test. The contrast between stained sieve tubes and other tissues is magnificent. Opinions differ on the test's value for routine inspection. Some consider it unreliable; others find it useful for diagnosing PLRV in tubers of primarily infected plants.

112

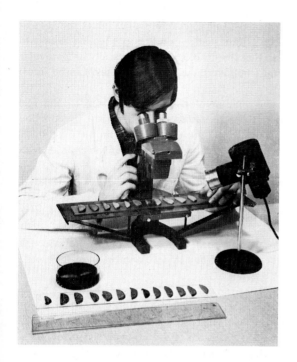

Fig. 32. Examining tuber slices for callose in sieve tubes.

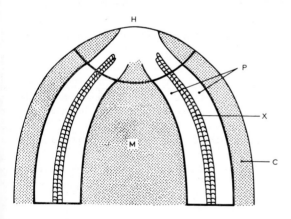

Fig. 33. Diagrammatic longitudinal section through the heel end of a potato. Sieve tubes containing callose are counted in the area surrounded by black lines. C: cortex. H: heel end. M: medulla. P: phloem. X: xylem.

9.2.2 Factors in excessive production of callose

In 'Bintje' potatoes, excessive callose sometimes is observed in medulla and cortex but not in the phloem bundle. Such tubers are very likely to be infected with PLRV and should be further examined.

The amount of callose in healthy and diseased tubers differs between varieties. Healthy 'Sientje' and 'Majestic' tubers contain so much that healthy and diseased tubers cannot be distinguished. Diseased 'Bintje' develops thick plugs but 'Eigenheimer' and 'Krasava' develop very thin strings. Callose production seems to depend on the phloem structure, so that the histology of each variety, in particular the form of the callose lumps, must be determined before the test can be introduced.

Little has been published on the amount of callose, as assessed by the Igel Lange test. The criteria classing a tuber as diseased are arbitrary. A common stipulation is that more than one callose plug must be detected in the sieve tubes of one section. No relation has been established with severity of infection or with strain.

Tubers harvested early may not yet have formed excessive callose. Formation in diseased tubers is stimulated by storage at a suitable temperature, $16°–20°C$, for at least 4 weeks. Other means, such as chemicals, stimulate callose production in healthy tubers too.

Tubers with primary infection usually form more callose than tubers with secondary infection. However, tubers infected late in development show no excess.

9.3 Inclusion bodies

Under certain conditions virus particles aggregate in the cell into inclusion bodies or X-bodies, which are visible with a light microscope. Little is known about the ability of potato viruses to induce viral inclusions. PVX and two strains of AMV sometimes produce amorphous inclusions in epidermal cells of host leaves. According to McWorther (1965), PVY does not produce inclusions but other workers have observed small granular inclusions. Viral inclusions have proved useful for identification of certain viruses. For potato, they do not yet have practical significance.

9.4 Further reading

Bode, O., 1962. Die Blattrollkrankheit der Kartoffel. Die durch die Virose bei der Kartoffel hervorgerufenen Veränderungen und die Möglichkeiten des Nachweises. Angew. Bot. 36: 86–116.

Bokx, J. A. de, 1967. The callose test for the detection of leafroll virus in potato tubers. Eur. Potato J. 10: 221–234.

Bos, L., 1970. Symptoms of virus diseases in plants. 2nd ed. (revised) Pudoc, Wageningen, 206 p.

McWorther, F. P., 1965. Plant virus inclusions. A. Rev. Phytopath. 3: 287–312.

10   Potato viruses: properties and symptoms

A. B. R. Beemster and A. Rozendaal

Because of how potatoes are propagated, and because of their wide distribution and importance in many countries, most of the numerous known potato viruses are worldwide. Some have been studied thoroughly and for a long time, so that much information is available. However their identification is not necessarily easy, since many potato viruses are known and, despite diversity in some respects, they often show similarities. In particular, symptoms in potatoes may overlap.

This chapter describes the main potato viruses and their diagnostic characteristics. The descriptions are not comprehensive but give sufficient information on such aspects as symptoms, host range, and vectors. It surveys fairly completely characteristics considered useful to those interested in potato viruses and emphasizes pathological aspects.

Viruses are grouped according to their mode of transmission. The group described in 10.5 includes some diseases that were long considered to be of virus origin but of which some are now known to be caused by mycoplasma. Since virologists have dealt with these diseases, they are included. Research still has to elucidate some problems before certain diseases can be ascribed to either viruses or mycoplasmas.

Although the nomenclature of viruses in general has been under discussion for many years, we still have no generally accepted system. Some potato viruses are known by several names, sometimes a tradition name alongside a systematic name. The description of each virus is headed by what the authors consider the most widely accepted name followed, as necessary, by current synonyms for the virus and for the disease it causes in potatoes.

Although some characteristics, in particular symptoms, vary, such variation cannot be indicated here. Complete description is almost impossible, since symptom expression depends on many factors, e.g. environmental conditions, strain, and variety.

10.1   Viruses transmitted by contact

10.1.1   Potato virus X
Synonyms: *Solanum* virus 1, Smith; potato latent virus, Burnett & Jones; healthy potato virus, vide E. M. Johnson; potato virus 16, J. Johnson.

Diseases: potato interveinal mosaic; potato mottle; potato simple mosaic; potato top necrosis; potato common mosaic.
German: leichtes Mosaik der Kartoffel. Spanish: mosaico leve; mosaico latente.

General. PVX is worldwide, occurring wherever potatoes are grown. As the virus generally evokes mild symptoms in potato plants, it was long considered as almost harmless to the potato. However, careful trials have shown yield depressions of over 10%, varying according to virus strains and potato variety. PVX is among the mildest potato viruses known. Potatoes affected by PVX may yield slightly fewer and slightly smaller tubers than those from healthy plants. Some necrosis-evoking strains may cause losses of over 50% in some potato varieties. Multiple infection with other potato viruses like PVA and PVY is much more damaging than single infection. Therefore PVX is always a potential danger.

Physical properties. TIP between 68° and 76°C, depending on the strain; DEP between 10^{-5} and 10^{-6}; SIDT at least 250 days; SIV several weeks. Particles thread-like; normal length 515 nm and diameter 13 nm.

Transmission. PVX is easily transmitted artificially by sap inoculation and by stem and tuber-core grafting. It spreads naturally by contact between healthy and infected plants and by carriage on farm implements, clothing and animal fur. Anything that has touched affected plants can be infectious. Healthy seed potatoes may be infected by contact between healthy and affected sprouts. Contact between roots may allow infection in the field but is of little importance.

Aphids do not transmit PVX; grasshoppers and other chewing insects can transmit it in the same way as clothing and fur. Recently transmission has also been reported by the fungus *Synchytrium endobioticum*. This fact seems unimportant for the spread of PVX.

PVX is transmitted easily to new tubers if the plant is infected early in growth. However, when potato plants are harvested soon after inoculation or when the infection takes place late in growth some tubers may be virus-free or partially infected.

Symptoms. In many varieties PVX evokes an interveinal mosaic i.e. a mosaic pattern visible only between the veins of the leaves (Plate 1). The mosaic is sometimes scarcely visible, if at all, depending on strain, variety and environmental conditions. Otherwise the potato plants show their normal habit of growth with flat leaves. Infected plants without symptoms are called carriers. It is important to know which varieties are carriers; since they are an important source of infection for varieties that react more severely.

Some virulent strains of PVX cause rugosity of the leaves or even crinkling, called PVX crinkle.

Infected plants with only mild symptoms in the upper leaves may show typical symptoms in the older leaves shaded by the top foliage; such older leaves do not

116

turn uniformly yellow but have a greenish banding of veins on a yellow background.

Some varieties react with certain strains in quite another way. After infection of such plants by tuber or stem grafting they react with moderate or severe top necrosis, a sort of hypersensitivity. Such a variety is field-resistant. Natural infection by sap evokes only a local reaction, such hypersensitivity prevents systemic infection.

Strains. Many strains are known differing in the symptoms they evoke either on potatoes or test plants. These strains can be classified, according to Cockerham, into four groups, which he called X^1, X^2, X^3 and X^4. Viruses of any one group are serologically related, but viruses of one group give no cross-protection against viruses of another, e.g. plants infected with PVX^4 are susceptible to PVX^3 and 'Eersteling' potatoes infected with PVX^2 can be infected very easily with PVX^3.

The groups X^1, X^2 and X^3 each evoke a hypersensitivity reaction in certain varieties but the X^4 group evokes only an interveinal mosaic in all varieties so far tested. Hence PVX^4 is also dangerous for varieties hypersensitive to any strain of the first groups. Fortunately strains of PVX^4 have not been found in the field so far.

PVX^2 is identical with the top necrosis virus originally described by Quanjer and with X^B originally described by Bawden as virus B. PVX^3 is common virus X and in the literature and in commerce is often called potato common virus X.

Test plants and other hosts. *Gomphrena globosa* has proved to be a useful test plant for PVX; 4 to 5 days after inoculation, local lesions appear on inoculated

Fig. 34. Systemic symptoms of PVX on 'White Burley' tobacco, 15 days after inoculation.

117

Fig. 35. Local lesions on *Capsicum annuum* 10 days after inoculation with PVX.

leaves as small, grayish spots, gradually increasing in size and becoming surrounded by a reddish zone (Chap. 8). *Nicotiana tabacum* (e.g. 'White Burley' or 'Samsun') is often used as a production host whence virus can be obtained and purified. The virus evokes vein clearing, mottling and ringspots in tobacco (Fig. 34) and some strains also local lesions and systemic necrosis. *Datura stramonium* reacts systemically; symptoms differ considerably between strains. *D. stramonium* is sometimes used to isolate PVX from a mixture of PVX and PVY, as *D. stramonium* is immune to PVY. *Capsicum annuum* develops local round distinct necrotic lesions different in shape from the lesions of PAMV (Fig. 35) (Section 10.2.4); systemic symptoms are milder than of PAMV.

Among other known hosts and host plants are *Lycopersicon esculentum, Nicotiana glutinosa* and *Chenopodium amaranticolor*.

Serology. High-titre antiserum can be prepared against PVX. The antiserum can be profitably used in routine tests by the agglutination or precipitin method.

10.1.2 Potato virus S

General. PVS was first described in 1951 from the Netherlands but proved to be widespread in commercial stocks in Europe, Canada and the United States, in fact wherever potatoes are grown.

Yield depression, about 10–15%, differs between varieties and between strains. Infected potato plants yield a higher proportion of small tubers.

Physical properties. TIP 55°–60°C; DEP 10⁻³; SIDT 11 months; SIV 2–3 days. Particles rigid to flexible threads; normal length 650 nm and diameter 12–13 nm.

Transmission. PVS can be transmitted by stem grafting, by tuber-core grafting, by sap inoculation and by contact between infected and healthy plants. Contact seems to be the only way PVS is transmitted naturally. It is uncertain whether the virus can be transmitted by aphids but at least some strains might be aphid transmissible. PVS usually spreads slowly in the field. But with some combinations of variety and strain, virus spread may be considerable. Tubers from newly infected plants may be partially infected.

Symptoms. Symptoms vary with strain, variety and the weather but not so much as with PVX. Typical is a deepening of veins on the upper side of leaves, which may become rugose (Fig. 36). In many varieties PVS evokes mild rugosity. Besides this, many varieties show a slight pendulousness of leaves and a more open stand of the crop. Very often only careful observation and comparison with healthy plants allow visual diagnosis.

Some varieties react with slight or distinct mottle and sometimes faint banding of veins. The most sensitive of them turn bronzy; their leaves may be severely rugose and may even develop necrotic spots on the upper surface. The most

Fig. 36. Rugosity of potato leaves caused by PVS (right).

virulent strains evoke severe bronzing and even leafdropping.

Some varieties, e.g. 'Bintje', flower much less freely when affected than when healthy.

Unlike healthy leaves, older leaves in the shade do not usually turn uniformly yellow but often have green or greenish-bronze spots. This spotting can sometimes be conclusive for diagnosis.

Cloudy weather may enhance symptoms that would not be seen in sunny weather.

Strains. Different strains evoke similar symptoms in potatoes but differ in host range. In the Netherlands a virulent strain has occasionally been found that evokes bronzy necrosis in many varieties, later accompanied by withering and dropping of the lower and middle leaves. Cross-protection tests proved that PVS was involved. The symptoms evoked by this strain are so easily recognized that visual diagnosis does not give any problem.

PVS is related to carnation latent virus and PVM (Section 10.2.3).

Test plants and other hosts. A really good test plant has yet to be found for PVS. The virus has few hosts and symptoms in those that react are variable, even with one strain.

Plants developing local lesions under certain conditions are *Chenopodium quinoa*, *C. amaranticolor* and *Gomphrena globosa*. The most widely used test plant, *Nicotiana debneyi*, evokes vein clearing about 20 days after inoculation, later becoming pronounced and then turning into vein banding and leaf mottling. Ultimately affected leaves become chlorotic and necrotic between veins.

Some other hosts also develop systemic symptoms, e.g. *Solanum rostratum*. *Datura metel* may be used to distinguish PVM (Section 10.2.3). PVS generally evokes only local symptoms in it.

Nicotiana tabacum, *N. glutinosa* and *Lycopersicon esculentum* are not susceptible to PVS, unlike most other potato viruses.

Serology. High-titre antisera can be prepared against PVS. Rabbits can be injected with (partly) purified preparations of PVS from potato. In commercial production of seed potatoes, a serological test is widely used for detecting PVS. Because of the vague symptoms of PVS in potatoes and other plants, a reliable serological test is of great importance.

10.1.3 Potato spindle tuber virus
Synonyms: potato spindling tuber virus, Schultz & Folsom; *Solanum* virus 12, Smith; potato virus 8, Johnson.
Diseases: potato spindle tuber, potato marginal leafroll.
French: tubercules en fuseau. German: Spindelknollenkrankheit der Kartoffel. Spanish: tubérculo puntiagudo.

Plate 1. Interveinal mosaic caused by a severe strain of PVX in 'Eigenheimer'.

Plate 2. Leafdrop streak in 'Eersteling' caused by PVYᶜ.

Plate 3. Mosaic symptoms of PVY^N in 'Burmania'.

Plate 4. Deformation of potato 'Mentor', caused by a PVM strain from 'Up to Date'.

Plate 5. Yellow flecking in 'Doré', caused by PAMV.

Plate 6. 'Jefta' potato plant with primary symptoms of AMV.

Plate 7. 'Spartaan' potato plant with primary symptoms of PLRV.

Plate 8. 'Bevelander' potato leaf with stem mottle.

General. Potato spindle tuber has been known in the United States since 1922. It is there an important disease in certain regions. Later it was found also in Canada, Argentina and parts of Europe (Soviet Union, Poland and Bulgaria).

Physical properties. TIP 65°–80°C; DEP between 10^{-2} and 10^{-3}; SIV 3–5 days. The virus has the properties of a free nucleic acid (double-stranded RNA).

Transmission and spread. PSTV spreads naturally by contact and by transfer on farm implements. Some insects like *Lygus pratensis* and *Melanoplus* spp. can also transmit the virus. Transmission by aphids has also been reported but confirmation is still needed. The virus can be artificially transmitted by stem and tuber-core grafting.
   It can be dispersed in seed and pollen as well as in tubers.

Symptoms. Potato affected by PSTV produce long spindly tubers, often deformed in other ways such as cracking. Symptoms in the haulm are usually slight. Plants stand erect and leaves are discoloured darker green. In warm weather symptoms are more pronounced than in cooler weather. Yields of tubers is 20–35% less in weight and quality is poor because of deformation.

Strains. Mild and severe strains are known. A special strain called potato unmottled curly dwarf virus has been described.

Test plants and other hosts. PSTV can be transmitted to some other hosts, most of which hardly react, if it all. 'Rutgers' tomatoes can be used as a test plant, reacting with stunting and some rugosity of new leaves. Decapitation of the inoculated tomato plants enhances the test.

Serology. PSTV-affected plants have specific antigenic properties but a reliable serological test has not yet been elaborated.

10.1.4   Tobacco mosaic virus
TMV, a highly infectious contact transmitted virus is found occasionally affecting potato. Usually the plants do not react except, in some varieties, for local lesions on inoculated leaves.

10.2   Viruses transmitted by aphids

10.2.1   Potato virus A
Synonyms: *Solanum* virus 3, Smith; potato mosaic virus, Holmes.
Diseases: potato common mosaic, Quanjer; supermild mosaic; potato veinal mosaic.
German: Rauhmosaik. Spanish: mosaico.

General. PVA has been little studied, perhaps because is usually evokes mild symptoms in most varieties. Thus it may seem less important than, for instance, PLRV and PVY. However it does deserve more attention, since it is widespread in certain varieties and, in combination with PVX, it also usually causes a severe disease known as potato crinkle. In combination with PVY, it also gives rise to a severe disease. Yield losses can be great in such combined infections.

The instability of PVA and its low concentration in the potato plant may also be responsible for the scantiness of data.

Physical properties. TIP 44°–52°C; DEP about 1:50; SIV 12–24 h. Particles are threads 730 nm long and 11 nm wide.

Transmission. PVA can be transmitted artificially by sap inoculation, by stem and tuber-core grafting and naturally by aphids, in which it does not persist and is stylet-borne. Aphids that can transmit PVA are: *Aphis nasturtii*, *Macrosiphum euphorbiae*, *Myzus persicae*, *Neomyzus circumflexus*. Of these *M. persicae* is responsible for most of the spread in the field.

Symptoms. In many potato varieties, PVA evokes mosaic, sometimes severe. The light parts of the mosaic are irregular, lying both on and between the veins; the dark parts of the mosaic are darker than of a healthy leaf (Fig. 37). In contrast to the interveinal mosaic caused by PVX, PVA causes typical veinal mosaic. Infected leaves as a whole look shiny. Veins later deepen and leaf margins become crinkled. The difference in growth of veins and lamina causes rugosity, sometimes severe. Infected stands usually look open because stems bend outwards. In sunny warm weather, symptoms are much less distinct than in cloudy cool weather or are even completely masked.

Some varieties like the Dutch 'Triumf' are almost symptomless under certain conditions and others like the Dutch 'Lichte Industrie' only show slight mottling. Infection of such varieties is dangerous for susceptible and sensitive varieties growing nearby.

Some varieties are field-resistant. After artificial infection by stem and tuber-core grafting, they do not react with mosaic but with top necrosis. Examples are the Dutch varieties Bintje, Eersteling, Record and Saskia. In contrast to PVX, all potato varieties that have proved hypersensitive to one strain of PVA are hypersensitive also to any other strain of the virus.

Strains. PVA strains differ in the severity of symptoms they produce in different varieties. They can be grouped as mild, moderate or severe, but they principally are of the same type. The old Dutch variety Triumf carries a very mild strain, 'Lichte Industrie' a mild one. The variety Juliniere carries a more virulent strain, which also deviates in other aspects, whereas 'Saucisse Rouge' carries the most severe strain. As the varieties that are hypersensitive react to the virulent strains with clearer symptoms, the PVA strain from 'Saucisse Rouge' is most

Fig. 37. Potato leaf of 'Voran' with mosaic caused by PVA.

useful for testing potato varieties for field resistance. The strain carried by 'Juliniere' evokes a typical kind of figure necrosis, together with a clear mosaic in some varieties, e.g. Furore, Paul Kruger (synonym President). The figure necrosis is different from all other types of necrosis caused by other viruses. The varieties mentioned are useful for cross-protection tests with PVA.

PVA shows some similarity with PVY, but their differences justify nomenclature as different viruses.

Test plants and other hosts. *Solanum demissum* 'A' used to be used as a test plant. It reacts with local necrotic lesions or systemic necrosis of the stem. However, symptoms of PVA in this plant are similar to those evoked by PVX so that further tests are necessary for identification.

PVA is now better detected with leaves of 'A6' (*Solanum demissum* × *S. tuberosum* 'Aquila'). Inoculated leaves of 'A6' develop local dark solid lesions. Although PVY and some other potato viruses also evoke lesions, those of PVA are different in size and shape and are most distinct after inoculated test leaves have been kept at 20°C. At that temperature, lesions of PVY are less clear (Chap. 8).

123

The Dutch variety Gelderse Rode is a useful test plant. After stem or tuber-core grafting this variety reacts with a special kind of top necrosis, which is much less severe than the top necrosis caused by strains of PVX[3]. Thus the two types can be easily distinguished. Another advantage of this variety is its tolerance to PVY[O] and PVY[N] strains, by which PVY and PVA mixtures can easily be detected.

PVA can be purified by culture in *Nicotiana tabacum* (e.g. 'White Burley', 'Samsun'). The concentration of PVA in its hosts is usually low. 'Samsun' seems slightly better than 'White Burley'. Virus concentration reaches a maximum in tobacco leaves about 6 weeks after inoculation and then gradually decreases to almost nil in older leaves. Tobacco reacts only by slight clearing of veins. Later a vague mottling and vein banding, which almost disappears afterwards.

The host range of PVA seems to be restricted to Solanaceae, of which a number of species are known to be susceptible. *Nicotiana glutinosa* reacts to inoculation with vein clearing, crinkling and develops local, chlorotic lesions. *Lycopersicon pimpinellifolium* which can also be used as a test plant reacts with both local and systemic, necrotic symptoms. *Nicandra physaloides* reacts with a more or less severe systemic mottle, necrosis and stunting.

Serology. PVA is weakly antigenic. An antiserum has been prepared with virus preparations from *Nicotiana tabacum*. The virus from affected tobacco could be identified serologically but identification of that from potato has proved impractical because of the low concentration of virus.

10.2.2 Potato virus Y

Synonyms: *Solanum* virus 2, Smith; potato virus 20, J. Johnson; potato acropetal necrosis virus, Quanjer; tobacco veinal necrosis virus, Bawden & Kassanis; potato leafdrop streak virus, Murphy; Tabakrippenbräune-Virus, Klinkowski.
Diseases: streak; potato leafdrop streak; potato stipple-streak.
French: bigarrure; frisolée. German: Strichelkrankheit. Spanish: mosaico severo.

General. PVY has long been studied in many parts of the world. It is still a major virus of potatoes because it spreads easily and depresses yield so much, up to 80%. Depression varies with variety and strain. Combinations with other potota viruses like PVA, PVX and PVS cause severe diseases sometimes destroying the crop. The severity of the synergistic effect, however, depends very much on the combination of viruses and potato varieties.

Physical properties. TIP ranges with strain, $52°-62°C$; DEP $10^{-2}-10^{-3}$; SIDT 15 years; SIV 48–72 h. Particles thread-like 730 nm long and about 11 nm wide.

Transmission. PVY is transmissible by sap inoculation, by stem and core grafting and by aphids. Most of the natural spread is by aphids.

PVY is a stylet-borne (non-persistent) virus. *Myzus persicae* is considered an effective vector and is often responsible for most spread in a potato field. Other aphids that can transmit PVY are: *Macrosiphum euphorbiae, Aphis fabae, A. frangulae, A. nasturtii, Cavariella pastinacae, Neomyzus circumflexus, Myzus certus, M. ornatus.*

Symptoms. Symptoms in potato vary widely with strain and variety. They range in severity from weak symptoms (some varieties are even symptomless) to severe necrosis and death of the infected plants. The Dutch variety Zeeuwse Blauwe infected with PVY^C reacts only with mosaic; 'Thorbecke' is a symptomless carrier of this virus. Mild mosaic and some rugosity occur in certain varieties with certain strains and many varieties react with crinkle symptoms. Any one variety may react differently with different strains. Sensitive varieties react with necrosis which may affect only some veins on the lower surface of the leaves or may form severe necrosis on leaves and stems. Such severe necrosis may ultimately cause older leaves to collapse and either drop from the plants (called leafdrop streak) or remain hanging (called palm tree type) (Plate 2). Yield capacity, of course, is reduced in either case.

Necrosis is usually more severe after primary infection than after secondary. Secondarily infected plants are less necrotic, but are dwarfed and brittle, with leaves wrinkled and bunched together.

Strains. Many strains, or rather groups of strains are known that can be distinguished according to the severity of systemic symptoms in potato, tobacco or other hosts. The main groups are called PVY^O, PVY^N and PVY^C. PVY^O comprises 'common' strains; PVY^N comprises the tobacco veinal necrosis groups, named after the symptoms evoked on the leaves of *Nicotiana tabacum*. PVY^N became a menace in Western Europe about 15 years ago and has since been thoroughly studied. It has been detected in many parts of the world.

In general, PVY^O evokes much more severe symptoms than PVY^N (Fig. 38, Plate 3). PVY^N proved to be much more dangerous than PVY^O, because in most potato varieties PVY^N spreads more rapidly in the field than PVY^O. This behaviour is due to several factors, viz. the overlooking of affected plants during roguing because of the vague symptoms; later appearance of symptoms in the season than those of other strains; rapid translocation of PVY^N from leaves to tubers; and the less marked mature-plant resistance towards PVY^N than towards other potato viruses.

PVY^C evokes severe stipple-streak symptoms in many varieties. Aphids may transmit it but transmit some strains of it only with great difficulty, if at all. Potato varieties differ widely in hypersensitivity reactions to the groups PVY^C, PVY^O and PVY^N.

PVY^C is characterized by its hypersensitivity reaction in many varieties.
1. After stem or tuber-core grafting, they react with severe stipple-streak necrosis and generally without any mosaic or crinkle. The necrosis is also severe in the stems and tubers. Tubers even show clear necrotic spots on the skin (eye disease).

125

Fig. 38. Crinkle caused by PVY^O, in variety Kwinta (right).

The progeny of such necrotic tubers is often completely healthy. Their hypersensitivity is so strong that the virus has been eliminated completely. The varieties reacting in this way are completely field-resistant.

2. However there are also varieties that react with similar symptoms in the leaves and tubers, but whose progeny is not healthy and develops typical secondary stipple-streak symptoms. Apparently the hypersensitivity reaction in such varieties is not strong enough to eliminate the virus. All the same, such varieties prove field-resistant.

3. A third group shows necrosis that is less pronounced than in Group 2. The progeny of plants of these varieties is infected. Such varieties may be susceptible in the field. They are highly sensitive and, to some degree, hypersensitive.

Thus many of the varieties tested have proved hypersensitive to several strains of PVY^C, so that field-resistant varieties can be bred fairly easily.

PVY^O is characterized by the presence of a hypersensitivity reaction in only some varieties, as under 3. The haulm shows the same type of stipple-streak necrosis and the tubers a necrotic reaction. The tubers never produce virus-free plants. This reaction, however, is accompanied by complete, or almost complete, field resistance.

Thus it is much more difficult to breed varieties that are field-resistant to PVY^O than to PVY^C (Section 15.2.1).

PVY^N. A hypersensitivity reaction of a variety infected with PVY^N can be found only exceptionally, if at all, so that the breeding of varieties hypersensitive to PVY^N seems as yet extremely difficult. Fortunately, the breeding of moderately or extremely resistant varieties seems possible.

126

All potato varieties reacting with a moderate or severe mosaic or crinkle after infection with PVY^C, PVY^O or PVY^N mostly prove to be slightly or moderately susceptible in the field.

Test plants and other hosts. Reliable test plants are 'A6' and *Solanum demissum* 'Y'. Among other test plants are: *Physalis floridana* which reacts with local or systemic symptoms; *Datura stramonium* is sometimes used to isolate PVX from a mixture of PVX and PVY. PVX evokes systemic symptoms, whereas PVY does not infect it. To distinguish the various PVY groups, certain varieties can be used, e.g. Eersteling (synonym Duke of York) reacts on inoculation with PVY^C with severe stipple-streak symptoms, whereas PVY^O evokes severe crinkling and PVY^N crinkling of a milder type.

Serology. An antiserum of high titre can be prepared against PVY. Animals may be injected with (partly) purified preparations from affected tobacco plants. Although PVY can be detected serologically, this is not routine; the reaction is sometimes difficult to assess and needs experience. The test is also impractical for routine use, because of the delay from mixing antibody and antigen until the reaction can be assessed.

10.2.3   Potato virus M
Synonyms: potato leaf rolling mosaic virus, Schultz & Folsom; potato paracrinkle virus, Salaman & le Pelley; potato virus E, Bawden & Smith 1933; potato virus K, Köhler; *Solanum* virus 7, Smith; *Solanum* virus 11, Smith.
Diseases: potato leaf rolling mosaic; interveinal mosaic; paracrinkle.

General. PVM has only recently been clearly described. As its nomenclature shows PVM has long been known. There may still be some confusion about its name but PVM is now commonly accepted. Older names are being abandoned, mainly because there is no proof whether earlier descriptions are of diseases caused by one or more viruses, e.g. PVM, PVS and PVX. Early work on the virus itself was inadequate for identification.

The economic significance of PVM is uncertain. With some strains, symptoms in certain varieties are certainly severe, so that PVM could sometimes severely depress yield. Although PVM has been reported from the United States and some parts of Europe it does not seem to have spread much until the last few years. Recent spread especially is observed in those varieties which are reacting with mild symptoms by the less virulent strains of PVM. It seems to be transmitted naturally much less often than most other potato viruses.

Physical properties. TIP 65°–70°C; DEP 10^{-2}–10^{-3}; SIDT 11 months; SIV 2–4 days. Particles are slightly flexible threads; 650 nm long and 12–13 nm wide.

Transmission. PVM can be artificially transmitted by stem and tuber-core grafting, and by aphids. Natural spread is probably mainly by aphids. PVM is stylet-borne (non-persistent). Known aphid vectors are: *Myzus persicae, Macrosiphum euphorbiae, Aphis frangulae, A. nasturtii.* Strains differ in efficiency of transmission by aphids; one strain is known which is not transmitted by aphids.

Symptoms. As for all potato viruses, symptoms depend on virus strain, variety and environmental conditions. Symptoms are masked at higher temperatures (about 24°C). Mild strains evoke a mosaic between the veins of the leaflet tips and some deformation of the leaves. This deformation is characterized by a twisting of leaflet tips, sometimes severe and some rolling especially of the top leaves. Only infection of very young potato plants leads to symptoms. When the plants are older, inoculation of them does not cause any symptoms. This perhaps because PVM is translocated slowly. Progeny of primarily infected potato plants are often only partially infected, hence perhaps partly the slow spread of PVM. As an indication of how symptoms of one strain vary between varieties the following few types of symptoms were obtained after inoculation of a mild strain originally found in some clones of 'Bintje'.
1. No or almost no symptoms, depending on the growing conditions, in the varieties Frühmölle, Green Mountain, Irish Cobbler, Ideaal, Paul Kruger (synonym President), Saskia, Sebago, Up to Date and USDA 41956.
2. Only mild mosaic and some deformation in the varieties Alpha, Arran Crest, Bintje, Climax, Gineke, Industrie, Juliniere, Katahdin, Fortuna, Furore, Maritta, Noordeling, Sirtema and White Rose.
3. Clear mosaic and more severe deformation of the leaves of the varieties Bevelander, Libertas, Majestic, Meerlander, Prinslander, Saco, Ultimus and Voran.
4. As 3 but, sometimes in certain environmental conditions, some necrosis of petioles and sometimes of veins in varieties Eigenheimer, Doré, Eersteling (synonym Duke of York), Friso, Koopman's Blauwe, Profyt, Rode Star and Ysselster.
   Other strains evoke different symptoms (Plate 4).

Strains. Strains of PVM differ in type and severity of symptoms and in transmissibility by aphids. Potato leafrolling mosaic, potato virus K, potato virus E and potato paracrinkle virus are now considered to be identical or strains of PVM. PVS (Section 10.1.2) is also slightly related but can be distinguished serologically. It was thought that PVS was not transmissible by aphids, whereas PVM was. But some authors claim that PVS is transmitted by aphids. Carnation latent virus, which is considered to be a strain of PVS, is indeed aphid-transmitted. On the other hand there are strains of PVM, such as an isolate of potato paracrinkle virus, which could not be transmitted by aphids.

Usually there is no cross-protection between different groups of PVM strains but symptoms evoked by two PVM strains together are slightly milder than those caused by the more virulent of the two alone in cross-protection tests. PVS provides no protection against PVM.

128

Test plants and other hosts. There are several suitable test plants. *Datura metel* reacts to PVM with symptoms ranging from local chlorosis to necrosis and later with systemic necrosis. PVS generally evokes local symptoms in *D. metel.*

Other test plants are: *Nicotiana debneyi*, which reacts with local brown ring-like necrotic lesions; *Solanum rostratum*, systemic symptoms; *Vigna sinensis*, local necrosis. Tomato can be used to separate PVM from PVS: it cannot be infected with PVS but becomes systemically infected with PVM but without symptoms. *Nicotiana tabacum*, *N. glutinosa* and *Physalis floridana* cannot be infected with PVM.

To distinguish strains of PVM, the best procedure is to use those potato varieties that react to mild strains with mild symptoms and to virulent strains with severe symptoms, e.g. 'Kennebec' and 'Prinslander'.

Serology. PVM is strongly antigenic and high-titre antisera can be prepared. Antiserum can be used for diagnosis. PVM and PVS are serologically related but do not share all antigenic groups and can therefore be reliably distinguished.

10.2.4 Potato aucuba mosaic virus
Synonyms: potato viruses F and G, Clinch et al.; potato pseudo-net necrosis virus, Quanjer et al.; potato tuber blotch virus, Loughnane & Clinch; *Solanum* viruses 8 and 9, Smith.
Diseases: potato aucuba mosaic; potato pseudo-net necrosis; potato tuber blotch.
Dutch: aucubabont; aucubamozaïek (aardappel). French: mosaic aucuba de la pomme de terre. German: Aukuba Mosaik der Kartoffel; Aukuba Gelbflecken der Kartoffel. Italian: necrosi pseudoreticulata; mosaico aucuba (patata). Spanish: mosaico necrótico; mosaico abigarrado de la patata; suedonecrosis reticular; mosaico aucuba (patata).

General. PAMV is named by Quanjer in 1921 after the bright yellow flecking especially of lower and middle leaves of certain varieties resembling the yellow flecks on leaves of *Aucuba japonica* var. *variegata*. The symptoms are especially clear in young plants. The virus is known from Europe and North America. The effect on yield seems small but the tuber necrosis found in some varieties with certain strains is more important economically.

Physical properties. TIP 60°–70°C; DEP 10^{-5}–10^{-6}; SIV 60–90 days. Physical properties vary even beyond these limits. Particles thread-like; 580 nm long, 11–12 nm wide.

Transmission. PAMV is transmissible by stem and tuber-core grafting and by sap inoculation. Although *Myzus persicae* is considered to be a vector of PAMV little is yet known about this aspect. As the virus is never widespread in potato fields, aphids are presumably inefficient vectors. Some workers have found that PAMV is transmitted by *M. persicae* only when the infective plant contains both

PAMV and PVA but in the Netherlands PAMV proved to be aphid-transmissible in the absence of PVA. PAMV may also spread naturally by contact between infected and healthy plants.

Symptoms. Symptoms differ between strains and varieties. Some groups of strains of PAMV can be differentiated by their symptoms.

One group, present in the Dutch variety Triumf and clones of 'Gloria' evokes only the yellow flecking in most varieties (Plate 5) and hardly any symptoms in some tolerant varieties. A few varieties, e.g. Bintje, are deformed and stunted, but not yellow-flecked. However a very mild strain belonging to this group evokes even in 'Bintje' yellow flecking without any deformation. Other varieties again react with necrosis in the tubers (pseudo-net necrosis) but these symptoms vary widely.

In 'Libertas', the tuber necrosis is always visible even with the mildest strain of the group at time of harvesting. The necrotic spots in the tubers generally appear during storage. At higher temperature, the necrosis develops earlier and is more severe than at lower ones.

In the same group are strains that do not evoke typical yellow flecking but a mosaic combined with bronzy necrotic spots between the veins, especially on

Fig. 39. Deformation of 'Pa-trones' potato with PAMV isolated from 'May Queen'.

lower leaves. These strains evoke a more severe pseudo-net necrosis in the tubers (visible by harvest) than others of the group.

Another group that can be even differentiated into subgroups evokes yellow flecking in some varieties, but evokes severe stunting, often combined with widespread top necrosis of the stems, in many other varieties. Tubers are usually deformed and much of the flesh is necrotic. Some clones of 'Gloria' contain a virus of this group, whereas other clones contain a virus of the first group.

A very remarkable strain carried by 'May Queen' evokes a severe stunting and deformation combined with a violet blue discolouration, caused by the development of a large amount of anthocyanin, in several varieties, e.g. Bevelander, Bintje and Patrones (Fig. 39).

Strains. As the differences in symptoms in particular varieties show, there are many strains. Originally potato virus F and PAMV (potato virus G) were described as different viruses but they are now, together with many other strains, considered to belong to PAMV.

Test plants and other hosts. Capsicum annuum is as yet the best test plant for PAMV. About 8 to 10 days after inoculation, all strains evoke vague grayish-

Fig. 40. Local lesions on *Capsicum annuum* 12 days after inoculation with PAMV.

131

Fig. 41. Mosaic symptoms on *Nicotiana glutinosa* after inoculation with PAMV.

brown irregular concentric lesions on the inoculated leaves (Fig. 40); lesions differ from those of PVX (Section 10.1.1). The lesions turn into sunken necrotic spots with a gray centre and brown-purple margins. Systemic symptoms develop later: first vein clearing and gradually more severe symptoms, such as deformation and necrosis. The plants often die especially at 20°–22°C. Severity depends also on strain. At lower temperature, there are only local symptoms.

Tobacco, e.g. 'White Burley', is susceptible but tolerant to the virus. *Nicotiana glutinosa* develops yellow blotches 12 days after inoculation (Fig. 41). The tomato 'Kondine Red' reacts with small round yellow spots on younger leaves.

The best way to differentiate the very complicated groups of strains is with certain potato varieties. Symptoms evoked in the test varieties differ more than those in the test plants mentioned above. 'Eigenheimer' reacts with yellow flecking, various types of mosaic, crinkle and even top necrosis, according to the strain involved.

Serology. Antisera can be prepared with clarified sap from potato. PAMV can be identified serologically but sometimes with difficulty when using the agglutination test. The precipitin test has proved reliable.

10.2.5 *Alfalfa mosaic virus*
Synonyms: lucerne mosaic virus, Smith 1957; alfalfa virus 1, Smith 1957; alfalfa virus 2, Pierce 1934; *Solanum* virus 10, Smith 1957; potato calico virus, Hunger-

ford 1922; potato tuber necrosis virus, Oswald 1950.
Diseases: potato calico; potato tuber necrosis.
German: Kalikokrankheit; Gelbfleckigkeit des Kartoffellaubes.

General. Potato calico disease caused by certain strains of AMV is not so wide-spread as many other potato viruses although AMV is known to be almost world-wide. The disease was first described in California, later in Italy and parts of Central Europe. The disease does not occur naturally in the Netherlands.

Physical properties. TIP 55°–60°C; DEP 10^{-3}–2×10^{-3}; SIV 3–4 days. The virus consists of five components of which three are bacilliform and two almost isometric. The different types of particles range in length from 25–60 nm.

Transmission. AMV can be artificially transmitted to potato by stem and tuber-core grafting, and by mechanical inoculation. Aphids known to transmit the virus are *Myzus persicae*, *Macrosiphum euphorbiae* and *Acyrthosiphon pisum*. The virus is stylet-borne and non-persistent. The virus spreads from lucerne to potatoes if aphids migrate from lucerne to potatoes. In the Netherlands potato calico disease does not occur naturally, although AMV is easily isolated from some legumes, such as lucerne, white clover and hop clover (*Trifolium agrarium*). The Dutch strains can be artificially transmitted to potatoes, where they evoke typical calico. Once potatoes are infected, aphids can transmit AMV to healthy plants. Presumably the virus does not spread naturally to potatoes because conditions in the Netherlands do not force the aphids to migrate from lucerne to potato. According to some workers, the virus is transmitted to progeny through tubers only to a limited extent. But Dutch trials have proved that complete infection of the progeny is common.

Symptoms. AMV evokes leafspots, yellow like those of PAMV, but they are much larger and sometimes a complete leaflet may show the yellow colour (Plate 6). The calico symptom is usually accompanied by necrosis and leaf defor-mation, which is severe with certain strains and in certain varieties. Inoculated leaves develop black necrotic lesions. The necrosis later spreads internally into the leaflet veins and petioles. Later stem necrosis develops and the leaflets become rugose and plants sometimes even die.

AMV does not always evoke necrosis. If not, the symptoms are irregular bright yellow blotches on the leaves. In progeny, secondary infection evokes calico and also slight dwarfing.

Some strains evoke widespread necrosis in all the leaves, causing streaking and dropping of leaves. Leaves formed later become distorted, puckered and folded along the midribs. When infection is systemic, cortical tissue of tubers just under the epidermis at the stolon end becomes necrotic. Necrosis later spreads through the whole tuber and is visible as dry corky areas scattered throughout the tuber. Unlike necrosis from some strains of PAMV in certain varieties (Section 10.2.4) this necrosis has usually become visible by harvest time. The necrosis is so wide-spread that an affected tuber often produces no plant or only a small weak one. Weak strains, however, do not evoke tuber necrosis in certain varieties.

Strains. Strains fall into two main groups: potato calico strains and potato tuber necrosis strains. Strains also differ in the severity of symptoms evoked in test plants and in physical properties.

Test plants and other hosts. AMV has a wide range of hosts. In *Phaseolus vulgaris* it evokes characteristic symptoms, which differ in severity with some strains. Inoculated leaves react with reddish-brown necrotic local lesions which are sometimes small and sometimes larger; the necrosis may spread to veins. *Vicia faba* reacts with characteristic blackening of the leaves and stem necrosis, which often kills the plant. *Nicotiana tabacum* reacts with yellow local lesions and systemically with vein clearing and mottling.

Serology. High-titre antisera to AMV can be prepared with purified virus from *Nicotiana tabacum*.

10.2.6 Potato leafroll virus
Diseases: potato leafroll; potato phloem necrosis.
French: enroulement. German: Blattrollkrankheit. Spanish: enrollado.

General. PLRV probably occurs wherever potatoes grow. PLRV and PVY are considered to be the main causes of what was called potato degeneration. Plants with PLRV generally produce smaller tubers. The depression in yield depends on environmental conditions, variety and strain.

Physical properties. TIP 70°–80°C; DEP 10^{-3}; SIV 3–5 days at 2°C. Particles polyhedral; about 23 nm in diameter. These properties were found for virus cultured in aphids.

Transmission. PLRV can be artificially transmitted by stem grafting but is difficult to transmit by tuber-core grafting. Plants cannot be infected by mechanical inoculation. Naturally PLRV is transmitted to potatoes only by aphids, of which *Myzus persicae* seems the most efficient vector and the most important economically. Other aphids known to transmit PLRV to potatoes are: *M. ascalonicus*, *Neomyzus circumflexus*, *Aulacorthum solani*, *Macrosiphum euphorbiae* and *Aphis nasturtii*. The aphid must feed a long time to acquire virus and to become viruliferous. This type of virus is known as circulative (Chap. 3).

Symptoms. Symptoms depend on strain, variety and environmental conditions, but in the main are of one type. This is the reason why this virus was not designed by a capital as with many other potato viruses because the latter may cause the

134

most different types of symptoms.

Symptoms of primary infection appear mainly in young leaves at the top of the plants. These leaves usually stand upright and are pale-yellowish and in some varieties tinged purple or reddish (Plate 7). Constituent leaflets of certain varieties are often rolled, especially at the base. Some varieties even react with an epinasty of the top leaves.

Symptoms of secondary infection are always more serious for the whole plant although less pronounced at the top of the plant than for primary infections. The whole plant often looks erect and may be smaller than a healthy one. Older leaves are rolled and higher leaves are palish. Basal leaves, in particular, are stiff and leathery. An iodine test on leaves demonstrates a heavy accumulation of starch. Older leaves are tinged purple, pronouncedly in some varieties. Older leaves of other varieties show severe necrosis especially at the margins.

The tubers of certain varieties react with an internal necrosis known as net necrosis, which can be seen when a tuber is cut. This symptom is common in certain varieties from the United States. Yield depression in primarily infected crops is much less than in secondarily infected crops. If primary infection takes place late in the season, there are neither primary symptoms nor yield depression. Tubers from infected plants sometimes develop thin sprouts known as spindling sprouts. This symptom is not consistent and depends on variety, strain and environmental conditions. Spindling sprouts is not diagnostic of PLRV.

As test plants cannot be used for routine testing, a histological test, the Igel Lange test, has been developed. Phloem of infected potato plants and of tubers

Fig. 42. *Physalis floridana*, showing vein banding and stunting after introduction of PLRV by *Myzus persicae*.

contains more callose than that of healthy material (Section 9.2.1).

As PLRV infections are always accompanied by phloem necrosis in stems and petioles, infection can be detected by microscopical examination, especially if lesions are stained with Diamant fuchsin.

Strains. Several strains have been detected, differing in severity of symptoms in potatoes and other hosts, in particular *Physalis floridana*. All strains give the same types of symptom.

Test plants and other hosts. Test plants cannot be used in routine testing for PLRV, unlike PVX or PVY. Test plants have to be inoculated by aphids and this procedure takes time and space. Test plants are, however, practical for small trials and the best is *Physalis floridana*. This plant is highly susceptible to the virus and 7–14 days after inoculation shows distinctive stunting, chlorosis and some rolling (Fig. 42). *Physalis angulata* can also be used but is less susceptible. *Datura stramonium* reacts with chlorosis and some leafroll.

Serology. So far, all attempts to prepare an antiserum against PLRV have failed.

10.2.7 Cucumber mosaic virus
CMV is a virus with a very wide host range and is stylet-borne and transmitted by a number of aphid species. It is rarely found in potato. The virus evokes yellowing of inoculated leaves of potato; systemic infection also causes a yellowing of leaves.

10.3   Potato viruses transmitted by other insects

10.3.1 Tomato spotted wilt virus
This virus is transmitted by *Thrips* spp. and causes necrotic spots and streaks on stems and leaves of potato and ultimately top necrosis. In dry hot conditions, the virus is sometimes widespread in potatoes. The virus is rarely tuber-transmitted. Plants from infected tubers are heavily necrotic after emergence and die before full development.

10.3.2 Andean potato latent virus
APLV occurs in potatoes from some parts of South America. It is almost symptomless in potatoes. It is serologically related to *Ononis* yellow mosaic virus and *Dulcamara* virus. The virus is transmitted through the seeds of infected plants. No insect vector is known; the flea beetle *Psylloides affinis* is known to be a vector of the related *Dulcamara* virus.

10.4   Soilborne viruses

10.4.1   Tobacco rattle virus

Synonyms: potato stem mottle virus, Rozendaal 1947; potato corky ringspot virus, Eddins et al. 1946; potato spraing virus, Eddins et al. 1946; tobacco 'partridge' virus, Quanjer 1943; tobacco virus 11, J. Johnson 1957; *Nicotiana* virus 5, Smith 1957.

Diseases: potato stem mottle; potato figure aucuba mosaic; potato sprain; potato spraing; potato corky ringspot; potato concentric ring necrosis.

Danish: rattle (kartoffel). Dutch: aardappelstengelbont; kringerigheid. French: tacheture de la tige (pomme de terre). German: Stengelbuntkrankheit der Kartoffel; Pfropfenkrankheit der Kartoffel; Mauchekrankheit in Tabak. Italian: rattle (patata). Spanish: abigarramiento del tallo (patata). Swedish: stengelbont.

General.   The virus and the diseases it causes in potatoes are known by different names in the Netherlands, Germany, Great Britain, Italy, Denmark, Ireland, Sweden, Norway, France and the United States. It occurs only on light and peaty soil, where it causes a serious disease called stem mottle or corky ringspot. The virus is usually local in a field and spreads slowly in a season. In certain years the infection rate can be very high depending on growing conditions, number and activity of the vectors.

Physical properties.   TIP 75°–80°C; DEP 10^{-4}; SIV about 4 weeks. Particles: two components, viz. rods 180 nm and 75 nm long, respectively, and about 25 nm wide.

Transmission.   TRV can be artificially transmitted by stem grafting and sap inoculation but sometimes less easily than many other viruses. Early investigators knew only that certain patches of soil in a field were infectious. It has since been found that various nematodes (Chap. 4) of the genus *Trichodorus* can transmit the virus. The virus persists in them for a long time. Its persistance in *Trichodorus* and its wide host range are responsible for the continuance of infectiousness in infested patches.

Symptoms.   Certain strains evoke potato stem mottle, a misleading name since the mottle is not on the stem but usually on leaves of only some stems. Sometimes, however, all stems of a plant are infected. The symptoms of stem mottle in potatoes vary in severity and type: a mottling of the leaves, in which the lighter patches are courser and more yellowish than in other types of mosaic; leaves are sometimes small and deformed (Plate 8). Sometimes leaves have bright-yellow stripes shaped like chevrons and arcuate and ring-like yellow patches. This symptom is called figure aucuba mosaic. The patches differ in shape from those of PAMV (Section 10.2.4). Leaves of certain varieties show necrotic patches also arcuate or chevron-like, often together with the mosaic. Petioles and stems also may show necrotic streaks. With some strains and varieties, tubers too may be necrotic and deformed. Plants may be severely dwarfed or stunted. The symptoms are most severe at low temperatures. Above 20°C, symptoms are completely or almost completely masked.

A severe disorder of tubers known by different names (Dutch: kringerigheid; English: spraing or sprain; German: Pfropfenbildung, Pfropfenkrankheit) has long been known. It usually occurs on the same type of soil as potato stem mottle and is now ascribed to certain strains of TRV.

The cut flesh or even the surface of affected tubers contains necrotic arcs and rings reminiscent of the necrotic symptom in leaves caused by potato stem mottle strains. More than 50% of all the tubers from plants affected by strains causing stem mottle produce infected plants. With strains causing spraing only 0–30% of the tubers produce infected plants.

Strains. Strains of TRV fall into two main groups: potato stem mottle strains and potato spraing strains. They evoke characteristic symptoms in *Nicotiana tabacum*. The number of TRV strains is very large.

Test plants and other hosts. *Nicotiana tabacum* is a good test plant for TRV. After mechanical inoculation specific arcuate and ring-like patterns appear on inoculated leaves. Some strains may become systemic in *N. tabacum*, evoking widespread necrosis on leaves and stem. TRV has a wide range of hosts. Only the roots of most of them become infected and then the virus is not translocated to aerial parts. The virus can best be detected in the soil by inoculating tobacco leaves with sap from roots of certain hosts, such as *Stellaria media*, which have been growing in the soil. Virus may be cultured for purification in *N. tabacum*.

Serology. High-titre antisera can be prepared against TRV. They have been used to establish the serological relationship between different isolates. Antiserum prepared with some strains react specifically only to a limited number of other strains.

10.4.2 *Potato mop-top virus*
Diseases: potato mophead, Loughnane & McKay, 1967; potato spraing (also TRV), Calvert & Harrison, 1966; potato concentric necrosis; potato yellow mottling, Todd, 1965; potato mop-top.

General. PMTV was first described recently and is known to occur in different countries. As the disease is in some ways similar to TRV, the virus was long overlooked as a separate entity. The discovery of PMTV has explained some problems associated with stem mottle and internal necrosis of tubers. PMTV occurs on heavier soils than TRV.

Physical properties. The physical properties of PMTV have not yet been established. There is some evidence that the particles are elongated.

Symptoms. The symptoms caused by PMTV differ widely between varieties and even from year to year because of environmental conditions. Plants grown from infected tubers may produce three main types of symptoms on one stem of a plant or sometimes all stems.
1. Mop-top symptoms: stems have shortened internodes and crowded leaves, whose leaflets are reduced in size with wavy or rolling margins ('Alpha').
2. Aucuba symptoms: irregular bright-yellow blotches, rings or line patterns, usually in the middle leaves. This figure aucuba is the most common symptom of PMTV.
3. Chlorotic chevrons which may be distinct or diffuse and ultimately become a distinct mosaic in the upper leaves.

Tuber progenies from infected plants may be either healthy or partially or totally affected. The symptoms in the tubers differ between varieties. There are usually cracks of different size, so that tubers are malformed. The tubers crack along brown surface blotches. When cut, the tubers show necrotic spots and sometimes also rings and arcs. Tubers infected from the soil may show distinct, slightly raised necrotic concentric rings 1–5 cm in diameter anywhere on the surface. If tubers are infected late in growth, there may be no symptom. Spraing, internal necrotic arcs and streaks, may extend from some of these superficially visible rings. External symptoms are usually more conspicious than internal ones.

Transmission. PMTV is transmitted naturally by potato powdery scab fungus (*Spongospora subterranea*). The fungus and other hosts may be responsible for the persistance of the virus in soil, even when no potatoes are grown. The virus probably spreads from field to field in spore balls of *S. subterranea* carried by tubers.

Test plants and other hosts. To test the infectiousness of soil, *Nicotiana debneyi* is used. It reacts with characteristic necrotic symptoms 5–6 weeks after planting in infected soil. PMTV in potato leaves can be detected, though not easily, by inoculation of sap into leaves of *Chenopodium amaranticolor*. Small diffuse chlorotic ring-like patches appear and gradually enlarge as rings and similar patterns from around the original lesion. Lesions may finally cover large sections of the leaves. Infection is never systemic.

Chenopodium quinoa develops chlorotic lesions. *Nicotiana tabacum* 'White Burley', *N. clevelandii* and *Datura stramonium* may develop necrotic oak-leaf patterns under glass in winter. PMTV can be easier detected from potatoes inoculating first to tobacco and thence 2 weeks later to *C. amaranticolor*.

10.4.3 Tobacco necrosis virus
Disease: potato ABC disease.

General. The ABC disease has been described in the Netherlands where it occasionally affects 'Eersteling' (synonym 'Duke of York') and some other varieties. A similar disease has been reported from the United States. Little is known about it.

Physical properties. Physical properties are probably identical with those of tobacco necrosis virus strains. TIP $72°-85°C$; DEP $10^{-4}-10^{-6}$; SIV about 20 days. Particles isometric; about 20 nm in diameter.

Symptoms. Only tubers react to TNV. The skin of harvested tubers shows dark-brown lesions with radial or reticular cracks. The lesions are circular or band-like and are only superficial. Besides the dark-brown lesions, there are light-brown patches of the same diameter as the radial cracks. During storage, blisters may develop, which later become sunken. Sometimes the blisters are already visible at harvest. The sunken lesions may cover most of the surface of the tubers. In fields where 'Eersteling' was affected, 'Rode Eersteling' proved also to be affected, showing similar symptoms in the tubers. In Italy, tubers of 'Sieglinde' also show brown spots with reticular cracks in the skin.

Test plants and other hosts. Inoculation from infected tubers onto *Nicotiana tabacum* 'White Burley' gives rise to necrotic local lesions, typical for TNV. The virus has a wide host range.

10.4.4 Tomato black ring virus
TBRV is transmitted by the nematodes *Longidorus elongatus* and *L. attenuatus*. It can infect potato, causing necrotic spots and rings on the leaves. The virus is related to the virus causing bouquet disease in Germany. Tubers from infected plants may or may not be infected (Chap. 4).

10.5 Agents transmitted by leafhoppers
Certain infectious diseases known from many countries were long considered to be evoked by circulative viruses. These agents are transmissible by leafhoppers but rarely with sap. They have a wide range of hosts. Common symptoms are yellowing and dwarfing.

Since the discovery of mycoplasma in aster affected by yellows in Japan in 1967 (Section 1.5) electron micrographs have shown that mycoplasma is associated with many such diseases. Similarities of symptoms and of the type of vector suggest that certain potato diseases are caused by mycoplasma. Different types range in size from less than 100 nm to more than 1 000 nm. Unlike bacteria and fungi they have no rigid cell wall but only a thin membrane. They can contaminate cell structures and certain types isolated from animals have been cultured in vitro.

In the Netherlands, we have had little experience with these diseases in potato; the following descriptions are summarized and formalized from the literature.

10.5.1 Potato yellow dwarf virus

Synonyms: potato virus 5, Johnson 1957; *Solanum* virus 16.
Disease: potato yellow dwarf.
German: Gelbzweigigkeit der Kartoffel.

General. PYDV is the only leafhopper-borne virus that is transmissible by sap. Unlike the diseases described in Section 10.5.2, the infectious agent seems indeed to be a virus. It is only known from the United States and Canada.

Physical properties. TIP 50°–53°C; DEP 10^{-3}–10^{-4}; SIV 12–13 h. Particles are bacilliform 380 nm long and 75 nm wide.

Transmission by vectors. There are two closely related but distinct forms of PYDV. One is transmitted by the leafhoppers *Aceratagallia* spp., including *A. sanguinolenta* and further only by *Agallia quadripunctata*. The other is transmitted by *Agallia constricta* and *A. quadripunctata*. Both forms are circulative and multiply in their vectors.

Symptoms. Potato plants show apical yellowing and necrosis; tubers have internal necrotic spots, malformation, cracking and dwarfing.

Test plants. In *Nicotiana rustica* PYDV causes primary lesions.
   Other hosts include *Trifolium incarnatum. Chrysanthemum leucanthemum* var. *pinnatifidum* is the principal source of infection for potato crops.

10.5.2 Aster yellows (mycoplasma)

Synonyms: aster yellows virus, Kunkel 1926; New York aster yellows virus, Kunkel 1932; Californian aster yellows virus, Kunkel 1932; *Solanum* virus 17, Smith; western aster yellows virus, Freitag 1956.
Diseases: potato purple dwarf, Sandfort & Clay 1941; potato apical leafroll, Schultz & Bonde 1929; potato haywire (Canada), Wright; potato late breaking, Raymer & Amen 1954; potato purple top wilt, Brentzell 1938.

Potato purple top wilt is evoked by some strains of aster yellows including California strains but not New York strains. It is transmitted by the leafhopper *Macropsis fascifrons.* Symptoms are yellowish-purple discoloration, inward rolling of apical leaves and later wilting of leaves. Aerial tubers form. Often only some of the tubers pass on the disease to progeny. Tubers commonly form thin sprouts.
   Potato late breaking too is due to strains of aster yellows and is transmitted by *M. fascifrons.* In plants from infected tubers, symptoms usually appear late in growth and are similar to those of purple top wilt.

10.5.3 Tomato stolbur (mycoplasma)

Synonyms: tomato stolbur virus, Ryzkov et al. 1933; stolbur virus, Ryzkov et al. 1933; classical stolbur virus, Valenta et al. 1961; southern stolbur virus, Valenta et al. 1961; metastolbur virus, Valenta 1959.

Symptoms of stolbur virus are similar to those of potato purple top wilt. Three groups of strains are known differing in vector: stolbur, transmitted by the leaf-hoppers *Hyalesthes obsoletus*, *Euscelis plebejus*, *Aphrodes bicinctus* and *Macrostelis laevis*; parastolbur, transmitted by *E. plebejus*; and metastolbur, for which no vector is known.

10.5.4 Tomato big bud (mycoplasma)

Synonyms: tomato big bud virus, Samuel et al. 1933; tomato blue top, Samuel et al. 1933; tomato bunchy top, Samuel et al. 1933; tomato rosette, Cobb 1902; tomato virescence virus, Hill 1943.
Disease: potato haywire (USA), Webb & Schultz 1958.

Tomato big bud, transmitted by the leafhopper *Orosius argentatis*, evokes symptoms in potato similar to purple top wilt.

Closely related is *Vaccinium* false-blossom (synonyms: cranberry false-blossom virus, Dobroscky 1929; Wisconsin false-blossom virus, Holmes 1948; *Vaccinium* virus 1, Smith 1957) transmitted by *Euscelis striatulus*.

10.5.5 Potato witches' broom (mycoplasma)

Synonyms: potato witches' broom viruses, Hungerford & Dana 1924; potato virus 11, Johnson; *Solanum* virus 15, Smith 1957; northern stolbur, Suhov & Vovk 1949.
Disease: potato witches' broom; potato dwarf shrub virosis, Sprau 1951.

Potato witches' broom has been found in various countries throughout the world. Some strains are known to be transmitted by the leafhopper *Ophiola flavopicta*. Symptoms differ from those of potato purple top wilt and differ between strains. Plants produce many axillary and basal branches, becoming bushy in habit. They have chlorotic simple small leaves and many minute tubers. Tubers from infected plants produce many sprouts soon after formation.

10.6 Further reading

Bode, O., 1968. Kartoffel. In: M. Klinkowski (ed.), Pflanzliche Virologie II. Die Virosen des europäischen Raumes I. 2. Aufl. Akademie Verlag, Berlin, p. 31–68.

Doi, Y., M. Teranaka, K. Yora & H. Asuyama, 1967. Mycoplasma or PLT group-like microorganisms found in the phloem elements of plants infected with mulberry dwarf, potato witches' broom, aster yellows, or Paulownia witches' broom. Nippon Shokubutsu Byori Gakkaiho 33: 259–266.

Fernandez Valiela, M. V., 1969. Introduccion a la Fitopatologia. 3rd ed. Vol. I: Virus. Instituto Nacional de Tecnologia Agropecuaria (INTA), 1011 p.

Gabriel, W., 1967. Nasiennictwo ziemniaka. Panstwowe wydawnictwo rolnicze i lesne. Warszawa, 414 p.

Gibbs, A. J., B. D. Harrison & A. F. Murant (eds), 1970. Descriptions of plant viruses. Commonwealth Mycol. Inst., Ass. appl. Biol., United Kingdom.

MacLeod, D. J., 1962. Mosaic and streak viruses of the potato. Canada Dept. Agric., Publication 1150. 80 p.

Martyn, E. B., 1968. 'Plant virus names. An annotated list of names and synonyms of plant viruses and diseases.' Commonwealth Mycol. Inst., Surrey, England, 204 p.

Rozendaal, A. & J. H. Brust, 1955. The significance of potato virus S in seed potato culture. Proc. 2nd Conf. Potato Virus Dis., Lisse-Wageningen 1954, p. 120–133.

Rozendaal, A. & D. H. M. van Slogteren, 1958. A potato virus identified with potato virus M and its relationship with potato virus S. Proc. 3rd Conf. Potato Virus Dis., Lisse-Wageningen 1957, p. 20–36.

Schick, R. & M. Klinkowski (eds), 1962. Die Kartoffel II. VEB Deutscher Landwirtschaftsverlag, Berlin, 2112 p.

Smith, K. M., 1957. A textbook of plant virus diseases. 2nd ed. Little, Brown and Co., Boston, 652 p.

11 Virus translocation in potato plants and mature-plant resistance

A. B. R. Beemster

A successful production of seed potatoes is only possible when environmental conditions are suitable to produce potato seed which is free or nearly free of viruses. The growth period of potatoes generally coincides with the period of activity of aphids which are the main vectors of some of the important potato viruses (e.g. PLRV and PVY). As climatic factors cause considerable differences in the species present, the time they are active and their numbers in different regions or countries, the aphid population must be monitored wherever seed potatoes are grown. Aphids can very efficiently transmit viruses from infected to healthy plants by their normal habit of feeding on the foliage of potato plants. Information is then needed whether any initial virus infection of a potato leaf ultimately will give rise to the infection of the potato tubers, and if so, how long it takes for a virus to reach the tubers from the initial site of infection of the leaves of these primarily infected plants. This information, in combination with data on aphid activity, is needed to establish when to harvest virus-free seed potatoes. The study of virus translocation in potato plants also provides information on the presence of viruses in various parts such as leaves, stems and tubers. Although such information is only incidental to the establishment of a harvesting date it may prove valuable for developing systems of virus diagnosis in different parts of the plant.

This chapter will discuss information on virus translocation in potato plants. Numerous factors influence the rate of virus translocation. It is difficult to make general rules. The general trends formulated must be treated with caution.

After examining general principles (Section 11.1) data will be described on different viruses (Section 11.2) and different potato varieties (Section 11.3). The significance of these facts for the seed-potato grower will be discussed under Section 11.4.

11.1 Translocation
When a potato leaf is inoculated with a sap-transmissible virus like PVX or PVY, virus does not immediately move out of the inoculated leaf. For a time it remains in the cells of the inoculated leaf and multiplies there most likely being translocated over very short distances from cell to cell. When the concentration of virus in the cells of the inoculated leaves has reached a level much higher than

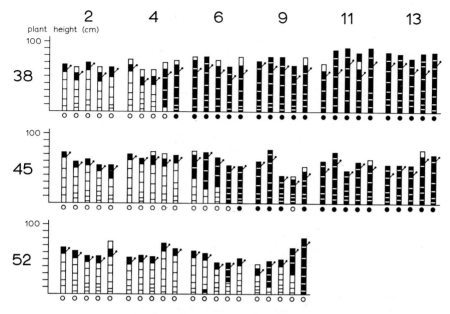

Fig. 43. Translocation of PVY⁰ through stems of 'Bintje' plants and to tubers after mechanical inoculation of leaves. Groups of plants were inoculated 38, 45 and 52 days after planting. Of each group five plants were tested for virus in different parts of stems 2, 4, 6, 9, 11 and 13 days after inoculation. The black dots attached to the schematic stems represent the position of the inoculated leaf on each of the plants and the circles underneath each stem represent tubers. Black and white indicate infected and healthy, respectively.

the initially introduced dose, the virus starts moving into the phloem and is rapidly translocated through the vascular system to other parts of the plant such as tubers and top.

PLRV is spread in the field entirely by aphids and aphids presumably introduce it directly into the phloem. Yet even this virus has proved to remain in the in-oculated leaf for a time before being translocated.

When potato plants are inoculated before or about the time tubers start to form, virus may move out of the inoculated leaf within 3 or 4 days. As the age of the plant at inoculation increases, the virus remains longer confined in the leaf. Long before full maturity, a stage is reached where hardly any virus leaves the inoculated leaf. This phenomenon is for the grower the most important feature of virus translocation in potato plants and is called mature-plant resistance. Its implications for the grower will be outlined later.

Figure 43 gives the results of a trial on translocation of a normal strain of PVY (PVY⁰) in 'Bintje' potatoes. The pattern of translocation through potato stems was established by cutting the stems into sections, each of them consisting

Table 4. Percentage of 'Bintje' tubers infected with PVY[O] harvested at different intervals after inoculation of leaves at different ages.

Days from inoculation to harvesting	Age of plants when inoculated (days)			
	38	45	52	59
2	.	0	0	0
4	.	0	0	0
6	.	4	0	0
9	86	27	0	0
11	88	53	0	0
13	80	34	0	16

of two nodes. These sections must be grown separately before they can be tested for virus. This procedure is the only suitable method for obtaining the data. Usually virus can be detected in the cuttings testing them using suitable diagnostic methods. With PLRV the tubers produced by the cuttings must be harvested later and tested by the tuber-index method.

Table 4 gives the percentages of infected tubers in the groups, already mentioned in Figure 43. There is a marked tendency for these percentages to decrease gradually with age of the plants at inoculation. Plants inoculated 59 days after planting (not in Fig. 43) showed an unexpected rise in the proportion of infected tubers 13 days after inoculation. Such irregularities sometimes occur and may be attributed to incidental differences in the physiological condition of the plants. Even so, the data presented in Figure 43 and Table 4 can be considered representative of what has been found in many trials with various potato viruses.

When the virus has started reaching the tubers of a potato plant all tubers are never simultaneously infected. When the tubers from a single plant are tested, both healthy and infected tubers are usually found. The longer the period between inoculation and harvest the more tubers are infected. When young plants are inoculated, the tubers eventually are usually all infected. However, if they are inoculated when the plants are already forming tubers healthy and infected tubers will be found, even after growth has ceased. The proportion of infected and healthy tubers depends on the period between inoculation and harvest. Even in a single tuber of a primarily infected plant differences can be demonstrated by cutting them into pieces called eye-cuttings, each with one eye. Usually both infected and uninfected eye-cuttings obtained from one single tuber are found when they are planted and tested. Here too, the percentage of infected eye-cuttings is usually higher the longer the period between inoculation and harvest. It was found that tubers stored at 4°C did not differ in the percentage of infected parts compared to tubers stored at 22°–24°C. This might indicate that virus is not translocated within partially infected tubers during storage. There are, however, indications that viruses can be transported within tubers when the tubers have been planted

146

and some of their eyes have developed into stems. This means that a partially infected tuber can give rise to a completely infected potato plant.

Information was also obtained on the question whether virus is translocated from the leaves to particular tubers and to a special part of them. It was found, indeed, that a large tuber is more often infected than a small one and that virus more frequently reaches the rose end of a tuber than the stolon end. This suggests that virus is moving passively in the stream of assimilates through the phloem bundles and that, like assimilates, more is translocated to large tubers than to small ones. Likewise more assimilates, and consequently also more virus, proved to be translocated towards the rose end.

Mature-plant resistance can be reversed by pruning. Of course potato plants are not pruned in practice. However the killing of haulms, which is common practice in some seed-potato growing areas, is in fact a kind of pruning. It may encourage multiplication and translocation of virus to tubers.

11.2 Differences between viruses in translocation

Virus translocation in potato plants seems to be similar for all potato viruses. It is difficult to find a reliable basis for comparing the rate of translocation of different viruses unless tests are carried out simultaneously, and with the same potato variety. This is especially true if differences are small. Even under like conditions, differences in the ways viruses can be transmitted may cause difficulty, e.g. PLRV can only be transmitted by insects, whereas PVX can be transmitted only by mechanical inoculation. The rate of translocation of PVY to tubers is higher by normal sap inoculation than by inoculation with aphids, presumably because aphids introduce much less virus than does mechanical inoculation. Diluted inoculum of PVY^O and PVY^N introduced mechanically gave the same result as virus introduced by aphids.

Table 5 gives the results of an experiment on translocation of PVX, PVY^O and PVY^N. In Table 6 those on PLRV.

PVY^N was translocated quicker than PVY^O and PVY^O quicker than PVX. Many experiments have shown that PVY^N is always very quickly translocated and that mature-plant resistance to this virus is reached late in growth. Differences

Table 5. Percentage of 'Bintje' tubers infected with PVX, PVY^O and PVY^N 24 days after inoculation from plants inoculated 7, 9 and 11 weeks after planting.

Virus	Period between planting and inoculation (weeks)		
	7	9	11
PVX	91	22	0
PVY^O	71	80	42
PVY^N	98	100	98

Table 6. Percentage of 'Bintje' tubers infected with PLRV when harvested at different intervals after inoculation of plants by aphids at different ages.

Age of plants when inoculated (days)	Days from inoculation to harvesting			
	10	17	24	31
37	29	41	44	31
44	3	22	14	31
51	0	9	30	34
58	0	2	0	5

between PVX, PVY^O and PLRV are much more variable and apparently depend on environmental conditions, method of inoculation and potato variety.

PVS is translocated to the tubers only when very young plants are inoculated, thus mature-plant resistance can be expected very early.

11.3 Differences between varieties in translocation

The review of translocation of different viruses was almost entirely based on trials with 'Bintje'. In some trials however, other varieties were compared. Varieties differ considerably in rate of virus translocation. The difference in translocation of PVX between 'Voran' and 'Bevelander' is marked (Table 7). Both are late varieties but, at 7 weeks of age, 'Voran' has a marked mature-plant resistance but 'Bevelander' not.

As early varieties generally start to form tubers earlier than late varieties, one might expect that mature-plant resistance appears sooner in early than in late varieties. But trials and practical experience show that varietal differences other than earliness are often overriding. The rate of virus translocation depends on the rate of multiplication; rates of multiplication probably differ between varieties. Whenever a virus multiplies more slowly in inoculated leaves, it is translocated to the tubers slower too. In plants with mature-plant resistance, viruses multiply at the site of infection much slower than in young plants. Consequently it will take longer for the virus to start moving from this site of infection. The rate of virus

Table 7. Percentage of infected tubers in different potato varieties harvested 10 days after inoculation with PVX.

Variety	Inoculation when 5 weeks old	Inoculation when 7 weeks old
Bintje	57	3
Eigenheimer	74	7
Voran	42	6
Bevelander	70	75

148

multiplication apparently varies between varieties by genetical factors and this ultimately will lead to differences in the rate of virus translocation and also to differences in the time when mature-plant resistance appears. Presumably this sort of difference between potato varieties determines how quickly a variety deteriorates with viruses.

11.4 Virus translocation and its significance for seed-potato growing
In the Netherlands it has been common practice for many years to fix a date for harvesting seed potatoes to keep them virus-free. In fixing the date, two bits of information are needed.

1. Date of infection of foliage may differ between viruses transmitted by contact (e.g. PVX and PVS) and by aphids (e.g. PLRV and PVY). Contact-transmitted viruses are controlled by clonal selection and multiplication (Chap. 17). For viruses transmitted only by insects, the date of appearance and the size of the aphid population in the field are assessed with Moericke traps (Section 3.4.1).

2. Period between infection and translocation to the tubers. In those regions where aphids are present at nearly the beginning of the season of potato growth, it is practically impossible to obtain virus-free tubers because only the complete absence of virus sources within and outside the crop could save tubers from infection. If climatic factors are unfavourable for aphids early in the season there is a better chance of harvesting virus-free seed potatoes. Mature-plant resistance may have some bearing for the grower in establishing the date of harvesting.

Mature-plant resistance in potato plants is detectable but not yet complete when tubers start to form. In greenhouse trials mature-plant resistance except to PVY^N, is usually almost complete 2–3 weeks after tubers start forming. In the field, therefore mature-plant resistance may be expected about 10 weeks after planting. In the Netherlands, mature-plant resistance may develop before aphids become numerous. Hence PLRV and PVY^O present little danger. However, it is dangerous because of the stringent requirements for seed potatoes, to suggest that early harvesting is futile. PVY^N may reach some tubers even after plants have been infected at a date considered safe for other viruses. In fact it may not be safe for other viruses; for instance, some plants may be retarded in growth or environmental conditions may prevent potatoes from reaching the stage of mature-plant resistance. Varietal differences in the date of tuber formation may play a role too.

If a date has to be fixed for harvesting any field, it would be useful if stage of growth could be recognized at which the mature-plant resistance is sufficient. In greenhouse trials with plants in pots under controlled conditions the number of days after planting is an adequate criterion though even then there may be differences in the order of about 10–15 days between different trials. In the field, however, development varies from year to year and from field to field with many factors.

For the moment the most practical way of making use of mature-plant resistance is to get the potato plants as soon as possible to a stage where foliage and shoots stop growing. At that stage there should be a high degree of mature-plant resistance. Several cultural measures promote this. But climatic factors cannot be changed. To get the plants to an advanced stage of growth in good time they must be planted as early as possible. The use of chitted seed will also favour early development of the plants and will promote an even stand.

Manuring needs special consideration. Here too, only general recommendations can be given about favourable conditions for plant development. In greenhouse trials a large amount of nitrogen delayed mature-plant resistance. Excess nitrogen favoured growth of the haulm and retarded tuber formation. Virus translocation in potato plants that had received high rates of nitrogen was the same as in very young potato plants until long after planting. Therefore high rates should be avoided in seed-potato growing.

Phosphorus is thought to have some influence too. So far field trials have been inconclusive but greenhouse trials suggest that high rates of phosphorus, applied before planting, favoured early and quick development of the potato plants; the potatoes acquired mature-plant resistance a bit earlier. This effect seems to occur only when nitrogen was restricted; phosphorus in combination with the high rates of nitrogen caused rank growth of foliage and delayed mature-plant resistance.

Enough nitrogen should be added for satisfactory production but excess must be avoided so that foliage has stopped growing by the time tubers are initiated. Enough phosphorus should be given, preferably before planting, to ensure early and quick development.

In years that climatic and other factors hinder production of virus-free seed potatoes, tubers may have to be tested before definite certification and classification. To ensure quick delivery of the seed potatoes, they must be tested as soon as possible after harvesting. As the tubers are then dormant, the tubers themselves ought to be tested. Ways of doing this have been described in Section 8.2. In such testing, remember that the virus may be restricted to certain parts of a tuber and to certain tubers of one plant. The virus concentration is probably very low in some tubers. Direct diagnosis in potato tubers is always difficult, especially if they have been infected late in growth.

The usual method of testing tubers is tuber indexing, very often after breaking the dormancy of the potato tubers. Eyes are cut from some tubers and are tested in various ways for different viruses. Do not take small tubers, because, if primarily infected, they are usually lighter infected than average. In crops with secondary infection, it has long been known that small tubers should not be selected as seed because they are usually the infected ones. But in rogued fields small tubers are usually less infected than large ones.

For the tests cut eyes from the rose end of large tubers because that end is more often infected than the rest of the tuber. This is already common practice because the terminal sprout grows more readily than laterals, when dormancy has been broken artificially.

The seed-potato grower wants both good yields and good quality. These desires are not always compatible because seed potatoes must often be harvested before yield is maximum and very often during an optimum period for tuber production. Therefore the farmer tends to delay harvesting until the final date fixed by the inspection service. This, of course, is not always possible, especially when areas are large. Instead of harvesting the tubers at the fixed date then farmers may destroy the potato haulm mechanically or chemically to prevent translocation of virus to the tubers. Even better is to pull the haulm, thus definitely ending any kind of translocation from the foliage or stems to the tubers. Killing the haulm chemically or mechanically very seldom completely and immediately kills aerial parts. If the haulm is not immediately killed, cut stems tend to produce new growth, which aphids find very attractive and often invade heavily. These aphids may introduce viruses that reach the tubers within a week, because viruses multiply and are translocated in such plants just as in very young plants. Even if growth is arrested, virus on its way to the tubers at the time of treatment may, according to greenhouse trials, reach the tubers even more quickly if defoliated. Tubers continue to be infected after incomplete killing of the haulms. Haulms must be killed rapidly and quickly. Haulm pulling seems safest, removing any chance of translocation from tops to tubers.

In conclusion knowledge on translocation of viruses and mature-plant resistance can be considered important for the growth and high quality seed potatoes.

11.5 Further reading

Beemster, A. B. R., 1958. Transport van X-virus in de aardappel (*Solanum tuberosum* L.) bij primaire infectie. Tijdschr. PlZiekt. 64: 165–262.
Beemster, A. B. R., 1961. Translocation of leaf roll and virus Y in the potato. Proc. 4th Conf. Potato Virus Dis., Braunschweig 1960, p. 60–67.

12 Incidence of infection in commercial crops and consequent losses

A. J. Reestman

For the production of seed potatoes of high quality, tubers used for planting should obviously be free from virus infection. Tubers used for growing potatoes for human (or animal) consumption or for industrial processing need not be completely free from virus.

The potato grower must consider the price of the seed potatoes as part of the production costs, and work out how much his yield would decrease if he buys seed potatoes of a lower quality grade. Many publications have been devoted to the losses caused by secondary infection. Viruses, like PVY, and PLRV alone or in combination with PVA, seriously affect plant growth, and some authors mention losses of up to 99%.

But even the viruses like PVM, PVS and PVX, which are generally considered to be less severe, may cause considerable losses. PVX has caused yield losses higher than 70% in 'Ackersegen'.

Usually losses are much less since yield loss is slightly correlated with inhibition of haulm growth of the particular plant but, if the haulms of one plant do not grow so much, adjoining plants make up for it. This is called compensation. Compensation is always partial and the degree of compensation depends, inter alia, on environmental conditions.

The worst a virus can do is to prevent infected seed potatoes from germinating, as sometimes happens with potato calico strains of AMV. Gaps appear in the crop. Section 12.2 will consider how healthy plants are influenced by a gap (i.e. by lack of competition). But first let us consider growth of one potato sprout.

12.1 Growth of individual stems

The main stem develops and extends rapidly, forming laterals at its base, especially if space is available and if nitrogen level is high.

After 15–20 leaves have formed, the stem usually develops flower buds in all varieties. At this stage, two laterals usually develop at the top of the main stem. Their leaves, together with those of other stems, may form a closed canopy, taking over photosynthesis from earlier formed leaves. They form the 'first storey'. Both laterals may form flower buds and two laterals whose leaves form a second canopy or second storey. Under favourable conditions, late varieties may form more than two storeys. Plants of such varieties can overgrow plants whose growth has been inhibited. Trials with alternate rows of an early ('Tanja') and a late ('Multa') variety proved that the yield of the late variety can be much higher than that of a monoculture of the late variety. Compensation by the late variety occurred after the early variety stopped growing.

12.2 Growth of the crop

Losses in trials with crops of nothing but diseased plants and of entirely healthy plants are not representative. Usually only a certain proportion of plants are diseased so that yield depends on interactions between plants.

In a potato field a gap is soon filled by haulms from surrounding plants, unless there is drought or the soil is unfertile. If weeds grow prolifically, they may fill the gap. If adjoining potato plants fill the gap, their yield increases. This increase in yield of plants next to gaps is also called compensation. If weeds get the upper hand, yield of adjoining plants may even decrease.

Losses cannot be assessed by adding the yields of diseased plants and healthy plants of a field or by using a factor for the decrease in yield of diseased plants in relation to the yield of healthy plants.

Stewart (1921) set out two trials on clay soil with rows 90 cm apart, and 24 000 (distance in the row 46 cm) and 30 000 plants per ha (distance in the row 37 cm), respectively. Plants adjoining gaps and in the same row yielded 46 and 54% more, respectively. The yields were low: 15 and 18 tons[5] per ha, respectively. Weeds did not occur. Livermore (1927) repeated the trials over 3 years, with 25 000 plants per ha (rows 90 cm apart, distance in the row 44 cm). Plants adjoining gaps yielded 46, 36 and 29% more, respectively, mean yields being 26, 22 and 27 tons per ha. In both Stewart's and Livermore's trials, gaps did not affect yield of plants in adjoining rows (90 cm apart). Then gaps of one plant in 10 caused losses from 4.6–7.1% of the yield.

In four trials in East Germany about 1960 with 40 000 plants per ha (rows 62.5 cm apart, distance in the row 40 cm), gaps were created by roguing early in the season. Compensation was observed in the four plants next to each open space of 78, 75, 92 and 77%, respectively, in the four trials.

In trials in the Netherlands over 3 years with 60 000 and 30 000 plants per ha, and rows 50–70 cm apart in the various trials, compensation for the lower plant density was usually very strong but depended on the size of seed potatoes. Smaller tubers compensated less than larger ones, mainly because of fewer main stems. The plant densities were rather high in these Dutch trials but they were laid out on fertile soils. Bodlaender & Reestman (1968) found compensation with plants and rows more than 90 cm apart. In almost all their plots of 10 000 plants per ha, the haulms completely covered the soil but later than at normal plant densities.

Potato plants compete to fill the gaps. Competition can also be seen between plants with different numbers of stems. Stewart (1921) found that plants with few

5. 1 metric ton = 1 000 kg.

153

stems yielded fewer but larger tubers than plants with many stems.

Reestman & de Wit (1959) even noticed competition between stems of one plant, especially at low plant densities. Stems from large tubers (thus producing many stems at the same place) yielded less than those from small tubers.

In a healthy crop, plants are never identical, even if chitted (= pre-germinated) tubers equal in size are planted at exactly the same depth. From emergence onwards, plants always differ in size, number of stems, leaf area, rate of growth and ultimately in yield, because of soil fertility and other environmental factors.

Even if plants start alike, differences develop as they grow. Growth rate of tubers depends on the degree to which the field is covered by potato foliage. Yield will be maximum when cover is complete for the longer part of the growing season.

Results of all trials show that a certain number of plants developing from healthy tubers may, unnoticed, become primarily infected. Particularly when studying differences in yield of diseased central plants and their healthy neighbours, this point has to be taken into account. If the primary disease also reduces yield, the losses reported in the literature and in this Chapter will be too high in comparison with a crop grown under conditions with smaller chances of infection. It is indeed very probable that primary infection with, for instance, PVY^O affects the yield unfavourably and that compensation by primarily infected adjoining plants can be less than by uninfected healthy plants.

Theoretically yields could be as high with partly diseased crops as with healthy crops, if both provide the same cover and if rates of photosynthesis and respiration were the same.

12.3 Effect of secondary infection with PLRV

In a crop with a certain percentage of plants secondarily infected with PLRV, the emerging plants vary more than in a healthy crop. Small plants yield less than the larger ones. In a trial with 'Voran' planted 50 cm apart in the row and between rows in fertile soil, 10% of the plants were diseased and each diseased plant was surrounded by healthy plants. Loss of yield was only 2%.

Yield of a healthy plant was found to depend on the number of diseased plants surrounding it (0, 1, 2, 3 or 4). Likewise yield of a diseased plant depended on the number of healthy plants surrounding it (also 0–4).

As all situations may occur in one field, it is difficult to assess compensation. However de Wit (1960) has developed a general formula for growth of mixed crops. It is applicable to trials with healthy plants and gaps (Fig. 44) or diseased plants. The formula consists of two parts, one for the yield of the healthy proportion of the plants (Y_H) and one for the yield of the diseased proportion of the plants (Y_D).

$$Y_H = K_{hl} \times Z_h (K_{hl} \times Z_h + Z_1)^{-1} \times M_H$$

and

$$Y_D = Z_1 (K_{hl} \times Z_h + Z_1)^{-1} \times M_D$$

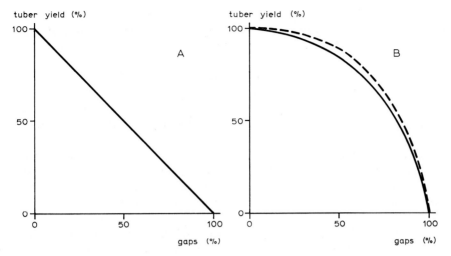

Fig. 44. Relation between yield and percentages of gaps (schematic). No compensation (A), with compensation (B; ———: small seed, – – – –: large seed).

in which M_H and M_D are the yields for a crop of only healthy and only diseased plants, respectively, and Z_h and Z_1 the proportion of healthy and diseased plants in the crop, respectively; K_{h1} is a constant. Total yield is the sum of the yield of the two components Y_H and Y_D.

A few plants with secondary infection hardly decrease crop yield but a high proportion of diseased plants usually causes large losses. If diseased plants grow to normal size but have a much lower rate of photosynthesis than healthy plants, the plants cover the ground but yield little. Hence yield would be depressed more than by gaps. However, Stewart (1921) found that the net loss (including the increase in yield of the two adjoining plants) from a gap was 40% and from a plant with PLRV 31%.

If the loss from PLRV is comparable to that from gaps, the loss could be diminished by planting more densely according to the known incidence of PLRV in the seed potatoes. Theoretically if 35% of the seed potatoes had PLRV, the same yield could be obtained by planting, say, 60 000 seed potatoes per ha, as by planting the usual 40 000 healthy ones per ha. The same result could be expected if, at 40 000 plants per ha, six main stems grew from each potato instead of four.

12.4 Effect of other viruses

With gaps or plants with secondary infection of PLRV, healthy plants may largely compensate losses. With other viruses causing mosaic, e.g. PVX, compensation seems less likely. Diseased plants develop normal foliage covering the ground until maturity, so that adjoining plants cannot compensate for diseased plants.

With PVY^O, however, field trials mentioned in the literature have shown that healthy plants may compensate for adjoining diseased plants. No adequate data are available on competition between plants in crops with milder viruses, e.g. PVM and PVS.

For PVA and PVY^N, scanty data are available. The effect of level of incidence of PVA on 'Green Mountain' was compared with that of PLRV and PVY^O. Losses increased with incidence. With 100% incidence, loss from PVA was much less (31%) than that from PLRV (62%) or PVY^O (63%). In Germany the effect was compared of level of incidence of PVY^N in four potato varieties. Yield decreased as incidence increased. Losses were greater when symptoms were more apparent. If symptoms of PVY^N appear late in growth and development of the haulm is not affected, there may be no compensation. Data from comparisons of 100% diseased with healthy plants may then be representative.

12.5 Effect of infection on weight, number and dry matter content of tubers

Secondary virus infection is often stated to influence the mean weight of tubers. Plants secondarily infected with PVA, PVM and PVX produce lighter tubers than healthy plants. Plants secondarily infected with PLRV and PVY produce fewer tubers than healthy plants, though less so than with PVA. This sort of information from plots with a certain proportion of diseased and healthy plants is not conclusively an effect of virus. Weight and number of tubers could partly depend on competition between plants.

Tubers from plants of 'Voran' and 'Record' with PLRV seemed to contain less dry matter than tubers from healthy plants. Dry matter content, however, also depends on plant density and time of initiation and maturity of tubers.

In some trials, I compared dry matter contents in diseased 'Voran' tubers of certain sizes. Small tubers from plants secondarily infected with PLRV had more dry matter than healthy tubers. Large tubers had less dry matter than healthy tubers. In total, dry matter was about the same in healthy and diseased tubers.

Plants stunted by PLRV contained more dry matter than diseased plants that had developed better.

12.6 Practical significance

Data on losses with secondary infection are extremely confusing, undoubtedly because environmental conditions and varieties differ between the trials. Certainly losses in a secondarily diseased plant can be compensated to some extent by adjoining healthy plants. The extent of this compensation probably governs losses in the field.

Gaps may be filled and diseased plants grown over early in growth before tubers start forming, e.g. by laterals from the lower buds of the stems.

When diseased plants prematurely stop growing, the other plants may grow over them. The situation is similar to that of a mixed crop of an early and a late variety (Section 12.1), in which yield may be higher than in a single crop at the same plant density. Indeed some of our trials (unpublished) with mixtures of

156

diseased and healthy plants substantiate this view. Diseased plants may also compensate for gaps, but usually less than healthy plants. Undoubtedly diseased plants of different vigour compete with one another.

Varietal differences or differences in plant density may be responsible for the large variation in published data for 100% diseased and 100% healthy plants.

It is impossible to predict the loss a farmer may expect if he plants seed potatoes with a certain proportion of diseased tubers, because competition between plants in the field is governed by environmental conditions.

Compensation does not occur and percentage loss is highest with infertile soil or drought, low plant density and few sprouts per tuber.

Compensation is highest with fertile soil and sufficient water, dense planting and many sprouts per tuber.

With high compensation, it is theoretically possible that, up to a certain percentage, the diseases would not reduce yield in weight. Even if the planting is dense or if diseased plants start forming tubers earlier than healthy plants, or if healthy plants grow for longer than diseased ones, slightly higher yields could be obtained. In the Netherlands where potato fields are usually completely covered by foliage when tubers start forming, conditions for compensation are usually good.

Losses from secondary infection are usually expressed as percentage of the yields of healthy crops. The farmer can ignore a 10% incidence of PLRV in his seed and a consequent loss of 2%, if the total yield is 20 tons per ha (loss 0.4 ton). But if environmental conditions are good and yield is 80 tons per ha, he would lose 1.6 tons per ha.

12.7 Further reading

Podlaender, K. B. A. & A. J. Reestman, 1968. The interaction of nitrogen supply and plant density in potatoes. Neth. J. agric. Sci. 16: 165–176.

Livermore, J. R., 1927. A critical study of some of the factors concerned in measuring the effect of selection in the potato. J. Am. Soc. Agron. 19: 857–896.

Reestman, A. J. & C. T. de Wit, 1959. Yield and size distribution of potatoes as influenced by seed rate. Neth. J. agric. Sci. 7: 257–268.

Reestman, A. J., 1970. The importance of the degree of virus-infection for the production of ware potatoes. Potato Res. 13: 248–268.

Stewart, F. C., 1921. Further studies on the effect of missing hills in potato fields and on the variation in the yield of potato plants from halves of the same seed tuber. N.Y. agric. Exp. Stn Bull. 489, 50 p.

Wit, C. T. de, 1960. On competition. Versl. landbouwk. Onderz. 66.8 (2nd ed., 1964), 82 p.

13 Therapy

Frederika Quak

Unlike insects, mites, nematodes, fungi and bacteria, viruses cannot be controlled by applying chemicals to host plants. Virus multiplication is intimately associated with normal metabolic processes in plants, so that virus inhibitors so far known have proved toxic to the plant. Moreover they cannot cure a whole plant: when treatment ceases, the virus soon recovers to its former concentration.

By killing the vectors (insects, nematodes, mites) with chemicals, the spread of some virus diseases can be alleviated (Chap. 14). However some viruses are transmitted mechanically or by insects immediately the insect starts feeding (stylet-borne viruses). Such viruses cannot be controlled by pesticides. Recently spraying with mineral oils proved to considerably reduce infection of certain crops with stylet-borne viruses (Section 14.2).

Fortunately few viruses are transmitted by seed of infected plants, so the seeds usually develop into healthy plants. But virus-free seedlings are useless for maintenance of clones, hybrids and varieties, including the potato.

Once infected (systemically), the disease is transmitted from generation to generation, and some potato varieties have over the years become completely infected. Probably all clonal crops are infected with one or more viruses, in particular with latent viruses hardly detectable by their symptoms. Occasionally one or more plants of a variety without virus can be selected by lack of symptoms.

Routine testing, either serologically or with indicator plants, may also provide plants free from virus. Selection of tubers and of clones have both considerably improved quality but favoured symptomless carriers of unknown viruses which could infect other varieties. Methods have been developed for freeing clones of infected varieties from one or more viruses: heat treatment or meristem culture. Cured or virus-free is used here in a limited sense of free from the viruses for which the plant is tested. Unknown viruses may remain.

The success of therapy depends on the virus to be eliminated and on characteristics of the plant material. Heat treatment is usually effective only against isometric and thread-like and not against rod-shaped viruses. There are four stages in curing operations.
1. Identification of virus(es) present in the clone.
2. Therapy.
3. Testing of treated plants.

158

4. Propagation and continued testing of cured plants under conditions that avoid reinfection.

13.1 Heat treatment

Diseased sugar-cane was already treated with heat before the cause of disease was known. In 1889, it was noticed in Java that sugar-cane suffering from sereh disease (now known to be caused by a virus) grew better after having been kept at 50°–52°C in water for 30 min. Later sugar-cane ratoon stunt also proved to be controlled in this way (2 h at 50°C).

In many parts of the world, several thousand tons of sugar-cane cuttings are now treated each year in large water baths before being planted. Hot air, usually at 35°–38°C for 2–4 weeks, is now commonly used for several crops.

For potato, heat treatment is of limited importance. In the 1920s, there were unsuccessful attemps to cure potato tubers of PLRV, PVX and PVY.

About 1950, PLRV proved to be heat-inactivated in tubers. Potato tubers soon die with heat but Kassanis found that 'Majestic' and 'Arran Consul' tubers remained viable after a considerable period at 37.5°C, if kept humid. He removed tubers after different periods in the incubator and stored them at 15°C until they sprouted. He then planted them in pots under glass. All plants from incubated tubers had typical symptoms of PLRV; some tubers incubated for 10–20 days showed typical symptoms, whereas others did not. None of the plants from tubers that survived 25 days or more in the incubator showed symptoms.

American workers reported that incubation at 35°C for 56 days or 36°C for 39 days completely eliminated PLRV from tubers of several potato varieties.

Some workers recommend fluctuating temperatures, particularly for eye cuttings which are more sensitive than whole tubers. Almost all eye-cuttings of 'Russet Burbank' survived periods of 4 h at 40°C, alternating with periods of 20 h at 16°–20° for up to 8 weeks. Tubers were completely cured of PLRV after treatment for 6 weeks.

In India, potatoes with PLRV were kept in a naturally hot thatched shed. For the first 2 months, average temperature was about 32°C and for the next 4 months about 29°. PLRV was completely eliminated in 6 months but significant reduction in virus content occurred much sooner especially in the first 2 months. Survival of tubers was 44–60%.

The proportion of PLRV-free tubers and tuber survival after heat treatment varies between varieties. Mutants may perhaps occur among plants from heat-treated tubers.

In general, heat causes the tubers to deteriorate. They may change in colour or sprout late or not at all, so that heat is less suitable for commercial use or for seed intended for immediate yield trials. However experience has shown that heat eliminates PLRV and PVY from small stocks of seed of special value, which could then be multiplied into improved clones.

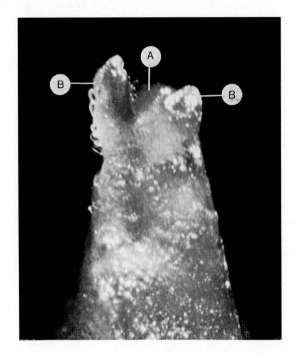

Fig. 45. Growing point of potato with meristem (about 0.1 mm in diam.) (A) and leaf primordia (B).

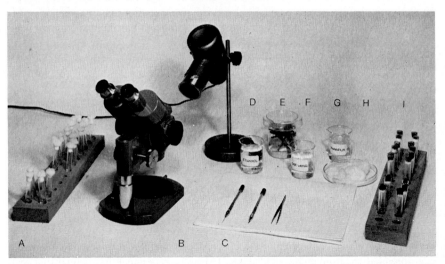

Fig. 46. Equipment needed for excising meristems: nutrient medium in tubes (A), microscope (× 10–40) and lamp (B), sterile filter paper, mounted needle, mounted fragment of razor blade and tweezers (C), ethanol (D), disinfected potato shoots (E), sterile water (F), Parafilm, disinfected in ethanol (G), ethanol-soaked cotton wool (H) and tubes, flamed and sealed with sterile Parafilm (I).

160

13.2 Meristem culture

Limasset & Cornuet (1949) found that the concentration of TMV in tobacco leaves diminished as they approached the tip. In half of the growing points or apical meristems, no virus was detectable. On this principle, Morel & Martin (1952) presumed that meristems of virus-diseased dahlia could be isolated and cultured aseptically in vitro in order to get healthy plants. After using various nutrient media, they succeeded in obtaining from meristems some plantlets 1–2 cm long but without roots. By grafting them onto young virus-free seedlings, they got healthy plants.

The technique has since been used to cure completely infected valuable varieties of some crops. Morel (1964) and Kassanis (1965) clearly describe the many difficulties that were encountered. The meristem is a dome of actively dividing cells, about 0.1 mm across and 0.25 mm long. The work must all be done under sterile conditions. Success depends on nutrient requirements that vary from species to species and sometimes even from variety to variety. Either a liquid or a solid agar medium is used with all necessary minerals, sugar, vitamins and growth substances.

Reviewing the literature, one is struck by the disparity of terminology. Besides 'meristem culture', the terms 'meristem-tip culture', 'tip culture', 'culture of shoot apices' or 'shoot tip culture' are used, partly depending on the actual size of the isolated pieces of tissue. As a rule, meristem of both main shoot and axillary buds are excised to the dimensions mentioned before. However the chances of growth are often so small that with the meristem one or two leaf primordia are excised too (Fig. 45). Such tips are up to 1 mm long. These have better chance of developing but are less likely to be free from virus.

13.2.1 Technique

For potato, take shoots from tubers germinating in light or darkness or segments from stems of full-grown potato plants. Apical and axillary meristems are protected by developing leaves to such an extent that disinfection may be superfluous. For mild surface-sterilization of shoots and defoliated segments of stem, dip them for some seconds in 96% ethanol, submerge them in a filtered solution of 50 g commercial calcium hypochlorite per litre water and rinse several times in sterile water. If no transfer room as used for mycological work is available, excise the meristems in normal dust-free laboratory space; the smallness of the isolates makes aerial contamination unlikely. A binocular dissecting microscope magnification 10–40 is required. Wipe the stage of the microscope with cotton wool dipped in ethanol after isolating each meristem. On one side of the microscope, place six to ten sheets of sterile (autoclaved) filter paper and two 100-ml beakers, one filled with ethanol the other with sterile water, in which to dip dissecting instruments before blotting them between the sheets of filter paper (Fig. 46).

To avoid microbial and viral contamination, frequently disinfect the working ends of mounted needles and fragments of safety razor blades in ethanol and then sterile water. Otherwise use a large stock of sterile needles and blades. Working under the microscope, snap off the immature leaves and leaf primordia with slight pressure from the needle. Transfer the excised meristem to nutrient medium in a culture tube by sticking the blade, to which it clings, in the agar and withdrawing it slowly. In liquid media the meristems are supported on a filter-paper bridge, partly immersed in liquid.

Culture tubes of various shapes and sizes have been used. Pyrex glass is recommended. Seal the tubes with aluminium caps. Cotton-wool plugs, flamed before being sealed with plastic seals such as Parafilm, effectively close the tubes, but have sometimes proved toxic to the excised meristem. Wash culture tubes thoroughly and boil them in glass-distilled water before use.

The nutrient medium is usually based on that developed by White (1934). Minor elements may be added according to Berthelot (1934) or Heller (1953). Iron may be given in chelate form, readily available to the plantlet.

The type and concentration of vitamins and growth substances vary between media. Root initiation is stimulated by α-naphthalene acetic acid (1 mg/litre). Gibberellins encourage elongation, while substances like kinetin, whether or not in certain proportion to adenine, may stimulate a dormant meristem to growth

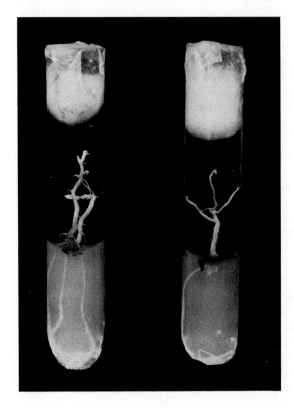

Fig. 47. Meristem cultures of potato (about natural size).

Fig. 48. Meristem culture of potato after transfer to soil.

and differentiation. Normal growth of potato meristems depends closely on the concentration of potassium and ammonium ions (Morel, 1964).

Autoclave the tubes containing nutrient medium at as low a temperature and as briefly as possible to achieve complete sterilization without destruction of certain constituents (e.g. 20 min at 105°C).

Plantlets from potato meristems are very slender with small scaly leaves (Fig. 47). When they are 2–4 cm long, transfer them to small pots containing a sieved compost mixture and cover with glass for some weeks (Fig. 48). As soon as the plants are big enough, take leaf samples and test them for virus, serologically or by inoculation onto indicator plants. Since it may take some time for traces of virus to build up a demonstrable concentration, repeated testing is essential before any clone may be declared free from a certain virus.

13.2.2 Factors in the success of meristem culture

There is no simple rule for the success of meristem culture, since it depends partly on the nature of the viruses present: some viruses are more readily eliminated than others. We found that all potato plants obtained from meristem and one leaf primordium were free from PLRV and 80% were free from PVA and PVY. Only one plant from about 500 was free from PVX. Of many plants grown from meristems of 'Eersteling', a symptomless carrier of PVS and PVX, only two had lost PVX but were still infected with PVS. Perhaps different viruses reach different distances up the meristem.

Success is also influenced by the composition of the nutrient medium. Both PVS and PVX were eliminated from 'Eersteling' by growing meristems on the

163

Table 8. Nutrient medium for potato meristems (Morel & Muller, 1964).

KCl	1 000	mg	Gibberellic acid		0.1 mg
$(NH_4)_2SO_4$	1 000	mg	$FeCl_3.6H_2O$[1]		1 mg
$Ca(NO_3)_2.4H_2O$	500	mg	Heller's solution of minor elements[2]		1 ml
$MgSO_4.7H_2O$	125	mg	Difco agar		6 g
KH_2PO_4	125	mg	Distilled water	1 000	ml
Sucrose	20	g			

1. Alternative: 5 ml of a stock solution of $FeSO_4.7H_2O$ 5.57 g, and Na_2EDTA 7.45 g in 1 litre distilled water (Na_2EDTA = disodiumethylenediaminetetra-acetate) (Murashige & Skoog, 1962).

2. Heller's solution of minor elements.

$ZnSO_4.7H_2O$	1 000	mg	$AlCl_3$	30	mg
H_3BO_3	1 000	mg	$NiCl_2.6H_2O$	30	mg
$MnSO_4.4H_2O$	10	mg	KI	10	mg
$CuSO_4.5H_2O$	30	mg	Distilled water	1 000	ml

improved medium devised by Morel & Muller (Table 8).

Several potato varieties and selections of importance in the Netherlands have been subjected to meristem culture. Results have varied between varieties. Within a year of excision PVS-free tubers of 'Red Pontiac' were obtained from several meristems. Other varieties required 2 years to reach this stage, and two selections of 'Kennebec' grew poorly and only produced plants containing PVS as before.

13.3 Meristem culture after heat treatment

Since few meristems develop and not all are virus-free, some workers have heat-treated plant material and then cultured larger meristem tips from them. Assuming that virus multiplication is inhibited, they excised meristem tips up to 1 mm long with two or three leaf primordia. As heat treatment may impede the metabolism and reduce growth of the meristems, trials were needed to discover how long meristems could be kept at high temperature and still develop in reasonable numbers, thus obtaining the maximum proportion alive and virus-free.

In Canada, PVS and PVX could be eliminated in this way from 'White Rose'. Plants were grown under continuous light with air temperatures fluctuating from 35° to 37°C and soil temperatures from 30° to 33°C. At intervals, axillary buds were excised and cultured. The size of the bud was of importance in virus eradication from buds taken after short or no treatment, but was of less consequence as the duration of the heat treatment lengthened. The proportion of PVX-free plants increased progressively with incubation until it reached 50% after 8 weeks and almost 100% after 18 weeks. PVS was more difficult to eliminate. Heat treatments of up to 8 weeks increased the proportion of plantlets free from PVS but longer incubation caused no further increase. Of the PVX-free plants, only about 20% were PVS-free.

164

A worker in New Zealand heat-treated 'Aucklander Short Top' plants infected with PVY and cultured shoot tips 0.5 to 2 cm long on a nutrient medium. PVY was eliminated from some of the plantlets. Similar treatment of PVX-infected 'Dakota' did not eliminate PVX.

13.4 Virus in meristematic tissue

As well as by its practical importance, meristem culture has intrigued plant pathologists by its theoretical interest. If the nature of the phenomena on which it is based were understood, its difficulties could easier be overcome.

Perhaps meristems are often free from certain viruses, because virus is unevenly distributed in a systemically infected plant (Chap. 11).

French workers surmised from the virus-inhibiting effect of certain growth hormones that a high concentration of hormones in meristems inactivated invading virus. This hypothesis has never been proved. Our infection experiments with suspensions of tobacco callus cells suggest a competition between cell division and virus multiplication. In actively dividing tissue, synthesis of normal nucleoproteins would prevail and later, during cell elongation, synthesis of viral nucleoprotein. Observations by Crowley & Hanson (1960) support this hypothesis. They correlated the length of the virus-free tip of a TMV-infected tomato root with the zone where mitosis occurred. A growth inhibitor in the medium causes shortening of the mitotic zone in the root tip. The virus-free zone diminished to the same extent.

Recently, however, virus particles have been observed in meristematic tissue. At first only Esau had observed TMV particles and even viral inclusion bodies in electron micrographs of mitotic cells but not from meristem. She used mesophyll of young tobacco leaves. Walkey & Webb (1968) studied apical meristems of *Nicotiana rustica*, systemically infected with cherry leafroll virus. They excised meristems, without leaf primordia, and homogenized each one in a drop of potassium phosphotungstate, which enhances the visibility of isometric virus particles. Under electron microscope, the homogenate clearly showed virus particles. Similar particles were enclosed in unbranched tubular structures of indeterminate nature. Unfortuately they did not culture any of the meristem, so that it is not known whether meristems of virus-infected *N. rustica* develop into virus-free plants.

According to Hollings, an excised carnation meristem contains carnation mottle virus in such a high concentration that he could demonstrate it with the local-lesion host *Chenopodium amaranticolor*. However after 30 h on nutrient medium, the meristem was no longer infectious. He concluded that contact with the nutrient medium eliminated virus particles originally present.

Hence differences in the ease with which viruses can be eliminated could be due to differences in inactivation on nutrient medium as well as to differences in distribution in the meristem. The composition of the culture medium might well be of importance in inactivating virus from the meristem as well as in the success of their culture.

There is no general explanation yet for all observations. However some hy-

165

potheses seem plausible for certain situations. The lack of a theoretical basis does not detract from the practical importance of meristem culture for therapy of clones.

13.5 Conclusions

Potato clones can be cured of virus diseases by heat treatment, meristem culture or a combination of them. Whether the prolonged work, including continued checking and culling during propagation, is worthwhile depends on the prospects of the plants obtained.

Cured clones are not immune. They are bound to be reinfected when released for normal production. The grower must constantly be on the alert for reinfection.

13.6 Further reading

Berthelot, A., 1934. Nouvelles remarques d'ordre chimique sur le choix des milieux de culture naturels et sur la manière de formuler les milieux synthétiques. Bull. Soc. Chim. biol. 16: 1553–1557.

Crowley, N. C. & J. B. Hanson, 1960. The infection of apical meristems of tomato roots with tobacco mosaic virus after treatment with ethylenediaminetetra-acetic acid. Virology 12: 603–606.

Heller, R., 1953. Recherches sur la nutrition minérale des tissus végétaux cultivés in vitro. Annls scient. natn. Bot. Biol. vég. 14: 1–223.

Hollings, M. & O. M. Stone, 1964. Investigation of carnation viruses. I. Carnation mottle. Ann. appl. Biol. 53: 103–118.

Hollings, M. & O. M. Stone, 1968. Techniques and problems in the production of virus-tested planting material. Scient. Hort. 20: 57–72.

Houten, J. G. ten, F. Quak & F. A. van der Meer, 1968. Heat treatment and meristem culture for the production of virus-free plant material. Neth. J. Plant Path. 74: 17–24.

Kassanis, B., 1965. Therapy of virus-infected plants. J.R. agric. Soc. 126: 105–114.

Limasset, P. & P. Cornuet, 1949. Recherche du virus de la mosaïque du tabac (Marmor tabaci Holmes) dans les méristèmes des plantes infectées. C.R. Acad. Sci. Paris 228: 1971–1972.

Morel, G., 1964. Régénération des variétiés virosées par la culture des méristèmes apicaux. Rev. hort. 136: 733–740.

Morel, G. & C. Martin, 1952. Guérison de dahlias atteints d'une maladie à virus. C.R. Acad. Sci. Paris 235: 1324–1325.

Morel, G. & J. F. Muller, 1964. La culture in vitro du méristème apical de la pomme de terre. C.R. Acad. Sci. Paris 258: 5250–5252.

Stace-Smith, R. & F. C. Mellor, 1968. Eradication of potato viruses X and S by thermotherapy and axillary bud culture. Phytopathology 58: 199–203.

Walkey, D. G. A. & M. J. W. Webb, 1968. Virus in plant apical meristems. J. gen. Virol. 3: 311–313.

White, P. R., 1934. Potentially unlimited growth of excised tomato root tips in a liquid medium. Pl. Physiol. 9: 585–600.

14 Control of aphid vectors in the Netherlands

A. Schepers

Since it became known that aphids transmitted potato viruses, attempts have been made to prevent viruses from spreading by killing or controlling aphids. In the Netherlands, Hille Ris Lambers made the first trials in 1938. Very frequent spraying with nicotine did not hinder virus spread, even when the aphids did not multiply. In the United States DDT or DDT mixtures, applied to prevent direct injury by aphids, sometimes also reduced PLRV infection. In England, Broadbent et al. (1956) inhibited spread of PLRV by spraying with a special DDT emulsion and some other insecticides. In one of our trials, the same emulsion almost completely stopped the spread of PLRV from secondarily infected plants.

However, by 1957 Dutch trials with DDT were discontinued for three reasons. First DDT had to be sprayed onto both the upper and lower surfaces of the leaves, a difficult procedure. Secondly DDT sprayed only onto the upper parts of the plants may reduce the counts of aphids in those parts, whereas in the lower parts they may increase as rapidly as ever. Thirdly systemic chemicals were released to growers in 1957. They kill aphids feeding on sprayed plants. For our trials with them, begun in 1951, we used Systox (Bayer; active substance Demeton). Since 1958, we have had trials with Meta-iso-Systox (Demeton-S-methyl).

14.1 Trials with Systox

Figure 49 shows the layout of some plants of our first trial with Systox. It was set out in an area where aphids were usually too numerous for seed potatoes to be grown. Each plot was enclosed by two dense rows of oats 15 cm apart. Hille Ris Lambers had found that this measure effectively prevented aphids spreading from plot to plot. Apterae were stopped and alates either 'jumped' short distances or flew further away without touching adjoining plots. Later trials were similar.

Two tubers were harvested from each plant, except the sources of infection and planted the next year in the same position in the plot. The parameter of disease incidence was the percentage of hills infected in the original plot. So the influence of the sources of infection on the health of the progeny could be exactly studied. Yield of tubers was estimated in 1951, 1952 and 1955.

Similar trials were with PVA, PVY[N] and PVY[O]. In other trials, van der Wolf (1964) and I (trials in 1958–61, unpublished) independently studied the effect of Systox in rogued plots.

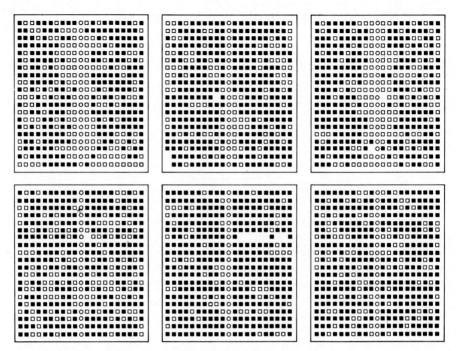

Fig. 49. Layout and results of some plots of the 1951-trial.
O: plants infected with PLRV the previous year.
□: primarily infected plants (2 tubers tested on each plant).
■: healthy plants.
upper blocks: control plots sprayed with water.
lower blocks: treated plots sprayed with Systox.
1951; 'Bintje'; 1 300 litre spray of Systox (1 ml/litre) at emergence and 2 000 litre every
10 days thereafter; plots of 20 × 21 plants 50 cm apart.

14.1.1 Effect on aphid counts

Aphids were counted in the trials in 1951, 1952 and 1955. We examined the
lowest leaf, a leaf halfway up, and the whole top of incompletely unfolded leaves
of one stem per plant. The number of plants sampled depended on aphid density.
Table 9 gives counts of *Myzus persicae*.

Apterae were never found in plots sprayed with Systox. Sometimes there were
a few alates and larvae on the leaves examined. Beat-sampling (Section 3.3.2) of
whole plants from treated plots confirmed the complete absence of apterae. Any
spasmodic larvae were all in the first stage of development: evidently they soon
died after feeding on the Systox-treated plants. When we put healthy alates on
treated leaves they died usually within 8 h, always within 24 h. Aphids did not
colonize plots treated with Systox during the whole season.

Table 9. Effect of spraying with Systox on counts of alatae (al), apterae (ap) and larvae (la) of *Myzus persicae* per 20 'Bintje' plants on different dates.

Date of count[1]	Systox									Control								
	1951			1952			1955			1951			1952			1955		
	la	al	ap	la	al	ap	la	al	ap	la	al	ap	la	al	ap	la	al	ap
1	0	0	0	1	0	0	0	0	0	30	2	4	8	2	2	6	0	1
2	0	0	0	0	0	0	0	0	0	324	1	42	51	3	16	54	0	4
3	0	1	0	0	0	0	0	0	0	1699	5	167	160	2	22	156	1	18
4	49	49	0	0	0	0	0	0	0	4234	156	322	465	4	59	378	4	54
5	8	4	0	0	0	0	0	0	0	80	12	80	990	9	95	538	2	52
6	0	0	0	0	1	0	0	0	0	27	0	27	698	13	130	48	1	3
7				0	0	0	1	1	0				577	0	70	15	0	1
8				0	0	0	0	1	0				21	0	0	2	1	1
9							0	0	0							2	0	1

1. Dates of counts. (Aphid counts on 10–80 plants, according to aphid density.)

	1	2	3	4	5	6	7	8	9
1951–	06–14	06–23	06–30	07–10	07–24	08–03			
1952–	05–17	05–28	06–06	06–16	06–23	07–06	07–13	07–21	
1955–	06–22	06–30	07–06	07–13	07–21	07–27	08–03	08–10	08–17

14.1.2 Effect on predators of aphids

In 1951, predator counts were much lower in Systox-treated plots than in controls. The difference may not be a direct effect of Systox, since the count of predators is a function of aphid density. Predators present during spraying would indeed be killed but, after the leaves have absorbed the poison, no residue remains. Newly arriving predators would not be at risk and could multiply as long as they had aphids to feed on.

14.1.3 Effect on spread of PLRV

Unrogued plots. Most of our trials were designed so that the effect of the virus sources could be examined exactly. In the trials depicted in Table 10, PLRV spread considerably from the virus sources to healthy plants in the plots sprayed with water but hardly at all in plots treated with Systox. In treated plots, PLRV-infected plants were evenly spread among the rows. Infection in these plots must therefore be attributed to spread from outside the field by viruliferous aphids. The high incidence in treated plots in 1951 may be because most of the alates arriving were carrying virus and because aphids were numerous (Table 9, Controls). Regular spraying with Systox can inhibit virus spread from secondarily infected plants within the field but does not prevent virus infection by aphids

Table 10. Effect of Systox on percentage of plants per row infected with PLRV at increasing distance from one row of secondarily infected plants (Row No 0).

		Row No											Avg
		0	1	2	3	4	5	6	7	8	9	10	
1951	Systox	100	18	25	18	25	25	21	29	27	22	.[1]	22.2
	Control	100	74	49	30	28	21	24	25	19	37	.[1]	34.1
1952	Systox	100	1	1	0	1	1	0	0	0	0	1	0.4
	Control	100	59	20	13	13	12	10	8	33	44	2	14.4
1955	Systox	100	10	4	1	1	3	2	2	4	5	3	3.5
	Control	100	91	54	27	19	8	8	6	6	10	6	23.5

1. No data available; in 1951 0.1% at 2 000 litre/ha (first spraying 1 300 litre/ha); in 1952 0.3%, 1 500 litre/ha; in 1955 0.1%, 1 125 litre/ha. Treatments were repeated 8 times in each season. Control plots were sprayed with equivalent amounts of water. Two tubers were taken from each plant in 1951 and 1955; in 1952 four tubers were taken from each plant at a first, two at a second, and one at a third harvest. If only one plant in the progeny proved to be infected with PLRV, the mother plant was still taken to be infected. Values averaged from three replicate plots.

coming from outside. From 1958 till 1961 49 similar trials were laid out throughout the Netherlands. Our conclusions have been confirmed by van der Wolf (1964) in the Netherlands and by British and German workers.

Rogued plots. In a trial in 1952, we unexpectedly found indications that Systox decreased the incidence of PLRV in rogued plots. This effect was confirmed in some trials between 1958 and 1961. The results of 13 trials in 1959, a year when aphids were plentiful, were particularly clear (Table 11). In the other years viruliferous alates were few and incidence in untreated plots was slight. In 1959 spraying once at emergence was almost as effective as spraying every 2 weeks. Van der Wolf (1964) confirmed these conclusions.

Systox may have reduced infection by the absence of aphids during roguing. No viruliferous aphids would be spread around while diseased plants were being pulled out and removed.

The high incidence of PLRV in treated plots shows that Systox may be of little value in a year when aphids are abundant. The similar incidence of PLRV in plots sprayed once and five times confirms that Systox does not reduce infection from viruliferous alates arriving from elsewhere later in the season.

14.1.4 Effect on spread of PVA and PVY

Transmission of non-persistent (stylet-borne) viruses like PVA, PVY^N and PVY^O is very different from that of persistent (circulative) viruses like PLRV (Chap. 3). An aphid can transmit them seconds after probing a diseased plant.

By their nature, stylet-borne viruses can be transmitted not only by potato

Table 11. Effect of Systox in rogued plots on percentage incidence of PLRV in daughter tubers.

Trial No	Harvested 15 to 22 June			Harvested 29 June to 6 July		
	untreated	Systox at emergence	Systox 5× at 2-weeks' intervals	untreated	Systox at emergence	Systox 5× at 2-weeks' intervals
1	10	5	3	15	18	5
2	11	10	6	13	17	10
3	68	11	18	20	21	26
4	10	11	6	22	9	14
5	19	13	14	51	24	36
6	18	9	10	37	32	24
7	78	60	50	81	87	76
8	4	6	3	16	10	11
9	.	32	20	.	32	73
10	6	3	3	22	12	10
11	18	18	11	72	52	49
12	47	24	23	49	62	55
13	73	59	51	86	77	59

1959; 'Bintje'; 1 ml Systox/litre at 1 300 litre/ha either once at emergence or five times at 2-weeks' intervals; values from two replicate plots; 1.5% of planted tubers secondarily infected; infected plants rogued as soon as inspector could see symptoms; two tubers sampled per plant; values averaged from two replicate plots.

aphids but also by other aphid species during brief visits to the potato plants. Spread of non-persistent viruses is difficult to prevent, since several hours pass before an aphid dies after imbibing systemic insecticides in sap of a sprayed plant. During this time, the aphid can visit many plants.

However a reduction in spread of PVY by spraying insecticides has sometimes been reported (Broadbent et al., 1956; van der Wolf, 1964). We studied the influence of Systox sprayings on the spread of PVY[O] in 1951 (treatment as in Fig. 49) and of PVY[N] in 1960 (Table 12).

In 1960 there was a considerable spread of PVY[N] in the plots, whether sprayed with Systox or not. Results were similar with PVY[O] in 1951. Our conclusion that spraying with systemic insecticides cannot prevent spread of PVY has been confirmed by British and German workers.

We studied spread of PVA in similar trials in 1955, 1957 and 1958. In 1957, the influence of the secondarily diseased plants stretched far across the plots (Table 13). In 1955 and 1958, spread was much less, only the first row or two being influenced by the virus source. Although Systox seemed to reduce spread of PVA in 1955, there was no effect in the other years. The general conclusion is that even frequent spraying with Systox does not reduce spread of PVA.

171

Table 12. Effect of Systox on percentage of plants per row infected with PVY^N at increasing distance from one row of secondarily infected plants (Row No 0).

Trial No		Row No						Avg
		0	1	2	3	4	5	
1	Systox	100	18	18	5	13	3	11.4
	Control	100	18	8	5	8	18	11.4
2	Systox	100	74	55	18	10	21	35.6
	Control	100	80	64	18	13	11	37.2
3	Systox	100	97	83	59	73	50	72.4
	Control	100	93	73	59	50	25	60.0

1960; 1 ml Systox/litre, 1 300 litre/ha sprayed 4 times (trials 1 and 2) and 3 times (trial 3) at 2-weeks' intervals from emergence; values averaged from two replicate plots; two tubers sampled per plant.

Table 13. Effect of Systox on percentage of plants per row infected with PVA at increasing distance from one row of secondarily infected 'Lichte Industrie' (Row No 0).

Variety		Row No											Avg
		0	1	2	3	4	5	6	7	8	9	10	
Eigenheimer	Systox 7×	100	95	77	59	37	22	23	22	2	6	24	38.7
	Control 7×	100	85	78	41	39	28	19	21	18	17	12	35.8
	Systox 10×	100	93	83	63	51	31	34	28	24	19	31	45.7
	Control 10×	100	98	78	35	57	43	29	24	32	29	36	46.1
Ysselster	Systox 7×	100	88	41	30	17	14	14	7	8	7	5	23.1
	Control 7×	100	68	50	26	29	16	13	17	10	11	5	24.5
	Systox 10×	100	81	43	27	25	28	15	10	7	10	7	25.3
	Control 10×	100	78	47	34	29	22	7	13	15	22	14	28.1

Incidence in August (7×) and October 1957 (10×); 1 ml Systox/litre, 1 000 litre/ha, sprayed every 10 days from emergence until haulms were dying; values averaged from three replicate plots; two tubers sampled per plant.

14.1.5 Effect on yield

In some trials we detected a slight increase in yield after regular spraying with Systox. In other trials, yield decreased slightly. In general we conclude that systemic aphicides have no effect on tuber yield in the Netherlands.

14.2 Miscellaneous trials

Mineral oil. In Canada, Bradley (1966) has obtained promising results in field trials. Regular spraying with mineral oil, either neat or emulsified in water, considerably reduced spread of PVY. Very frequent spraying, however, reduced tuber yield. There have been no trials in the Netherlands.

Aluminium foil. In a preliminary trial in 1966 with 'Multa' potatoes planted in July, incidence of viruses was the same in plots with and without aluminium foil covering the ground between the rows. Aphids, however, were scarce that year. The principle is that aphids are discouraged from landing by the ultra-violet light reflected off the foil. The technique is of little use in crops that cover the foil by a certain stage; positive results have been obtained in low or open crops (Johnson et al., 1967).

Soil insecticides. In small tests with Disyston (Bayer) we found that a soil-applied insecticide remaining potent for a certain time after emergence can be as effective as early sprayings, if it is applied at planting.

14.3 Practical conclusions

Our trials have proved that spraying with systemic insecticides can completely prevent PLRV from spreading from secondarily infected plants in the field. Only one or two treatments are necessary after the plants have emerged. By then, the secondarily diseased plants can be rogued.

Spraying after roguing is of little use, since it does not prevent infection from viruliferous alates arriving from elsewhere. Pulling up or killing of haulms or lifting remain the most effective ways of preventing infections after roguing.

Because of how stylet-borne viruses are transmitted, systemic insecticides have little or no effect against their spread. Healthy seed and careful roguing should keep them in check.

Nowhere in the Netherlands has application of aphicides become routine. Aphicides are not normally used on seed potatoes. Only in years when the crop is late or aphids are early and present before emergence are growers advised to use systemic insecticides. The policy is discussed in Section 3.6. The use of an aphicide just before roguing has been advised to prevent spread of virus by aphids falling off the infected plants.

14.4 Further reading

Bradley, R. H. E., 1966. Spread of potato virus Y curtailed by oil. Nature 209: 1370–1371.

Broadbent, L., P. E. Burt & G. D. Heathcote, 1956. The control of potato viruses diseases by insecticides. Ann. appl. Biol. 44: 256–274.

Hille Ris Lambers, D., A. J. Reestman & A. Schepers, 1953. Insecticides against aphid vectors of potato viruses. Neth. J. agric. Sci. 1: 188–201.

Johnson, G. V., A. Bing & F. F. Smith, 1967. Reflective surfaces used to repel dispersing aphids and reduce spread of aphid-borne cucumber mosaic virus in Gladiolus plantings. J. econ. Ent. 60: 16–18.

Schepers, A., A. J. Reestman & D. Hille Ris Lambers, 1955. Some experiments with Systox. Proc. 2nd Conf. Potato Virus Dis., Lisse-Wageningen 1954, p. 75–83.

Wolf, J. P. M. van der, 1964. Virus transmission and vector control in seed potatoes. Höfchenbr. Bayer PflSchutz-Nachr. 17: 113–184.

15 Breeding for resistance

H. T. Wiersema

Breeding is undoubtedly the oldest way of combating virus diseases in potato. Before anything was known about viruses, degeneration of the potato was attributed to ageing, to wearing out of the stocks by continual asexual or vegetative propagation. According to this hypothesis, which was probably first advanced by van Bavegem in 1782, sexual reproduction was necessary to rejuvenate and restore the yield capacity of the stocks. Since then, new varieties have been raised from true seed by many gardeners and growers.

The hypothesis was wrong but the method based on it worked well, because most potato viruses, except PSTV, are not transmitted by true seed.

Sooner or later, new varieties contracted virus diseases, so that breeders had to keep working to maintain the health of potato stocks. In this way the occurrence of virus diseases has stimulated potato breeding.

The pioneers of potato virus research were well aware of the importance of breeding resistant varieties. Oortwijn Botjes (1920), in his classical paper on PLRV, wrote: 'One of the best methods of controlling the disease is to breed varieties of low susceptibility'. He continued: 'Susceptibility can be assessed by planting healthy tubers between two rows of infected tubers and estimating the proportion of infected hills by testing the tuber progeny. By comparing these proportions with those of known varieties grown under the same conditions, the susceptibility of new varieties can be determined'. Resistance to infection, not only to PLRV but also to other viruses, is still assessed by Oortwijn Botjes' field exposure test.

The type of resistance in which in the field only a small proportion of plants becomes infected is here called resistance to infection. Resistance to infection and its opposite susceptibility denote the difficulty or ease with which varieties catch a disease when exposed to infection. Varieties exist over the whole range from resistant to susceptible.

Tolerance and its opposite sensitivity refer to the severity of symptoms in an infected plant and are thus also a criterion of the effect of the virus. Some varieties are very sensitive: they react with severe symptoms and give only a low yield. Others are more tolerant (less sensitive) and react with very weak symptoms while yield is hardly affected.

Resistance to infection and tolerance to disease are independent properties.

Varieties with the same resistance to a particular virus may differ widely in tolerance. Likewise varieties with the same tolerance may differ widely in resistance.

Resistance and tolerance are inherited independently: breeders can select for both characteristics. Breeding for resistance aims to keep virus out of the plants. Breeding for tolerance aims to limit the effects of virus after it has entered the plant. Resistance to infection is preferable. Infection of tolerant varieties is difficult to detect. To breed tolerant varieties is to create sources of infection. Tolerance is often strain-specific. Varieties tolerant to one strain of a virus may be sensitive to other strains of the same virus.

Some varieties are so sensitive — hypersensitive — that the virus is restricted to the site of infection so that no systemic infection occurs. Murphy (1936), another potato virus pioneer, was the first to realize the importance of hypersensitivity in breeding for resistance.

A third type of resistance: extreme resistance (= immunity) was found by Schultz & Raleigh (1933) in a seedling that was resistant, even after graft inoculation, to all strains of PVX.

To combat the major virus diseases, potato breeders try to incorporate one of these three types of resistance in new varieties: resistance to infection (Section 15.1), hypersensitivity (Section 15.2) or extreme resistance (Section 15.3). Soilborne viruses will be considered separately (Section 15.4).

15.1 Breeding for resistance to infection
Resistance to infection is only partial. It does not fully protect the plant against infection. The resistance is uniform: it gives a similar protection against all strains of a virus. The nature of resistance is unknown but the evidence suggests that it is complex.

Like other characteristics, e.g. yield and quality, resistance is influenced by environmental factors. Varieties that can be readily infected with the sap-transmissible PVA, PVS, PVX or PVY at 20°C or more are hard to infect or completely escape infection at 15°C or less. These viruses usually spread more in a hot season or in countries with a hot climate.

Resistance varies with age too. If plants are inoculated when young, they normally show a higher proportion of infected hills in their tuber progeny than if inoculated later. This decrease in susceptibility with increasing age of the plant is commonly called 'mature-plant resistance' (Section 11.1).

Potatoes can be bred for resistance to infection to most potato viruses.

15.1.1 Potato leafroll virus

Inheritance. Not much is known about the inheritance of resistance to PLRV. Breeding experience suggests it is determined by many genes with additive effect. Some resistant varieties derive from crosses between less resistant parents. Usually a higher proportion of resistant offspring is obtained by crossing unrelated resistant parents than by inbreeding. Resistance can be increased by intercrossing resistant types but is decreased by outcrossing with susceptibles.

In addition to sources of resistance within *Solanum tuberosum* resistant paren-
tal material has been derived from *Solanum demissum*, *S. andigena*, *S. acaule*,
S. chacoense and *S. stoloniferum* used in backcross programmes for resistance
to other diseases. For example, *S. demissum*, used in breeding for resistance
to *Phytophthora infestans*, occurs in the pedigree of 'Apta', 'Aquila' and 'Schwalbe'. By intercrossing this material of diverse origin, presumably with different
genes for resistance, breeders in different countries have obtained highly resistant seedlings. However few have yet been placed in variety lists, because the
organoleptic quality of most is unsatisfactory. It can be improved by outcrossing
with high-quality varieties, most of which, however, are highly susceptible to
PLRV. Quality is also determined by many genes. Thus the breeder must combine
two polygenic characteristics and this is a slow process requiring large breeding
populations.

Method of testing. Seedlings and varieties are still tested at the Foundation for
Plant Breeding, Wageningen on principles described by Oortwijn Botjes (1920).
The field exposure test was modified by Baerecke (1961).

Each year plant healthy tubers of the seedlings and varieties under test between
rows of PLRV-infected tubers. Alternate every row of infected tubers with two
rows so that each plant on test has a diseased neighbour. Choose a variety that
is moderately tolerant to PLRV as source of infection. If possible, it should be
resistant to PVY in order to decrease the spread of this aphid-transmitted virus.

Since the numbers of *Myzus persicae*, the main vector of PLRV, may vary
considerably within a field, even over short distances, there should be from 4 to
20 or more random replicates of 2-tuber plots of each variety or seedling. Early-
generation seedlings being tested for the first time could not be replicated more
than four or five times because of the many plants that must be tested and because
of the limited supply of tubers. Few seedlings survive these tests and tests for other
economically important traits. When more tubers are available in later years, more
replicates are possible.

Include two or more standard varieties different in resistance for comparisons.
To compensate for the small number of replicates of the early-generation seedlings, plant many plots, at least 40, of each standard variety to ensure a reliable
basis of comparison.

For reliable infection data, ensure that tubers are healthy and rogue out any
secondarily infected plants.

Harvest the field when most of the plants are mature. Keep a 10-tuber sample
of each 2-hill plot to be planted in the evaluation field the next year. Retain
about the same proportions of large, medium and small tubers as occur in the
entire plot. Formerly it was recommended that the tubers of each hill be kept
separate. This is not necessary because a hill is not a plant, but a group of plants
arising from separate sprouts of the tuber.

Field tests to estimate the proportion of infected tubers are more reliable than the Igel Lange test, which does not always give reliable results when plants are infected late in the season (Section 9.2.1).

In the evaluation field, plant all tubers of one clone or variety together in one plot. Record all diseased hills during growth before the plants have fully developed. Diseased plants are easily detected by their retarded growth. Record also the severity of the symptoms. High sensitivity to PLRV may retard or prevent infected tubers of some clones or varieties, e.g. 'Apta' and 'Carla', from emerging. Missing hills are therefore considered infected. They may, however, be due to diseases such as dry rot (*Fusarium* spp.). If in doubt, dig up and examine the seed tuber. If it is hard and has not rotted, it can be assumed that PLRV is involved.

A difficulty of the field exposure test is the variability of infection from plot to plot and from season to season. Reasons include variability from place to place in aphid infestation and from year to year in time when infestation reaches its peak. The parameter is percentage of hills infected. When viruses do not spread much, for instance because vectors are few, seedlings of high and moderate resistance cannot be distinguished. Percentage infection is low or nil in both. If viruses spread much, moderately resistant seedlings are indistinguishable from the highly susceptible ones since both are almost completely infected. A good differentiation is possible only when the percentage of infected hills is 10–20 for the highly resistant and 90–100% for the highly susceptible. The tests should be laid out in an area where virus usually spreads a lot. In the Netherlands, spread of PLRV is usually below the desired range.

An early aphid infestation normally results in a higher percentage of infected hills than a late one, because of mature-plant resistance. When the aphid peak

Table 14. Percentage of PLRV-infected hills in the tuber progeny of varieties and seedlings after a field exposure test.

Variety or seedling	1964	1965	1966	1967	Variety or seedling	1964	1965	1966	1967
Aquila	97	13	39	68	SVP[3] 60–2172	44	0	0	37
Burmania	85	2	9	66	60–1–41	12	6	0	6
Schwalbe	53	0	10	28	60–35–375	40	0	0	4
MPI[1] 49540/2	25	0	4	18	61–1–5	40	0	0	4
Bintje	84	34	78	75	61–1–21	.	2	18	5
Penobscot	.[2]	28	10	36	61–19–428	70	4	4	18
SVP[3] 54–44	79	.	9	30	61–29–75	.	2	16	35
54–121	85	.	5	36	61–74–167	.	4	0	2
58–02	.	0	2	3					

1. Max-Planck-Institut (Köln).
2. No data available.
3. Stichting voor Plantenveredeling (Foundation for Agricultural Plant Breeding, Wageningen).

comes late in the growing season, the drop in infection of early varieties is greater than of late varieties. If aphids tend to appear late in the area of the test, tubers should be planted late. Premature defoliation by *Phytophthora infestans* may cause a low percentage of PLRV infection. Preventive spraying against this disease is advisable. Because of the variable factors, a reliable assessment takes at least 3 or 4 years. I have used a sheltered area in the woods near Wageningen where the virus normally does spread. A few of the seedlings tested were resistant to PLRV. As standards the resistant varieties, in order of increasing resistance, Aquila, Burmania, Schwalbe and Max-Planck-Institut (MPI) 49540/2 were sued. Burmania is a resistant Dutch variety (Table 14). The others are of German origin. They are commonly used as standards in other countries. Penobscot is a moderately resistant variety recently released in the United States. For comparison we included in the test Bintje, a moderately resistant variety.

15.1.2 Other viruses

Breeding for resistance to infection to PVA, PVS, PVX or PVY is much easier than to PLRV. Some commercial varieties are highly resistant to them. Other types of resistance to these viruses, such as hypersensitivity and extreme resistance are also available and are easier to introduce.

Testing for resistance to these viruses is similar to that for PLRV. In the exposure tests for PVS or PVX, infected plants are alternated in the row with the plants to be tested, because the viruses spread by contact only.

PVA, PVS, PVX and PVY do not always produce clearly visible symptoms. Serological tests or indicator plants are necessary to estimate the percentage of infected hills in the tuber progeny.

15.2 Breeding for hypersensitivity

This form of resistance is based on extreme sensitivity of the plant cells to virus. If a hypersensitive variety becomes infected in the field, not only the infected but also the surrounding cells die quickly. The dead tissue presumably forms a barrier against further spread within the plant. Hypersensitive varieties are completely resistant to infection in the field. In Britain, such varieties are said to be field immune. If, however, plants of a hypersensitive variety are artificially infected by grafting infected scions onto them, necrosis appears near the shoot apices, spreads to the stem, and kills the growing point and ultimately the whole plant. This top necrosis may well be due to a continuous supply of virus from the diseased scion.

Hypersensitivity is usually tested by graft inoculation, because top necrosis is a more reliable criterion for hypersensitivity in potatoes than the local lesion reaction.

15.2.1 Potato viruses A, X and Y

Resistance of hypersensitive type is found in many cultivated varieties. It is controlled by a single dominant gene inherited in a tetrasomic pattern (Cockerham, 1943; Cadman, 1942). Hypersensitivity to PVA, PVX[B], PVY[C] and PVX is determined by the genes N_a, N_b, N_c and N_x, respectively. PVX[B] is a strain of PVX.

N_c controls only the unimportant strain PVY^C of the economically important PVY. The drawback of this type of resistance in cultivated varieties is that resistance is strain-specific. Varieties resistant to one strain may be susceptible to others. This phenomenon is well known for rusts of cereals and flax and for *Phytophthora infestans* (R gene resistance) in potatoes. Whenever a resistant variety is cultivated widely, a new race of the parasite arises to attack it.

Potato virus X. The fungi mentioned can be differentiated into races by the reaction of a set of varieties. For *Phytophthora infestans*, potato varieties carrying different R genes are used. Cockerham (1955) differentiated the strains of PVX into groups 1, 2, 3 and 4, by means of varieties carrying none ($n_x n_b$), either one ($N_x n_b$ and $n_x N_b$) or both ($N_x N_b$) of the genes N_x and N_b determining top-necrotic response (Table 15).

Strains of Group 1, to which only varieties of the $n_x n_b$ genotype are susceptible, often occur together with strains of Group 2 or 3.

Group 2 comprises PVX^B strains. The widely grown variety Eersteling is a carrier and used to be an important source of infection. Since 'Eersteling' was freed of virus (Chap. 13), this group of strains has become much less important economically.

To Group 3 belong the common strains of PVX. Economically this is the most important group.

Of Group 4 only one strain has been described in the literature. It has not been found in commercial potatoes. This dangerous strain, to which the $N_x N_b$ varieties are susceptible, can easily be obtained by grafting a PVX^B-infected scion onto an $N_x N_b$ variety (Cockerham & Davidson, 1963; Rozendaal, 1966). The grafted plants react with top necrosis. However many plants of their tuber progeny react unusually with moderate or severe mottle. All $N_x N_b$ varieties tested were susceptible to the strain in these plants.

Presumably PVX^B mutates easily, because strains of Group 3 can likewise be obtained by grafting onto $n_x N_b$ varieties.

Table 15. Interrelationship of genes for hypersensitivity and strain groups of PVX (Cockerham, 1955).

Variety	Genotype	Strain group			
		1	2	3	4
Arran Banner	$n_x n_b$	s	s	s	s
Epicure	$N_x n_b$	R	s	R	s
Arran Victory	$n_x N_b$	R	R	s	s
Craigs Defiance	$N_x N_b$	R	R	R	s

R = hypersensitive
s = susceptible

More than half the varieties cultivated carry the gene N_b, e.g. Bintje, Climax, Furore, Jubel, Katahdin, Libertas, Maritta, Pontiac, Record, Sebago, Voran.

The gene N_x, which determines the top-necrotic response to the common strain of PVX (Group 3) is far less common and has been found only in some British varieties, e.g. Arran Crest, Craigs Defiance, Epicure, King Edward and Ninety-fold. 'Craigs Defiance' and some of its derivatives, 'Pentland Dell', 'Ulster Knight' and the Dutch varieties Ambassadeur and Commandeur carry both the genes N_x and N_b.

Potato virus A. The gene N_a, determining hypersensitivity to all strains of PVA is present in about half the varieties cultivated, e.g. Bintje, Climax, Eersteling, Grata, Irish Cobbler, Katahdin, Record, Saskia, Sientje, Ulster Prince, Up to Date. All the N_x varieties mentioned are hypersensitive to PVA. The gene N_a is closely linked with the gene N_x and both genes are carried by these varieties on the same chromosome. This linkage is very convenient for the breeder since seedlings bred for hypersensitivity to PVX are usually hypersensitive to PVA as well.

Potato virus Y. The gene N_c determining top-necrotic response to PVY^C is found in about half the varieties cultivated, e.g. Avenir, Burmania, Eersteling, Epicure, King Edward, Maritta, Majestic, Sientje, Voran.

These varieties are, however, not hypersensitive to the more important PVY^O and PVY^N strains.

A few varieties possess al four genes N_a, N_b, N_c and N_x for hypersensitivity, e.g. Ambassadeur, Commandeur, Craigs Defiance, Craigs Snowwhite and Ulster Knight. The main reason that these genes have been used in breeding for resistance is that they were readily available in commercial varieties. Since no genes for hypersensitivity to the PVY^N and PVY^O strains are available and since this type of resistance is only strain-specific, breeding for extreme resistance or immunity is preferred by most breeders nowadays. In breeding for extreme resistance (Section 15.3), only two genes are needed to obtain complete protection against all strains of PVA, PVX and PVY.

15.2.2 Potato virus S
Baerecke (1967) found hypersensitivity to all strains of PVS in the Bolivian *Solanum andigena* 'Huaca nahui' Plant Introduction (PI) 258907. The top-necrotic response is governed by a single dominant gene N_s. Hypersensitivity to PVS is preferable to the high resistance to infection found in 'Saco'. This variety transmits its resistance to only a few of its offspring. Moreover hypersensitivity to the disease is much easier to test than resistance to infection.

15.2.3 Practical significance of hypersensitivity
The danger of the appearance of new races or strains of pathogen that overcome hypersensitivity seems to be much less for PVA, PVS, PVX and PVY than for

Phytophthora infestans or the cereal rusts. Varieties carrying the genes N_x or N_a have been grown for more than a century, without resistance-breaking strains appearing in the field. In potato breeding, hypersensitivity to viruses still seems a valuable type of resistance.

15.3   Breeding for extreme resistance
Extreme resistance (= immunity) is the best type of resistance. It protects plants against all strains of a virus, even after graft inoculation. Breeding for this type of resistance is easy, because the way of testing is simple and inheritance is by one gene. Only two genes are required to give extreme resistance to PVX, PVY and PVA.

15.3.1   Extreme resistance to potato virus X
Schultz & Raleigh (1933) first discovered extreme resistance in potato in the seedling USDA 41956, which has the Chilean variety Villa roela in its pedigree. It has proved resistant to all strains of PVX yet tested. 'Saco' and 'Tawa' released in the United States, are both derived from this seedling.

The *S. andigena* clone Commonwealth Potato Collection (CPC) 1673, resistant to race A of the golden nematode, *Heterodera rostochiensis*, is extremely resistant to PVX. The two traits are inherited independently each by a single dominant gene. Seven of the nine varieties resistant to *H. rostochiensis* that are in the 1971 Dutch descriptive list of varieties are extremely resistant to PVX: Alcmaria, Amaryl, Ehud, Maryke, Prevalent, Prominent and Rector.

S. acaule has also been used as a source of extreme resistance to PVX. Repeated backcrosses in Germany have yielded 'Anett' and 'Saphir'.

Cockerham (1958) and Ross (1961) found that a single dominant gene X_i usually governed extreme resistance to PVX in *S. acaule*. The alleles X_n and x gave hypersensitivity and susceptibility, respectively. X_i was dominant over X_n.

The genetic relationship between extreme resistance and hypersensitivity suggests that extreme resistance is an extreme form of hypersensitivity. Normal inoculation evokes no reaction in extremely resistant varieties but heavy inoculation of leaves of extremely resistant seedlings from *S. andigena* backcrosses with PVX from a spraygun caused necrotic spots. Unlike hypersensitive plants, graft-inoculated extremely resistant plants were not systemically infected but occasionally leaves showed necrotic spots.

Traces of PVX were sometimes recovered from graft-inoculated extremely resistant plants, especially from roots. In double grafts with an intermediate extremely resistant scion, virus passes readily from the infected top scion to the susceptible stock but is rarely recovered from leaves of the intermediate. Presumably PVX is translocated but does not multiply in extremely resistant plants.

15.3.2   Extreme resistance to potato viruses Y and A
Extreme resistance to PVY and PVA is controlled by one dominant gene. Cockerham (1958) and Ross (1961) found that the reaction of *S. stoloniferum* to either

virus is governed by three alleles, like that of *S. acaule* to PVX. Plants extremely resistant to PVY are extremely resistant also to PVA. In backcross programmes for extreme resistance to PVY and PVA, seedlings with good commercial qualities have been obtained from *S. chacoense* and *S. stoloniferum* and some are being tested in various countries. It is likely that varieties can soon be released.

15.3.3   Methods in testing for extreme resistance

Preliminary screening of seedlings. Extreme resistance permits the screening of very young seedlings. Thousands of seedlings can be inoculated with a spraygun in a very short time (Fig. 50; Timian et al., 1955; Wiersema, 1961).

Sow in boxes in a greenhouse. As soon as two true leaves have formed, spray the seedlings with inoculum of PVX, PVY or both, according to the resistance anticipated, from a distance of 2–5 cm at a pressure of 1.5–2 kg/cm². To prevent carborundum settling out, shake the spraygun slightly during spraying or, if it is the gravity-cup type, force air through the fluid in the cup by closing the air cap with a finger. For clear quick symptoms, grow the plants at 20°–22°C. About 3 weeks after inoculation, discard plants with symptoms. Transplant healthy-looking seedlings into pots. About 90% of them are extremely resistant. The great advantage of this method is that most of the susceptible seedlings can be discarded before they take much greenhouse space.

The test is too severe to use in selecting for hypersensitivity. Even in testing for extreme resistance to PVY and PVA, fewer seedlings survive the massive inoculation than anticipated, about 30% in backcrosses instead of 50%. Survival of spray-inoculated older plants reaches the expected 50%.

Fig. 50. Inoculation of seedling plants at the cotyledon stage with PVY from a spraygun.

Preparing inoculum. For tests against PVX, use PVX$_5$ (Timian et al., 1955), to which susceptible seedlings react with local necrosis in 5–11 days and with systemic symptoms in 10–15 days. For tests against PVY and PVA, use a necrotic strain, e.g. PVY^O. Necrosis appears in 7–10 days and susceptible plants usually die or show distinct symptoms within 3 weeks.

Multiply the virus in young 'White Burley' tobacco grown in 20-cm pots. Protect the tobacco against contamination by placing 8–12 pots in an aphid-proof cage watered from the outside. Harvest mature leaves showing clear symptoms: large ringspots for PVX$_5$ and vein banding for PVY^O.

Mince the leaves in a blender or liquidizer. Strain the sap through nylon cloth. If not needed directly, freeze and store it at $-20°C$ for up to a few months. Dilute with 2–5 times its volume of water and, just before use, add about 12 g 400-mesh carborundum per 100 ml diluted sap.

Prolonged storage of viruses. To maintain the virus strains constant, tobacco leaves infected with PVX$_5$ and PVY^O may be dried and stored indefinitely. Take pieces of leaf about 2 cm $\times$ 2 cm 3 weeks after inoculation. Place each piece in a folded filter paper, turn over the edge twice and fasten it with a paper clip or seal it with a crimper. Record data, such as strain No and date, on the envelope. Dry it slowly at $4°C$ in a can or other container between layers of blue silica gel that turns pink when moist. When dry, transfer to a preserving bottle containing silica gel and covered with a glass lid and rubber ring. Store at $4°C$. Inoculum to infect 'White Burley' plants can be made by grinding a dried leaf in a mortar with some water.

Final testing of seedlings. To confirm the extreme resistance of the seedlings after 2 years or more, graft scions of them onto tomato stocks inoculated with PVX or PVY from a spraygun when young. To allow examination of tuber progeny, graft also infected scions onto the seedlings to be tested. In tests against PVY, use PVY^N as well as PVY^O. Plants with extreme resistance to PVX normally show no symptoms when grafted on PVX-infected stocks. With PVY small necrotic spots often appear on the lower leaves, but the upper part of the plant does not show symptoms and virus cannot be recovered from it. About 5 weeks after grafting, all plants that look healthy are tested for virus: for PVX by the serological test (Section 7.2) and for PVY with 'A6' test plants (Chap. 8).

15.4 Resistance to soilborne viruses

Soilborne diseases are difficult to control directly. To breed resistant varieties is often the only alternative.

Of the soilborne viruses of potato, TRV is undoubtedly the most important (Section 10.4.1). Breeders have worked against this virus since the turn of the century.

Recently Calvert & Harrison (1966) found that another soilborne virus, PMTV (Section 10.4.2), may induce tuber and haulm symptoms similar to those of TRV.

The physiological disorder 'Eisenfleckigkeit' again evokes similar symptoms.

In a field test on varieties and seedlings, it is sometimes difficult to tell which of the three diseases is involved. Two or even all three may occur on the same field.

15.4.1 Tobacco rattle virus

TRV has a wide host range and varies considerably. Some strains even differ in particle size and serological reaction. Potato varieties react quite differently to different strains. Resistance is specific. Strains differ in their ability to become systemic in the potato. This property depends also on environmental conditions and variety. Some strains usually cause spraing and are rarely transmitted through the tubers (Section 10.4.1). Others evoke only mild primary lesions in tubers but are more often transmitted through the tubers and cause stem mottle in the progeny. Spraing is thus mainly more important in ware and stem mottle in seed crops. There is, however, no sharp difference between the spraing and the stem mottle strains. A strain that is systemic in one variety may be not in another.

The incidence of spraing and the type of symptoms caused by TRV vary considerably in one field from year to year. Of the environmental factors, moisture content of top soil seems important. The nematode vectors are sensitive to desiccation. When the top soil dries out, they move deeper into the soil and feed on roots only. Spraing appears only when infective nematodes of the genus *Trichodorus* feed on the growing tubers (van Hoof, 1964). Early infection gives more severe symptoms.

The strain specificity of resistance to TRV is a serious problem to the breeder. It has long been known that certain varieties, e.g. Ambassadeur, Gineke, Libertas, Noordeling, Sientje and Voran, are resistant when grown in some sandy soils but susceptible in peaty soil. Two values were given for resistance to TRV of such varieties in the annual editions of the Dutch variety lists 1942–60. Later, however, varietal reaction proved also to differ in fields with the same soil type, even when close together.

Van Hoof (1964, 1968) showed that TRV is so variable that almost every infested field harbours its own strain that is effectively transmitted by the race of *Trichodorus* vector in that field. Results apply only to the field used for a resistance test. Varieties resistant to every strain cannot be bred until a general type of resistance is found. Until then the aim must be resistance to as many strains as possible.

Inheritance and nature of resistance. Little is known about the inheritance of resistance. General experience is that more seedlings are resistant to spraing from crosses between resistant parents than between susceptible ones. 'Bintje' and 'MPI 19268' are especially good parents.

Harrison (1968) tested 14 potato varieties in a TRV-infested field in Norfolk. Varieties that reacted with severe spraing had a lower incidence of stem mottle in tuber progeny than varieties acting with milder spraing symptoms. Only two varieties, Arran Pilot and Bintje, were not affected by either spraing or stem mottle; no virus could be transmitted from the tubers to test plants.

King Edward, however, another variety not affected by spraing, proved susceptible to stem mottle. The virus could be transmitted from its tubers, which showed only small brown flecks. The absence of spraing is evidently due to tolerance of the tubers to primary infection.

Harrison supposed that TRV has been carried with infected seed tubers of this widely grown variety to many areas where the virus is now established. However, this is unlikely because establishment at a new site requires the right race of nematode vector (Section 4.3.2).

We may speculate on the nature of resistance. Potato is more sensitive to TRV than other susceptible plant species tolerating infection. The severe, often necrotic, reaction, which demonstrates a high sensitivity, restricts translocation and prevents infection becoming systemic. The inverse relationship between severity of spraing and incidence of stem mottle also shows that extreme sensitivity may be the cause of resistance. The strain specificity supports this hypothesis because sensitivity, tolerance and hypersensitivity to other viruses are strain-specific (Section 15.1).

The resistance of such varieties as Arran Pilot, Bintje, Climax and Surprise, which escape infection on many infested fields but not on all, can perhaps be ascribed to a very high sensitivity or hypersensitivity. The leaves of these varieties react to inoculation from a spraygun with sharp necrotic spots while more susceptible varieties react with stem mottle.

Besides varying in sensitivity to disease, varieties presumably also vary in resistance to infection. This type of resistance, which is not strain-specific, can usually be assessed as for PLRV by determining the proportion of infected hills in the tuber progeny of exposed plants. But since TRV is only partly transmitted through seed tubers, this method cannot be used.

Testing for resistance to spraing. Plant replicates of two or more tuber plots of each seedling and variety under test in a field where spraing regularly occurs. Replication is necessary because infestation is usually irregular. Include a few standard varieties such as the resistant variety Bintje and the highly susceptible variety Eigenheimer in the test. At harvest, slice a few tubers from each hill, and evaluate the seedlings and varieties according to severity and incidence of tuber symptoms and number of tubers affected. Usually three or more years of testing are necessary to assess resistance reliably.

For the test choose a field infested with a strain that induces severe spraing in many varieties. Seedlings and varieties resistant in such a field are often resistant in fields infested with milder strains.

In the Netherlands older seedlings are then tested by the Institute for Research on Varieties of Field Crops (IVRO, Wageningen) in fields in different districts. The figures for resistance in the Dutch variety lists are based on results of these tests. Varieties with a high figure, such as Avenir, Bintje, Civa, Climax, Eba, Jaerla, Multa, Nascor, Noordeling and Surprise, are resistant to spraing in many fields. In other fields, some of them are susceptible and others resistant. This varies for the different fields. The farmer, however, usually knows or soon discovers which varieties are resistant in his fields.

Testing for resistance to stem mottle. Plant seedlings and varieties in a field infested with a stem mottle strain of TRV. Evaluation of primary tuber symptoms and further procedure is as for spraing. Plant five or more tubers from each hill in a field free from TRV in the next year. Estimate the percentage of infected plants and the proportion of infected stems of these plants during growth and examine the harvested tubers of affected plants for secondary symptoms.

Incidence of stem mottle varies considerably from year to year. Although different test plots have been planted in infested fields in recent years, any incidence of stem mottle in the progeny was too low for reliable conclusions. Apart from what Rozendaal (1947) reported in the earliest publication about stem mottle, little is known about the resistance of the Dutch varieties to stem mottle. He pointed out that varieties highly resistant to stem mottle, e.g. Bintje, Climax, Gineke, Noordeling and Surprise, are also resistant to spraing. 'Bevelander', 'Eersteling', 'Eigenheimer' and 'Mentor' are susceptible to stem mottle and spraing.

Stem mottle is not a serious problem in the Netherlands because most seed potatoes are grown on clay soils, which are too heavy for the nematode vector. On infested soils, only resistant varieties are grown for seed. There seems little danger of TRV being carried to a new site with infected seed.

15.4.2 Potato mop-top virus
Occurrence and symptoms of PMTV are similar to those of TRV. It is, however, also found on heavier soils where *Trichodorus* is absent.

The host range of PMTV and its fungus vector *Spongospora subterranea* seem to be the same ten species of Solanaceae, of which *Solanum nigrum*, potato and tomato are the most common in Western Europe.

PMTV and its vector can be established on a *Spongospora*-free site by planting seed infected with both vector and virus. Incidence and severity of symptoms on tubers and haulms depend on environmental conditions.

The reaction of different varieties has been studied in field tests in Ireland. Calvert (1968) has assessed varietal reaction on a susceptibility index, based on the percentage incidence, and on the severity of primary symptoms in haulms and tubers and of secondary symptoms in tubers. Of the varieties tested, King Edward was the least and Arran Pilot the most susceptible.

Since 'Arran Pilot' is resistant to spraing caused by TRV, spraing symptoms in this variety are good evidence for the presence of PMTV. 'Arran Pilot' is therefore usually included in field trials.

So far nothing is known about the inheritance of resistance.

15.5 Further reading

Baerecke, M. L., 1961. Erfahrungen mit einjährigen Kartoffelabbauversuchen unter starken Blattrollinfektionsbedingungen. Z. PflZücht. 45: 225–253.

Baerecke, M. L., 1967. Ueberempfindlichkeit gegen das S-Virus der Kartoffel in einem bolivianischen Andigena-Klon. Züchter 37: 281–286.

Cadman, C. H., 1942. Autotetraploid inheritance in the potato: Some new evidence. J. Genet. 44: 33–52.

Calvert, E. L., 1968. The reaction of potato varieties to potato mop-top virus. Rec. agric. Res. Minist. Agric., N.Ireland, 17: 31–40.

Cockerham, G., 1943. The reaction of potato varieties to viruses X, A, B and C. Ann. appl. Biol. 30: 338–344.

Cockerham, G., 1955. Strains of potato virus X. Proc. 2nd Conf. Potato Virus Dis., Lisse-Wageningen 1954, p. 89–92.

Cockerham, G., 1958. Experimental breeding in relation to virus resistance. Proc. 3rd Conf. Potato Virus Dis., Lisse-Wageningen 1957, p. 199–203.

Cockerham, G. & T. M. Davidson, 1963. Note on an unusual strain of potato virus X. Scott. Pl. Breeding Stn Rec., p. 26–29.

Dutch descriptive list of varieties (46ste Rassenlijst), 1971. IVRO, Wageningen. 320 p.

Hooker, W. J., C. E. Peterson & R. G. Timian, 1954. Virus X resistance in potato. Am. Potato J. 31: 199–212.

Murphy, P. A., 1936. Nature and control of potato virus diseases. Nature 138: 955.

Oortwijn Botjes, J. G., 1920. De bladrolziekte van de aardappelplant (Die Blattrollkrankheit der Kartoffelpflanze). Doctoral thesis, Wageningen, 136 p.

Ross, H., 1961. Ueber die Vererbung von Eigenschaften für Resistenz gegen das Y- und A-Virus in Solanum stoloniferum und die mögliche Bedeutung für eine allgemeine Genetik der Virusresistenz in Solanum Sect. Tuberarium. Proc. 4th Conf. Potato Virus Dis., Braunschweig 1960, p. 40–49.

Rozendaal, A., 1947. Ziekten van het stengelbont-type bij de aardappel. Tijdschr. PlZiekt. 53: 93–101.

Schultz, E. S. & W. P. Raleigh, 1933. Resistance of potato to latent mosaic. Phytopathology 23: 32.

Timian, R. G., W. J. Hooker & C. E. Peterson, 1955. Immunity to virus X in potato. a) Studies of clonal lines. Phytopathology 45: 313–319. b) Studies of segregating seedling populations. Phytopathology 45: 445–450. c) Selection of immune plants in the breeding program. Am. Potato J. 32: 411–417.

Wiersema, H. T., 1961. Methods and means used in breeding potatoes with extreme resistance to viruses X and Y. Proc. 4th Conf. Potato Virus Dis., Braunschweig 1960, p. 30–36.

16 Dutch techniques of growing seed potatoes

D. E. van der Zaag

Between 1965 and 1970, about 22 000 ha in the Netherlands was under seed potatoes, almost 17% of the total area under potatoes. In other European countries, the percentage is lower, e.g. United Kingdom 15%, Denmark about 11%, West Germany about 7%, France about 4% and Belgium less than 1%. During the period, less than 5% of the total area under seed potatoes in the Netherlands was rejected. Annual production of certified seed was about 450 000 tons, of which 400 000 tons were sealed and sold and the rest was used by the growers. Between 1965 and 1970 about 270 000 tons of certified seed was exported to more than 50 countries; 75% of the total was to Belgium, France, West Germany, Italy and Switzerland. The rest was exported to Mediterranean countries, South America and Asia. Other European countries with important exports of seed potatoes are the United Kingdom, the Republic of Ireland, Denmark and France. In the years 1962–6, they exported about 57 000, 43 000, 20 000 and 60 000 tons, respectively. Total exports from all these countries were thus less than from the Netherlands.

Dutch varieties are widely grown in many countries, the old variety Bintje being the most widely known. New varieties such as Alpha, Climax, Patrones and Sirtema are, however, becoming increasingly well known in many parts of the world. Figure 51 shows changes in area under seed potatoes of the most important varieties.

16.1 Principles of growing seed potatoes

16.1.1 Health

The whole technique of growing revolves around health. To maintain health, the crop must be early, the plants must be uniform and there must be little or no haulm growth in the second half of the season.

To prevent spread from plants with secondary infection these plants must be rogued before aphids arrive. The crop must for roguing again be fairly early. Roguing requires an even crop stand. It is much easier to recognize plants with mild symptoms in an even stand than in an uneven stand.

The significance of mature-plant resistance is discussed in Chapter 11. Long ago, seed growers knew by experience that crops with much haulm growth, espe-

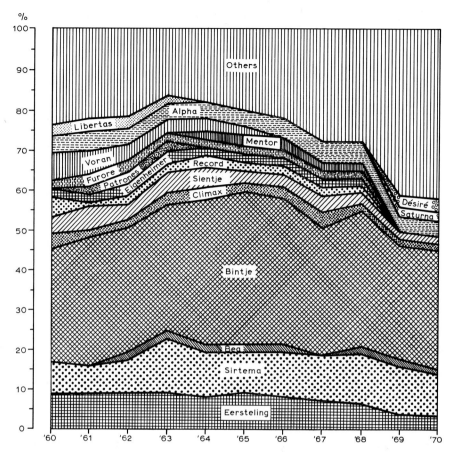

Fig. 51. Changes in area under seed potatoes of the more important varieties (more than 2% of the area).

cially late in the season, could be heavily infected. In contrast to crops of ware or industrial potatoes, haulms of seed potatoes must grow quickly early in the season and hardly at all later. Efforts to obtain an early uniform crop with moderate haulm growth succeed only if the seed is healthy and well prepared. Seed growers therefore plant only seed of the highest grade by health. Although we are here concerned with viruses, remember that fungi, bacteria and pests may need control too (Section 16.7). Fortunately they are no great problem in areas of the Netherlands where seed potatoes grow. The most important ones for Dutch seed growers are *Phytophthora infestans*, *Rhizoctonia solani* and common scab (*Streptomyces scabies*).

16.1.2 Yield

The profit from a crop depends very much on the yield. For a reasonable return,

189

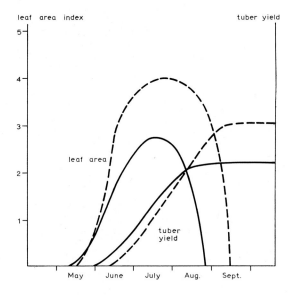

Fig. 52. Scheme of the relationship between foliage and tuber growth of two types of plants. Vigorous growth of foliage and late growth of tubers (A: – – – –), moderate growth of foliage and early growth of tubers (B: ———).

yield of seed should exceed 20 or 25 tons tubers per ha in total.

In Western Europe, tuber yields are high if sufficient foliage is formed before tuber initiation. Continued growth of foliage until late in the season does not stimulate early tuber growth, but provides a long period over which tubers continue to grow (Fig. 52A). For tubers to grow early, growth of foliage must be rapid at first but should soon slow down. Chitting and moderate rates of nitrogen give such a crop. Normally it ceases growth early in the season, so that yield rises to an early but low maximum (Fig. 52B). At one extreme, foliage may grow too rank and retard tuber growth, so that even late in the season yield is not high. Rank foliage may be destroyed by *Phytophthora infestans* before the end of the season. At the other extreme, tuber growth may start so early that there is too little foliage for sufficient tuber growth. The crop is early but yield suffers.

Stimulators of haulm growth are long days, high temperature, low light intensity, moist soil rich in nitrogen, and physiologically young seed tubers with no sprouts or young ones. The opposite conditions stimulate tuber growth.

Dutch growers must normally kill the haulms at the end of July or the beginning of August to prevent spread of virus by winged aphids. Seed potatoes require far less nitrogen than potatoes grown for other purposes. Growers prefer tubers that have been stored at about 5° or 10°C, so that they are well sprouted and therefore physiologically old when planted. Daylength, temperature and light intensity can be manipulated only by adjusting the date of planting.

16.1.3 Size grades of tubers
For 'Bintje', the price relation for the grades 28–35 mm, 35–45 mm and 45–55 mm during 1962–6 averaged about 10:7:5. Growers profit more from small seed.

Figure 53 shows changes in size grades of 'Bintje' during growth. Other varieties grown in the Netherlands have a similar pattern. Although total yield increases with time, the yield of small tubers decreases. The loss in the size range 28–45 mm is generally less than a third of the gain in tubers > 45 mm. The price of tubers

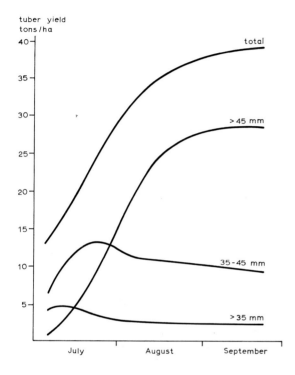

Fig. 53. Changes in proportions of 'Bintje' tubers of different size-grades.

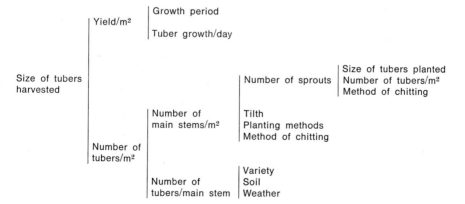

Fig. 54. Factors and parameters governing size of tubers per m².

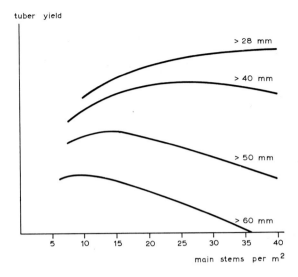

tuber yield

> 28 mm

> 40 mm

> 50 mm

> 60 mm

5   10   15   20   25   30   35   40

main stems per m²

Fig. 55. Relation of number of main stems per unit ground area to yield of tubers of different sizes (data from Reestman & Bodlaender).

> 45 mm, even for ware, is normally more than a third of the price of the grade 28–45 mm, for seed, so that growers gain nothing by killing haulms to gain small tubers, unless in health of the seed.

The size of tubers harvested depends on many factors and parameters, chiefly the number of main stems and yield. Each parameter is governed by the factors enclosed by the brace (Fig. 54). Figure 55 shows the relationship between number of stems and yield of tubers in the various grades. The number of stems depends on size of seed tubers, methods of chitting and planting, tilth and other soil conditions, and plant density. Maximum returns demand attention to all these factors. Seed should be chitted and planted carefully so that each plant forms many strong main stems.

16.2   Winter storage and preparation of tubers

16.2.1   Dormancy

Eyes of tubers do not normally sprout until several weeks after harvest. The length of dormancy depends on variety, weather and soil conditions, maturity and temperature and composition of the air around the tuber during dormancy. Varieties vary widely in length of dormancy. For 'Alpha' it is long and for 'Eersteling' it is short. Dormancy is much shorter after a hot dry season than after a cool wet season. An immature tuber usually has a slightly longer dormancy than a mature tuber.

Dormancy of some varieties, e.g. Voran, can be shortened by storage in constant warmth. Other varieties, e.g. Alpha, require a fluctuating temperature. More oxygen and less carbon dioxide in the air decrease the length of dormancy. In modern stores, tubers can normally be kept dormant until they are graded in the

192

autumn. By then, it is so cool outside that the store can easily be kept at 4° or 5°C. Seed for tropical or subtropical planting in October or November should be kept warmer or at fluctuating temperature, according to variety.

16.2.2 Dipping

To prevent sprouts or stems being killed and sclerotia forming on new tubers by *Rhizoctonia solani*, most growers disinfect tubers. Usually after grading in autumn, they dip tubers for 5 min in a solution of methyl mercuric benzoate (0.3 g/100 ml) or 4 and 6 chlorphenylphenol (1.5 g/100 ml). Disinfection of seed does not control infection from *R. solani* living in the soil.

16.2.3 Storage and chitting

After grading and dipping, tubers are placed in chitting trays (Fig. 57), each containing 10–12 kg of seed. These trays are placed in a glazed chitting house (Fig. 56) or in a well insulated store kept between 2° and about 5°C by ventilating with outside air. Several Dutch growers prefer to keep it just below 4°C to prevent sprouting until the end of February, which is possible in a well designed store.

Other growers prefer to maintain it slightly warmer with sufficient light to ensure that some sprouts are produced by January; these are then removed by hand. Tubers of many varieties show apical dominance, so that only one or two sprouts grow. If they are removed, more start growing. Diseased or otherwise unsatisfactory tubers can simultaneously be removed, but shortage of labour has made this method difficult.

Tubers kept cool, so that they remain sprout-free, can normally be heat-shocked at 15°–20°C at the end of February or the beginning of March. After a few days of heat, sprouts become visible and the temperature is gradually dropped.

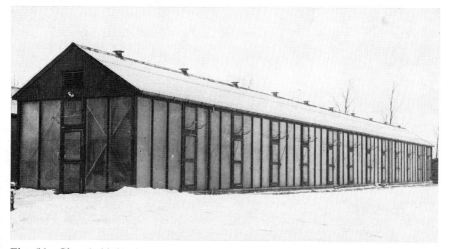

Fig. 56. Glazed chitting house. (From Office of Joint Services, Wageningen.)

193

Fig. 57. Chitting trays outdoors under polythene sheeting. (From Institute for Research on Storage and Processing of Agricultural Produce, Wageningen.)

Stores must be adequately lit. In glazed chitting houses, this is no problem but insulated rooms must be artificially lit. If tubers have sprouted by the end of February, they should be desprouted before giving them the heat shock.

For short strong sprouts suitable for fully automatic planting, growers carefully turn the tubers over in the chitting trays once or more. For extra strong sprouts, growers are increasingly placing chitting trays outdoors for the last few weeks before planting. Others place the trays outdoors immediately after the heat shock and protect the tubers against night frost by covering the stack of trays with polythene sheeting (Fig. 57). This method can give good results but severe night frosts or strong winds may cause damage. Over the years Dutch growers have paid considerable attention to chitting. It has paid dividends in an adequate number of stems per tuber and in early uniform crops.

16.2.4   Tuber cutting

Dutch growers prefer to plant whole seed; cutting is rare. If they cut, they cut only tubers over 50 mm diameter. Such tubers are cut in half. Tubers are best cut a few weeks before planting. The two parts of the tuber are left pressed together, so that the cut remains moist and heals rapidly.

16.3   Manuring

The cropping season for seed potatoes is brief in the Netherlands. To obtain a reasonable yield, the plants must have adequate supply of minerals. Soil conditions and manuring should encourage rapid early haulm growth.

194

16.3.1 Green manure
Most seed growers have their arable land under cereals, sugar-beet and potatoes. To maintain the tilth, clover or ryegrass is often ploughed in as green manure before the potato crop. A loose crumb structure is essential for seed potatoes.

16.3.2 Nitrogen
Nitrogen governs the whole pattern of potato growth. It stimulates haulms and retards tubers. Excessive rates are therefore dangerous for the crop. At the other extreme, too little results in too little haulm growth for tubers to grow. The plant's nitrogen supply comes partly from nitrified organic matter and partly from fertilizer. The supply from organic matter depends on the amount and type of organic matter in the soil, and on the weather during the previous winter and during growth. As the weather is uncertain in Western Europe, the amount of nitrogen from the soil cannot be predicted. The grower cannot accurately gauge how much nitrogen he must apply in spring.

On loamy soils[6], many growers apply about 120 kg N/ha for seed potatoes, sometimes only 100 kg and up to 150 kg. On sandy diluvial soils, the rates are normally lower than 100 kg per ha, as on these soils haulms are in general more vigorous than on loam.

A few weeks before or just before planting the nitrogen is all broadcast as nitrate or as nitrate and ammonium. Though most growers prefer nitrate, it has not been proved that this is better for seed potatoes than the mixture of nitrate and ammonium.

16.3.3 Phosphorus
The rate of phosphorus depends on the soil; on many fields, it is about 100 kg P_2O_5/ha. Some growers and scientists supposed that phosphorus promoted resistance but there is no evidence. Neither is there proof that vigour of progeny is influenced by larger dressings than normal.

Apply phosphorus in a readily soluble form, e.g. superphosphate (containing 16–18% P_2O_5).

16.3.4 Potassium
Like phosphorus rate, potassium rate can be decided from soil analysis. On some areas of loamy recent alluvium, hardly any is required. Many soils require 200–300 kg K_2O/ha. All potassium is supplied as K_2SO_4, for KCl may change leaf colour, blurring symptoms of virus disease.

16.3.5 Magnesium and trace elements
Most soils require only nitrogen, phosphorus and potassium for seed potatoes.

---

6. As used in this chapter, loam, loamy soils = Dutch zavel, zavelgrond. Potatoes are grown on loamy soils with up to 25% (w/w) lutum (particles < 2 μm).

Fig. 58. Power-driven harrow. (From Institute of Agricultural Engineering and Rationalization, Wageningen.)

Fig. 59. Semi-automatic planter with chitting trays. (From Institute for Research on Storage and Processing of Agricultural Produce, Wageningen.)

But sandy soils and some loamy soils may need extra magnesium. Some loamy soils need a dressing of manganese.

16.4 Seedbed preparation

All loamy soils must be ploughed in autumn, preferably when dry. Sandy soils may be ploughed in autumn or spring. On heavy-loamy soils, the seedbed is prepared in such a way as to avoid clods and to conserve moisture.

Clods are a major hindrance to machine-harvesting. Clods are man-made. Most of them form during seedbed preparation and other tillage. Growers on loamy soils now take great care to avoid clods in the seedbed.

The seedbed must be sufficiently moist for sprouts to grow. A dry seedbed causes slow and irregular emergence.

The soil must be fairly firm. Sandy soils sometimes form a deep loose seedbed. A tuber planted shallow is more likely to remain dry in a loose soil than in a firmer soil. In a loose soil, planting depth tends to be irregular.

For rapid and undisturbed growth, it is very important that there is no compact layer under the seedbed. Such layers may be formed by compaction by tractor wheels and implements used for seedbed preparation.

16.4.1 Loamy soils

The structure of loamy soils is liable to damage by tractor wheels. The seedbed should not be prepared until the soil is dry enough, usually in April. To prevent the soil from drying out, tubers are usually planted the same day. With power-driven harrows (Fig. 58), a deep clod-free seedbed can often be prepared in one operation. With normal trailed harrows, the tilth is rarely as deep and more than one harrowing is often necessary.

On clay soils, some growers prefer to use a rotary cultivator and a planter. A light harrow roughly levels the field and the rotary cultivator prepares seedbeds 35–40 cm wide along the projected rows, just before the planter. After planting, the rotary cultivator loosens the soil between the rows. Seedbed preparation and planting are almost simultaneous.

16.4.2 Sandy soils

Sandy soils are almost always ploughed in spring, even if they have already been ploughed in the autumn. If ploughed a few days before planting, the soil is too loose. Growers plough a while before planting or roll the land, so that by the time of planting the soil is firm.

16.5 Planting

Dutch growers are advised to aim for at least 30 main stems per m², although few fields reach this density. With careful management of tuber size, chitting, seedbed and planting, an average of five stems per plant is possible. Without it, many varieties hardly reach four. To achieve the aim, there must be about 60 000 plants per ha. In some areas, rows are 66 or 67 cm apart and in others 75 cm,

Fig. 60. Fully automatic planter. (From Institute of Agricultural Engineering and Rationalization, Wageningen.)

Fig. 61. Rotary cultivator. (From Institute of Agricultural Engineering and Rationalization, Wageningen.)

so that tubers must be planted 25 and 22 cm apart in the row, respectively. Despite the lower density actually achieved in most fields, there has recently been a distinct increase in number of stems per m².

Tubers used to be planted rather deep, as in many other countries. They are now usually planted with the upper part at ground level of the smooth soil. Unless rules for seedbed preparation are rigorously applied, the soil dries out too much for rapid sprouting. If the soil is too dry, tubers must be planted deeper.

16.5.1 Potato planters

Crops used to be planted either by hand or with a semi-automatic planter. Either way, the seed was planted carefully. Fully automatic planters are now increasingly used.

In semi-automatic planters, tubers are transferred by hand from the chitting tray to the cups of the planter (Fig. 59). With a three-row planter, four men can plant about 2.5 ha per day. This type of planter has been widely used in the Netherlands. But shortage of labour is forcing growers to switch to fully automatic planters. With a fully automatic planter, a few men can cover a large area. With a three-row machine, two men can plant about 4 ha per day. Many growers use two-row machines (Fig. 60), though three-row machines are still popular. However fully automatic planters damage more sprouts. Rough planting may cause an uneven emergence and very often fewer strong main stems per plant.

16.5.2 Sprout damage

In fully automatic planting, sprouts are usually damaged when chitting trays are emptied into the hopper and while the chain of cups is passing through the hopper.

Seed growers restrict damage by emptying the trays carefully into the hopper, by never filling it full, by running the planter slowly, and by aiming for strong sprouts during chitting. Even with all precautions, more than 15% of the sprouts are often injured. If one sprout is knocked off, the plant from that tuber usually has one stem less. Plants from tubers whose sprouts have all, or almost all, been damaged have more, but thinner, stems than plants from undamaged tubers. So even if a fully automatic planter is used carefully with suitably chitted tubers, fewer stems grow than if tubers are hand-planted. If used carelessly, more sprouts emerge than from hand-planted tubers; however the stand is not uniform and tubers form later.

16.6 Crop tillage

The purpose of crop tillage is to build up a well shaped ridge without clods and to kill weeds.

Usually the crop is tilled several times before the foliage closes over the drills. Growers are now trying to make the ridge in one or at most two operations because of a shortage of labour, to conserve moisture and to avoid root damage. To loosen sufficient soil, the rotary cultivator (Fig. 61) may be run between rows

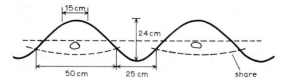

Fig. 62. Diagrammatic cross-section of an ideal ridge.

15 cm
24 cm
50 cm | 25 cm | share

or, on lighter soil, small spring-tine harrows, may be mounted in front of the ridging plough.

The convex top of the ridge (Fig. 62) should be at least 15 cm wide. If flat or hollow, rainwater may not run off and spores of *Phytophthora infestans* may be washed into the ridge.

The ridge should be at least 20 cm high, to give sufficient room for the new tubers and to leave a layer of soil above them. Such a layer helps to prevent green tubers and blight.

The base of the ridge must be 40–45 cm wide. The tuber should be at least 2 cm above the bottom of the furrow, to avoid wet rot (*Erwinia* spp.) after heavy rain.

The furrows must be at least 20–25 cm wide for tractor wheels to pass without compacting the loose soil of the ridges.

Weeds are normally killed during ridging or while the ridges are being harrowed and earthed up again. Herbicides have been little used on seed potatoes in the Netherlands. On sandy soils, DNOC (dinitro-orthocresol) is sometimes applied before emergence. Soil-acting herbicides have not been recommended for routine use on seed potatoes in the Netherlands. On the loamy soils, where most seed potatoes are grown, weeds are no problem.

16.7 Control of pathogens
The whole purpose of the special growing of seed potatoes is to produce a pathogen-free crop, in particular free from viruses.

16.7.1 Virus diseases
Plants with secondary infection by a virus can normally be rogued before vectors arrive. Successful roguing requires that plants be uniform, few parent tubers be infected, the weather be mild and moist and supply of minerals be adequate to enhance the symptoms, and the roguer be expert at recognizing virus symptoms.

Many farms begin roguing as soon as the plants are 15–20 cm high. Each week thereafter, according to the incidence of infected plants, the field is again checked. Infected plants are carefully dug up. The whole plant, including parent tuber and any new tubers, is placed in a bag of dense weave to prevent any aphids escaping. If aphids arrive before roguing is complete, insecticides may be used (Chap. 14).

16.7.2 Streptomyces scabies
Many loamy soils suitable for potatoes are calcareous. Common scab can be a

200

problem, especially in a dry summer. Several growers have been successful in controlling common scab with irrigation. If the ridge is wet while tubers are being initiated and for a few weeks thereafter, the number of tubers heavily attacked by scab is markedly reduced. *Streptomyces scabies* occurs in all soils. Experiments in the Netherlands did not show that, infection of the parent tuber has an influence on incidence in progeny.

16.7.3 *Phytophthora infestans*
Late blight is common in the Netherlands and most varieties are susceptible. Until haulms meet in the row, blight is rare. Susceptible varieties are then sprayed every week or two according to the weather. Spells of weather favouring the disease are forecast on the radio. Haulms of seed crops are usually destroyed late in July before late blight has become widespread. If on loamy soils, almost all plants should happen to have some infected leaflets earlier, growers are advised to kill the haulm immediately to prevent blight from spreading to the tubers.

Zineb or maneb (zinc or manganese ethylenebisdithiocarbamates) are used for the first two or three sprayings. Because they do not damage leaflets, roguing is easier. Later in the season, when blight becomes dangerous and roguing is almost complete, mixtures of maneb and organotin compounds have proved successful. Crops are sometimes sprayed from aircraft, but ground-spraying is much more usual.

16.8   Haulm destruction
To prevent viruses from being spread by aphids and to prevent blight, haulms are destroyed in the second half of the season. NAK fixes the dates by aphid flights, grade and variety (Section 3.6).

16.8.1 *Methods of haulm destruction*
Haulm destruction can be done in various ways.

By lifting the crop. Although the most radical method, this early lifting has some big disadvantages. Generally the skin of the tubers is not suberized sufficiently; many injuries can occur to the tubers during fully automatic harvesting. During storage, those damaged tubers can dry out. Thus early lifted tubers cannot be stored so well. This method of haulm destruction is used only for small clones lifted hy hand.

By haulm pulling. The stems with foliage and the subterranean parts of the stems are pulled from the tubers. The tubers will stay some time in the soil for the skins to suberize. This method of haulm killing is excellent for the certification scheme. However it demands much hand labour; therefore haulm-pulling machines have been developed that do the work with favourable results. However the culture of the crop (planting distances, form of the ridges) must be adjusted to the pulling machine and the machine has a low capacity.

With a flame thrower. In the United States, haulms have for several years been destroyed by burning with a flame thrower. This method has been tested in the

Netherlands since 1966. The flame thrower is mounted on a tractor. The green developing foliage burns quite well. The leaves are killed more rapidly than by spraying chemicals. The speed of the tractor must be adjusted to the development of foliage. In a lush crop, the tractor may not go more than 2.5 km/h. In mature dying crops, it may go a bit faster.

By spraying chemicals. Spraying with chemicals must be done in such way that the haulms are destroyed and no young shoots develop by the lifting date. Spraying can be used in two ways: the foliage is first damaged with some piece of equipment (e.g. harrow) and remaining stems are sprayed or foliage is sprayed directly without damaging it.

An advantage of the first way is that the grower can start spraying later than if he uses the second way. However young shoots develop more readily in a damaged than in an undamaged crop. Usually spraying must be repeated, especially in fields with late varieties. Haulm destruction gives no problem if plants are mature. The reaching of maturity is therefore important.

DNOC (dinitro-orthocresol) dissolved in mineral oil is often used as spray, sometimes also pentachlorophenol dissolved in mineral oil or calcium cyanamide. However, as calcium cyanamide yields unfavourable results, its application is not recommended. Sodium arsenite, formerly often used, is no longer recommended.

DNOC can be sprayed on all types of soil, since the chemical is destroyed in the soil rapidly. The rate is 40 litre DNOC in 800 litre water per ha.

Pentachlorophenol acts very rapidly but it kills only those parts of the plants that it touches. It hardly penetrates. It rapidly kills mature crops that show no vegetative growth. The rate is 80 to 120 litre pentachlorophenol in 800 to 1 000 litre water.

It is better to spray the haulmkillers with plenty of water, 800 to 1 000 litre per ha or, if haulms are cut, at least 500 litre. During dry periods, the foliage must be moist when sprayed, thus in the morning or evening. During warm and dry periods the action of the chemicals is least, the danger of poisoning the greatest. Haulm destruction prevents tuber infection by *Phytophthora infestans* but encourages attack of the tubers by *Rhizoctonia solani*. To avoid a large attack of *Rhizoctania*, lift the crop within 14 days of haulm destruction.

16.9   Harvesting

Harvest as soon as the tubers' skins are firm enough and the connection between tubers and stems is sufficiently loose, usually 10–14 days after destroying haulms.

Harvesting has become increasingly mechanized over the past 10 years. Before, almost all seed potatoes were lifted by machine and picked by hand. Early harvesters incorporated a bagger and now most harvesters lift the potatoes in bulk into trailers, which are in turn emptied onto conveyers in the store.

16.9.1   Harvesters

A popular machine for seed potatoes is a single-row harvester with a hopper holding about 1 200 kg. With a yield of 40 tons tubers and soil per ha, the ma-

Fig. 63. Two-row harvester with trailer.

chine can harvest 400 m of row without stopping. For long fields, a harvester filling a trailer running alongside is preferable (Fig. 63).

Two important characteristics of harvesters are working speed and tuber damage. Speed depends largely on field conditions. Under good conditions, a one-row machine harvests 1–2 ha per day and a two-row machine about 2–4 ha. With the machines usual in the Netherlands, tuber damage depends more on how the harvester is adjusted and used than on its type. In general, harvesters do no more damage than lifters with hand-picking.

16.9.2 Transport

Transport potatoes from the field to the store in self-emptying four-wheeled trailers or tipping carts. The self-emptying trailers have a roller at the front or the back that draws a chain or a canvas sheet along the bottom of the trailer. They discharge their load into the hopper of the conveyer that takes the tubers into the store. The system handles tubers smoothly and provides a regular flow. Tipping carts are quicker but rougher on the tubers. With the irregular flow, the hopper must be large enough to take almost the whole load.

In the store, screens remove soil, and conveyers transport the potatoes into bins. Tubers are not size-graded before storage.

16.10 Storage

During the last 15 years, potato stores have changed out of all recognition. Before, seed was commonly stored in the field in small clamps, which were ideal for spread of fungi and bacteria. The clamps were often so warm that many varieties sprouted before grading in autumn. Seed was of poor quality. The change to store houses has been a great improvement.

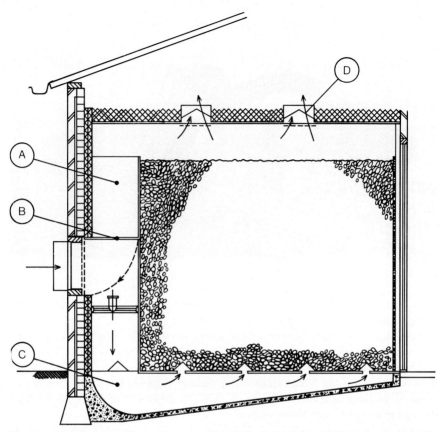

Fig. 64. Cross-section of a potato store. Ventilation channel inside (A); shutter in inside ventilation channel (B, horizontal position at inlet of air from outdoors; vertical position to ventilate in the store); channel to distribute the air (C); self-closing shutter (D). (From Institute for Research on Storage and Processing of Agricultural Produce, Wageningen.)

A modern store is ventilated and insulated (Fig. 64). Tubers are stored 3–3.5 m deep and a fan blows outside air up through them. If the tubers need cooling, the fan blows cool air through at night. If they need drying, the fan blows dry air through during the day. The walls and roof are insulated to prevent uncontrollable heat changes.

Many growers have built a potato store in an existing barn; others have a separate one. Some growers transport their seed to central stores (Fig. 65) belonging to a co-operative or a private firm, who takes charge also of grading and marketing.

16.11 Size-grading
Grading is the last stage of growing seed potatoes. The tubers are separated into

204

Fig. 65. A central potato store. (From Institute for Research on Storage and Processing of Agricultural Produce, Wageningen.)

the size ranges 28–35, 35–45 and 45–55 mm. With such small ranges, the difference between the smallest and largest tuber in a bag is not great. Mis-shapen, damaged, green or otherwise unsuitable tubers are picked out.

If growers store their seed on the farm, their own workers usually do the grading. Of recent years, more and more farms use only one or two workers, and co-operatives and private firms marketing the crop have taken over the grading. These operate big modern grading plants. Some growers have continued grading on the farm by mechanizing the transport of the tubers from the bin to the grader. The main cost is the work of picking out unsuitable tubers.

The crux remains to grow, harvest and store tubers in a way that gives few rejects.

16.12   Further reading

Burton, W. G., 1966. The potato. H. Veenman & Zonen NV, Wageningen, 382 p.
Ivins, J. D. & F. L. Milthorpe (eds), 1963. The growth of the potato. Butterworths, London, 328 p.

17 Inspection and quality grading of seed potatoes

J. Hiddema

In the Netherlands a committee of three first inspected seed potatoes in 1908. They recorded crop growth and varietal purity. With the discovery of PLRV in 1917 and later of mosaic viruses, inspectors started checking for virus diseases.

Certified seed soon proved to produce a much better crop than the uncertified. Merchants and agricultural societies in several regions established inspection services. Each service issued inspected seed with its own certificate and lead seal.

Lack of legislation made fraud easy. In the Netherlands and other countries, pressure grew to found one inspection service with one lead seal and one certificate. On 26 May 1932, the Vereeniging Nederlandsche Algemeene Keuringsdienst: Netherlands General Inspection Service (NAK) was founded.

The government directed NAK to inspect agricultural and horticultural crops. Only seeds and seed potatoes provided with certificates and lead seals could be exported. Later the restriction was extended to trade within the Netherlands.

In 1942, NAK split up into four services: General Netherlands Inspection Service for Field Seeds and Seed Potatoes (NAK), General Netherlands Inspection Services for Trees (NAK-B), for Ornamentals (NAK-S) and for Vegetables (NAK-G). The board of NAK represents breeders, traders, growers and consumers. But NAK is under government supervision. Regulations for inspection have to be approved by the Minister of Agriculture. Directives for inspection and certification are given by the central office in Wageningen. The directives are put into effect by eight regional inspection services.

17.1 Aim of inspection

A batch of potatoes is suitable for seed, if it can produce strong healthy plants that yield well. Seed must therefore be healthy too. Seed may be used either for propagation or for ware and industrial potatoes.

For propagation, the seed must be checked for health more rigorously; it must be almost free from disease agents transmitted through tubers. Viruses and some fungi and bacteria must be absent. The checks for virus need not be as rigorous for seed intended for ware potatoes, for which the seed grower can aim rather for yield than for health (Chap. 12).

The production of good seed potatoes is dependent on a well organized and thorough inspection. Their impartiality and expertise are a guarantee to the grower.

206

17.2 Quality grading
The 1908 inspection graded crops into: excellent, marked 10; good, 9; and medio-
cre, 8. Later the figures were replaced by the letters A, B and C. In 1935, it was
decided to add an extra letter A to groups A and B, when lifted early. Thus seed
potatoes were graded AA, A, AB, B and C. In 1948, clonal selection was introduced. Consequently in 1953, seed potatoes were graded, in descending order,
S, SE, E, A, B and C. In 1967, the European Economic Community issued directives for the seed-potato trade. They established two categories: basic seed, meant
for the production of seed potatoes; and certified seed, meant for the production
of ware and industrial potatoes. Grades S, SE and E fall into the category basic
seed and grades A, B and C into certified seed.

17.3 Parameters determining grade
The grade of seed potatoes depends on: grade of the initial material; results of
field inspection; lifting date; and results of tuber indexing.

17.3.1 Initial stock for seed-potato crops
Until 1947, the grower was free in his choice of initial stock. NAK set no
standards. Any grade could be presented for grading and was certified by field
inspection. In 1920, some prominent growers had started clonal selection. The
inspection services encouraged this by giving approved clones a preferential certificate. A disadvantage was that little was then known of transmission of viruses.
Later, early lifting was introduced as a means to improve tuber health. Voluntary
clonal selection diminished and deviant plants appeared by mutation in the clones.
Mild virus diseases such as PVS and PVX became prevalent.

To overcome these difficulties, compulsory clonal selection was introduced in
the Netherlands in 1947.

Clonal selection is selection of clones meeting varietal characteristics (e.g. yield
capacity, type) and free from tuber-transmissible diseases.

Clones are propagated from a single plant, whose tubers (the initial clone) are
kept together as seed for the first-year clone.

This procedure is repeated five times producing second-year, third-year, fourth-
year and fifth-year clones. The tubers are always stored and propagated separately
from other clones. If clones are certified, 3rd, 4th and 5th year stock falls into S
(Fig. 66). Clones are selected on farms approved by the NAK. For approval,
grower and the farm both need to fulfil certain requirements. The grower must
be experienced with seed potatoes and the farm must be free from sources of
infection. One farm may select not more than four varieties. Special directives are
issued for clonal selection of carrier varieties and for distances between varieties
with a view to chance of infection.

NAK keeps close control on clonal stocks during selection. Tubers are checked
each season. The crop is inspected in the field and tested for viruses in the
laboratory during growth. Central and regional fields check the clone for varietal
characteristics.

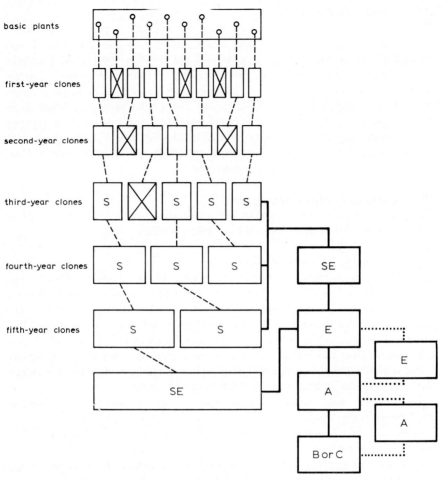

Fig. 66. Scheme of clonal propagation of seed potatoes.

⊠ Rejected at field inspection, serological test, judgment on type or tuber indexing.

————: crop is passed to the grower;

......: crop is replanted by the grower;

S, SE, E, A, B and C: quality grades of seed potatoes.

Clonal designation includes name of variety, province of the inspection service, farm No, year of initial clone and clone No, e.g. Bi.Fr.25-70-12 designates 'Bintje' clone from Friesland Farm 25 initiated in 1970, Clone 12.

Tests on the clones are for PVM, PVS and PVX. These viruses generally evoke such mild symptoms, that they are difficult to detect in the field. Other tests are for PVA and PVY, since in some varieties these viruses also evoke only mild symptoms.

PVM, PVS and PVX are detected serologically (Chap. 7), PVA and PVY by the 'A6' leaf test (Section 8.4). Clones are checked during growth. Tests are most reliable in the Netherlands 8–11 weeks after planting, i.e. 15–30 June.

The youngest completely unfolded leaf of each plant is taken to the laboratory in a plastic bag, which is opened immediately. Leaves can be stored 1 or 2 days at 4°–15°C in the open bags.

Of the first-year clones, all stems of each plant are tested. Of the 2nd-year clones, about half the plants are tested; in the 3rd, 4th and 5th year, 100 plants. Each test uses sap from two leaves. In the 1st and 2nd year, clones are rejected if only one virus test is positive. Positive tests in older clones affect their grading.

Varietal type of clones is checked both regionally and centrally. Every year, the central service of NAK lays out a clonal field and optionally the inspection services do too. A clone cannot be classified S unless at least one sample of it has grown on the central field. The plots of 21 plants are under continuous observation by trained inspectors, who check for diseases and for varietal type. Deviant clones and clones with deviant plants are rejected as basic seed.

Compulsory decline in grade. A grower intending to produce superior seed must grow grade S. Despite the health of the crop, the harvested tubers are never graded higher than SE. In later years, the grower's stock is automatically degraded further. So after 5 years his tubers, irrespective of their health, are no longer certified for seed.

These rules oblige the grower to replenish his stock regularly by buying tubers of grade S. There are two exceptions. A farmer, who buys SE seed, may propagate it for 2 years as grade E, assuming it meets other requirements. The same holds for grade A derived from grade E. By compelling growers to use grades S, SE and E, NAK has ensured that all seed comes from a recognized clone.

17.3.2 Field inspection

Grade is governed by the field inspection as well as by grade of the parent stock. Field inspection starts as soon as possible, usually early in June. The growers must have started roguing diseased plants before field inspectors start work. They inspect each crop at least three times: the second inspection is soon after the first and the last is just before haulm destruction. Field checks cover the following eight main parameters. The assessment is, to some degree, subjective.

Authenticity of the variety. The inspector checks that plants belong to the variety named in their schedule.

Varietal purity. Deviant plants and plants belonging to another variety are considered impurities. The standards of purity are strict. Grades S, SE, E and A may not contain any mutants or deviants; purity must be 100%. Grades B and C must be 99.95 and 99.9% pure, respectively.

Tuber-transmitted diseases and pests can be caused by viruses, fungi, bacteria and nematodes. Inspectors look especially for virus diseases. The other diseases are less prevalent in the Netherlands. Directives for inspectors relate mainly to the occurrence of viruses. The inspector checks whether the grower has rogued

Table 16. Factors applied by inspectors in assessing incidence of diseases at the first (1st) and the later inspections. (Data from NAK.)

	Basic seed				Certified seed		
	S and SE		E		A and B		C[1]
	1st	later	1st	later	1st	later	
Potato stipple streak, crinkle	32	64	16	32	16	32	6
Severe mosaic	32	64	16	32	8	16	6
Mild mosaic	32	64	16	32	1	1	0
Leafroll	8	32	8	32	8	32	6
Aucuba mosaic, stem mottle	4	8	4	8	2	4	6
Verticillium wilt	1	1	1	1	1	1	0
Suspect	1	2	1	2	1	2	0
Gaps	0.5	0	0.5	0	0.5	0	0
Blackleg[2] (*Erwinia atroseptica*)	0		0		A:10 and B:20		30

1. Grade C need be inspected once.
2. Allowable incidence of infected plants per ha.

the crop well. He searches through the field to determine whether health attains the figures for the highest grade the crop can reach. At four places in the field, he examines 100 plants and counts how many are diseased. The figure for each disease is multiplied by a factor, which is the same for almost all viruses in basic seed but differs between viruses in certified seed according to the harmfulness of the disease. Since virus incidence increases as the crop grows, the factor for later inspections is higher than that for the first (Table 16).

The sum of the products (incidence × factor) is the disease index of the field. Maximum index for the different grades are: S and SE 2; E 3; A 4; B 8; C 12. If the index exceeds 12, the crop is rejected.

Diseased plants are loaded heavier than gaps to encourage growers to rogue early and thoroughly. If gaps exceed 6%, a crop cannot be certified for basic seed. Its stand is irregular and any juvenile plants can be infected more readily. With SE seed, of which 4% was infected or suspect, completely different certification is possible, if the crop is rogued carefully, carelessly or not at all (Table 17).

After the first inspection, roguing must continue. If not, Crop II in Table 17 would be rejected at the second inspection (Table 18). The disease index at a later inspection can be higher, but never lower, than at an earlier inspection.

The crop is also scrutinized for symptoms of *Erwinia atroseptica*. If present, crops are not graded S, SE or E. They can be graded A, B or C, respectively, if there are no more than 10, 20 or 30 diseased plants per ha.

Stand of the crop. Potato crops, that are dressed too heavily with nitrogen

210

Table 17. Some crops with 4% diseased or suspect plants and gaps to show their disease index and grading, if they are from SE parent tubers. I: rejected, absence of gaps shows that the crop had not been rogued. II: graded B. III: graded E.

		S and SE			A and B		
		incidence (%)	factor	index	incidence (%)	factor	index
I	Mild mosaic	1	32	32	1	1	1
	Leafroll	2	8	16	2	8	16
	Suspect	1	1	1	1	1	1
	Gaps	0	0.5	0	0	0.5	0
	Total			49			18
II	Mild mosaic	1	32	32	1	1	1
	Leafroll	0.5	8	4	0.5	8	4
	Suspect	0.5	1	0.5	0.5	1	0.5
	Gaps	2	0.5	1	2	0.5	1
	Total			37.5			6.5
III	Mild mosaic	0	32	0			
	Leafroll	0	8	0			
	Suspect	0	1	0			
	Gaps	4	0.5	2			
	Total			2			

Table 18. Results of a second inspection of crop II of Table 17, if it was not further rogued. The crop is rejected.

	A, B and C		
	incidence (%)	factor	index
Mild mosaic	1	1	1
Leafroll	0.5	32	16
Suspect	0.5	2	1
Gaps	2	0	0
Total			18

grow rank. Symptoms of viruses are obscured. Likewise plants with deficiencies (e.g. of potassium) are difficult to assess. Either way, the grading may be reduced.

Stray plants from previous crops in fields with basic seed are taken as infected with viruses. The number of such plants is added to the number of virus-infected plants. In fields for certified seed, stray plants are taken as varietal impurity.

Rhizoctonia solani, Phytophthora infestans, and other diseases and injuries that obscure symptoms in foliage reduce the grade or cause rejection.

Maturity of the crop is an important factor. In an immature crop, viruses spread more than in a mature crop (Chap. 11). Immature crops are not certified as basic seed.

Surroundings as a source of infection. A crop is graded lower if an adjoining field can act as a source of virus infection. Sometimes only part of a crop nearest to the source of infection is reduced in grade or rejected a strip 10–25 m wide, next to the source of infection.

17.3.3 Lifting dates

Viruses transmitted by aphids during growth can be prevented from being translocated to tubers by timely killing of infected haulms (Chap. 3). For many years, the NAK has fixed lifting dates for different groups of varieties. At these dates, all haulms must be destroyed or the crop must be lifted. Lifting dates differ at the basis of an advice between regions, varieties, grades and years. Since basic seed must be free from all virus diseases, no chance may be taken with it. Lifting dates are set so early that the chance of tuber infection is nil. For certified seed, requirements are less stringent and lifting date can be set slightly later.

As soon as aphid flights bring danger, the NAK central office suggests lifting dates. They are passed on to regional inspection services by phone. The inspection services inform the growers as soon as possible. The information chain takes time and the growers must be given time to destroy the haulms adequately. Lifting dates are never fixed earlier than about 10 days after large flights of aphids have been monitored.

The 'suggested' lifting date is, in fact, compulsory for grades S and SE but is sometimes merely a suggestion for grade E. Regional services have three options. They may make the suggested date compulsory for all grades; if haulms are not killed by the date, the grade of the crop is reduced. They may fix a compulsory date some days later; if haulms are killed after the suggested date but before the compulsory date, crops retain their grade as long as indexing demonstrates the health of the tubers. If the services fix no compulsory date, grading, except for grades S and SE, depends on the field inspections and on tuber indexing. If a grower intends to destroy haulms (Section 16.8), he must tell the inspector 3 days before. The inspector can permit haulm destruction after thorough examination of the crop. If the crop no longer meets requirements, it will be graded lower or rejected as seed. The inspection service checks the success of haulm destruction. The entire stem must be killed by the lifting date. If part of the haulms survive or if young shoots are present, the grade is dropped.

17.3.4 Tuber indexing (Control after harvesting)

Despite the care, field inspection yields no guarantee for health. Lifting dates sometimes misfire for some fields.

212

Sampling. An extra safeguard is tuber indexing. Because of the many samples to be checked, samples of only 200 and 100 tubers are taken from crops for basic and certified seed, respectively. Such small samples give only a rough assessment of virus incidence. The inspector collects the tubers while walking in a letter B through the field. Tubers should be of medium size.

In principle all inspected seed is indexed for PLRV, PVA, PVM, PVS, PVX and PVY.

Indexing policy. Under special circumstances, NAK may exempt crops. General exemption can be granted, for instance: if initial tests show that indexing places almost all crops in the same grade as field inspection; if few aphids are present during growth; or if haulms are destroyed before the suggested lifting date.

In many years, indexing policy depends largely on whether growers have complied with suggested lifting dates. If indexing is done, the resulting grade supersedes the grade assessed in the field.

Seed of all varieties graded in the field as S and SE is indexed, even though harvested before the suggested lifting date.

Seed of almost all varieties graded E in the field is indexed, if haulms are destroyed after the suggested lifting date. If haulms are destroyed before the suggested lifting date, seed can be granted the grade assessed in the field. Some varieties, highly susceptible to one or more viruses, must be indexed, even though picked or haulm-killed before the suggested lifting date.

Seed graded A, B and C in the field can be granted these grades, if the haulms are destroyed before the suggested lifting date. Crops whose haulms are destroyed after the suggested date are always indexed.

Laboratory methods. The sampled tubers may be submitted directly to the Igel Lange test (Section 9.2.1) for checking for the presence of PLRV or are treated with either Rindite or gibberellic acid to break dormancy and to grow plantlets from them. These plantlets are grown in greenhouses; about 6 weeks after planting they are checked for the presence of mosaic visually or for the presence of PVA and PVY with the 'A6' leaf test (Section 8.4).

Rindite is a mixture of ethylene chlorohydrin, dichloroethane and carbon tetra-chloride (7:3:1 by volume). Store whole tubers in hermetically sealed rooms for 2 days at 25°C. Place the Rindite (0.8–1.0 ml/kg tubers) on filter paper at the bottom of containers or cells holding the tubers. The Rindite may not touch the tubers. Treat only tubers whose skin has suberized. Store freshly harvested tubers for some days at a high humidity and at 20°–24°C to suberize their skins. Avoid injured tubers; the vapour enters the tuber through the wounds and rots them quickly. After treatment keep the tubers in the dark or in diffuse light at about 20°. To prevent rootlets from forming, the store must not be too humid.

Dormancy can be broken readily in the varieties Bea, Climax, Eigenheimer and Sientje, less easily in Bintje, Désirée, Eersteling, Patrones and Sirtema, and with great difficulty in Alpha, Libertas, Ostara, Primura and Saskia. If no sprouts develop within a week of treatment, the tubers may be treated again.

Gibberellic acid (GA) is used as follows. Excise an eye from each tuber apex with a melon scoop. Place eyes from one sample of tubers in a coarsely woven bag and immerse them in aqueous GA (1 mg/litre) for 10 min; 10 litres of solution is sufficient for 2 000 excised eyes.

To prepare the GA solution, dissolve 1 g GA in 10–15 ml ethanol, and make up with water to 1 litre. Dilute this stock solution to 1 mg/litre when needed. Change the solution regularly during use.

To grow plantlets from tubers to test them, NAK uses gibberellic acid to break dormancy. Plant the excised and GA-treated eyes directly in a greenhouse. Cover them with a little soil to uniform depth to obtain an even crop. Water regularly before and after planting.

When the plantlets come up about a week after treatment, decrease the amount of water to avoid infection by *Phytophthora infestans*. Spray with a fungicide to prevent it.

Spraying with the growth inhibitor B9 (NN-dimethyl N'succinic acid mono-hydrazide) to prevent etiolation, to which some varieties are prone. The spraying rate and frequency depend on variety and soil type. Techniques with B9 are still being worked out. Plantlets sprayed with B9 form larger leaves and show clearer symptoms than unsprayed plantlets. About 4 weeks after planting, the plantlets have developed so much that the first symptoms of PVA, PVX and PVY show. Examine the plantlets after 3–4 weeks, and continue inspection until 6 weeks after planting. The number of plants with mosaic does not increase thereafter. Plantlets of some varieties show very mild mosaic, especially if infected with PVA or PVY^N. Some varieties, such as Doré, Primura and Sirtema, need to be checked also by the 'A6' leaf test.

17.4 Results of inspection

NAK tells the grower the result of each inspection as soon as possible either in writing or verbally. A written report is given, if the inspection leads to drop in grade and when the inspection leads to a final grading.

If the grower contests an assessment, he can apply to the regional inspection service for a new inspection by an independent committee. The party proved wrong pays costs. The grower can also appeal against an inspector's or a regional committee's decision to an appeal committee instituted by NAK. Experts examine the disputed crop. Their decision is final. Again, the party in the wrong pays.

17.5 Bulk inspection and certification

Approved crops are lifted, transported and stored under NAK supervision. The grower must inform the inspection service when he starts preparing the crop for transport. The inspector assesses the tubers for diseases and defects.

Each consignment is sampled for diseases and defects noticed at the preliminary inspection. When the seed is ready and if it meets all standards, each bag or crate is certified and sealed by the inspector or under his supervision. The inspector issues white certificates and labels for basic seed of grades S, SE and E, and blue certificates and labels for certified seed of grades A, B and C. NAK keeps records of all certificates issued.

All certificates and labels are printed with the NAK mark and mention the variety, quality and size grades, region, type of soil, grower's No, year of harvesting and weight of the bag or crate.

Once the seed is certified, labeled and sealed, it can be sold for planting. Each year about 400 000 tons of seed are sealed; about 8 million certificates, labels and seals are issued.

Descriptions of potato varieties mentioned in previous chapters

These data have been taken from J. A. Hogen Esch & H. Zingstra, 1969, Geniteurslijst voor aardappelrassen (List of origin of potato varieties), IVRO, Wageningen and from 46ste Rassenlijst, (46th Descriptive list of varieties), 1971, IVRO, Wageningen.

Numbers from 1 to 10 after the resistance of some varieties to viruses are taken from the 46th Descriptive list of varieties, 1971. A high number means a high resistance (low susceptibility); a low number a low resistance (high susceptibility) to a certain virus; a number around 5 means a moderate resistance (moderate susceptibility).

The letters refer to the countries where the potato varieties originated or are included in a varietal list or where they are grown.

A Austria, AL Algeria, AUS Australia, B Belgium, BG Bulgaria, BR Brasil, CDN Canada, CH Switzerland, CL Ceylon, CS Czechoslovakia, CY Cyprus, D(BR) West Germany, D(DR) East Germany, DK Denmark, E Spain, ET Egypt, F France, GB(EW) England & Wales, GB(IRL) N.Ireland, GB(SC) Scotland, GBY Malta, GR Greece, H Hungary, I Italy, IL Israel, IND India, IR Iran, IRL Eire, IRQ Iraq, IS Iceland, J Japan, L Luxemburg, MA Morocco, MEX Mexico, N Norway, NL Netherlands, P Portugal, PA Panama, PAK Pakistan, PL Poland, R Roumania, RA Argentina, RI Indonesia, RL Libanon, S Sweden, SF Finland, SU Soviet Union, TU Tunisia, USA United States, YU Yugoslavia, YV Venezuela.

Ackersegen. Bred Germany 1929 from Hindenburg × Allerfrüheste Gelbe. A-B-DK-E(synonym Sergen)-F-GR-I-P-PL(synonym Dar)-TU. Insusceptible to PVA; highly susceptible to PVY. Used to be important in Germany.

Albion. Bred NL 1911 from Thorbecke × Fransen. Highly susceptible to PLRV and to PVY[C]; insusceptible to PVA and to PVX. No longer grown commercially.

Alcmaria. Bred NL 1969 from Sirtema × (Saskia × Commonwealth Potato Collection (CPC) 1673-20 × Furore). NL. Moderately susceptible to PLRV (6), to PVA (6), to PVY (5) and to spraing (5); insusceptible to PVX.

Allerfrüheste Gelbe. Bred Germany 1922 from Industrie × Seedling 155/06. A-D(BR)-E-I(synonym Tonda di Berlino)-NL. Moderately susceptible to PLRV (6), to PVX (6) and to PVY (7).

Alpha. Bred NL 1925 from Paul Kruger × Preferent. B-DK-E-ET-GB(EW)-GB(IRL)-GB(SC)-GBY-GR-I-IL-IR-MA-MEX-NL-P-PA-PL-RL-S-YV. Moderately susceptible to PLRV (4), to PVX (4) and to spraing; slightly susceptible to PVY (6.5).

Amaryl. Bred NL 1963 from Saskia × (Commonwealth Potato Collection (CPC) 1673-20 × Furore). B-NL. Insusceptible to PVA and to PVX; moderately susceptible to PVY

216

(5.5); slightly susceptible to spraing (7).

Ambassadeur. Bred NL 1957 from Black 1256 × Libertas. F-IRL-NL. Moderately susceptible to PLRV and to PVY; insusceptible to PVA and to PVX.

Anett. Bred D(BR) 1964 from *Solanum demissum* hybrid × *S. acaule* hybrid. D(BR). Insusceptible to PVX; slightly susceptible to PVY.

Apta. Bred D(BR) 1951 from variety W × Hindenburg. A-D(BR)-L. Slightly susceptible to PLRV and to PVY.

Aquila. Bred Germany 1942 from variety W × unknown variety. BG-CS-PL-S. Slightly susceptible to PLRV, to PVY and to spraing.

Arran Banner. Bred GB(SC) 1927 from Sutton's Abundance × Sutton's Flourball. AL-B-BG-CY-E-ET-F-GB(EW)-GB(IRL)-GB(SC)-GBY-GR-IL-IR-IRL-NL-P-PL-RL. Highly susceptible to PVX; moderately susceptible to PVY.

Arran Consul. Bred GB(SC) 1924 from President × Flourball. CDN-GB(EW)-GB(IRL)-GB(SC)-P. Moderately susceptible to PLRV and to PVY; carrier of PVX.

Arran Crest. Bred GB(SC) 1928 from Epicure × Flourball. Insusceptible to PVA and to PVX; moderately susceptible to PVY.

Arran Pilot. Bred GB(SC) 1930 from May Queen × Pepo. DK-GB(EW)-GB(IRL)-GB(SC)-IRL-P. Moderately susceptible to PLRV and to PVY; carrier of PVS; slightly susceptible to spraing.

Arran Victory. Bred GB(SC) 1918 by self-pollination of Abundance. GB(EW)-GB(IRL)-GB(SC)-IRL-P. Moderately susceptible to PLRV and to PVY.

Aucklander Short Top. No data.

Avenir. Bred NL 1957 from A 42 × Voran × Katahdin. B-CH-CY-DK-E-F-GB(EW)-GB(IRL)-GB(SC)-GR-I-NL-RA. Slightly susceptible to PLRV (7); moderately susceptible to PVA, to PVX and to PVY (6).

Béa. Bred NL 1954 from Ari × (Belle de Fontenay × Katahdin). DK-F-I-NL-YU. Moderately susceptible to PLRV, to PVA and to PVX (6); slightly susceptible to PVY (7.5).

Bevelander. Bred NL 1925 from Bravo × Preferent. NL. Slightly susceptible to PVY; fairly susceptible to stem mottle. No longer grown commercially.

Bintje. Bred NL 1910 from Munstersen × Fransen. A-B-BG-BR-CH-CS-D(BR)-DK-E-F-GB(EW)-GB(IRL)-GB(SC)-I-IRQ-IS-L-NL-P-PAK-PL-R-S-T-USA-YU. Slightly susceptible to PLRV (7), to spraing (9) and to stem mottle; insusceptible to PVA; moderately susceptible to PVY (5).

Bliss Triumph. Bred at unknown place 1878 probably from Peerless × Early Rose seedling. CDN-USA. Carrier of PVS and PVX.

Burmania. Bred NL 1957 from Pimpernel × Libertas. NL. Slightly susceptible to PLRV (8), to PVA (7), to PVY (9) and to spraing (7); moderately susceptible to PVX (6).

Carla. Bred D(BR) 1960 from Apta × Oberarnbacher Frühe. B-CH-D(BR)-F-P. Slightly susceptible to PLRV, to PVY and to spraing.

Civa. Bred NL 1960 from Bintje × (Saskia × Frühmölle) × NV Kweekbedrijf CIV, Ottersum (CIV) 49-901. B-D(BR)-NL. Moderately susceptible to PLRV and to PVX (6); insusceptible to PVA; slightly susceptible to PVY (7).

Claudia. Bred F 1955 from Craigs Defiance × Aquila. AL-E-ET-F-I-IL-P.

Climax. Bred NL 1955 from Bintje × Record. A-B-CS-D(BR)-F-NL. Slightly susceptible to PLRV (7.5), to spraing and to stem mottle; insusceptible to PVA; moderately susceptible to PVX (6) and to PVY (4).

Commandeur. Bred NL 1963 from Black 1256 × Libertas. B-F-NL. Slightly susceptible to PLRV; insusceptible to PVA and to PVX; fairly susceptible to PVY.

Craigs Defiance. Bred GB(SC) 1938 from Epicure × Pepo. Insusceptible to PVA and to PVY; fairly susceptible to PVY.

Craigs Snowwhite. Bred GB(SC) 1947 from *Solanum demissum* hybrid × Craigs Defiance. Insusceptible to PVA and to some strains of PVX and PVY[C].

Dakota. No data.

Désirée. Bred NL 1962 from Urgenta × Depesche. A-AL-B-CH-D(BR)-E-GB(EW)-GB(IRL)-GB(SC)-L-NL-P-PAK-R-TU-YU. Moderately susceptible to PLRV (5) and to PVX (6); slightly susceptible to PVA (7) and to PVY (8).

Doré. Bred NL 1947 from Eersteling × (Record × Mulder K 101). B-DK-NL. Slightly susceptible to PLRV (7) and to spraing (8); highly susceptible to PVA and to PVY (2); moderately susceptible to PVX (6).

Duke of York. See Eersteling. GB(EW)-GB(IRL)-GB(SC)-IRL.

Eba. Bred NL 1966 from Eersteling × Bato. B-CH-F-NL. Slightly susceptible to PLRV (7), to PVY (8) and to spraing (9); insusceptible to PVA.

Eersteling. Bred GB(SC) 1900 from Early Primrose × King Kidney. A-B-BG-CH-CS-D(BR)-DK-F-GB(EW)-GB(IRL)-GB(SC)-L-NL-P-YU. Slightly susceptible to PLRV; insusceptible to PVA; moderately susceptible to PVY (4), to spraing (4) and to stem mottle.

Ehud. Bred NL 1965 from Panther × Karna 149. NL. Moderately susceptible to PLRV (6), to PVA (7) and to PVY (5.5); insusceptible to PVX.

Eigenheimer. Bred NL 1893 from Blauwe Reuzen × Fransen. B-I-NL-P-PAK-RI-SF. Moderately susceptible to PLRV (6), to PVA (4), to PVX (4), to PVY and to spraing.

Epicure. Bred GB(EW) 1897 from Magnum Bonum × Early Regent. GB(EW)-GB(IRL)-GB(SC)-IRL-SU (synonym Epikur). Insusceptible to PVA and to PVX; carrier of PVS.

Flava. Bred D(BR) from Erdgold × Fransen. Moderately susceptible to PLRV; carrier of PVS; fairly susceptible to PVY. Not longer grown commercially.

Fortuna. Bred D(BR) from Ella × *Solanum andigenum* hybrid. D(BR). Slightly susceptible to PLRV; insusceptible to PVA and to PVX; carrier of PVS. No longer listed.

Friso. Bred NL from Rode Star × Alpha. Fairly susceptible to spraing. No longer listed.

Frühmölle. Bred Germany 1925 from Sämling 118 × Richter's Jubel. B-D(BR)-D(DR)-NL. Fairly susceptible to virus diseases, e.g. spraing.

Furore. Bred NL 1930 from Rode Star × Alpha. B-NL. Moderately susceptible to PLRV (5), to PVA (6), to PVX (6), to PVY (6.5) and to spraing (4).

Gelderse Rode. Bred NL from unknown parents. Insusceptible to PVA and to PVX; carrier of PVS and PVY[C]. No longer grown commercially.

Gineke. Bred NL 1950 from Ultimus × Record. B-CL-NL. Moderately susceptible to PLRV (6), to PVX (6) and to PVY (4); insusceptible to PVA.

Gloria. Bred NL 1928 from Alpha × Bato. Formerly NL. Carrier of PAMV. No longer grown commercially.

Grata. Bred D(BR) 1955 from Ackersegen × Flava. A-B-D(BR)-ET-I-MA-P-S-TU. Slightly susceptible to PLRV; insusceptible to PVA; fairly susceptible to PVY.

Green Mountain. Bred USA 1885 from Dunmore × Excelsior. CDN-RA-USA-YV. Moderately susceptible to PLRV; fairly susceptible to PVA; carrier of PVS and PVX.

Ideaal. Bred NL 1917 from Epicure × Fransen. F. Slightly susceptible to PLRV and to spraing; insusceptible to PVA; moderately susceptible to PVY.

Industrie. Bred D(BR) 1900 from Zwickauer Frühkartoffel × Simson. F. Fairly susceptible to PLRV and to PVY; carrier of PVS; slightly susceptible to spraing.

Irish Cobbler (synonym Cobbler). Bred USA from unknown parents (probably a mutant of Early Rose). CDN-GR-R-USA. Insusceptible to PVA; carrier of PVS and PVX; moderately susceptible to PVY.

Jaerla. Bred NL 1969 from Sirtema × Max-Planck-Institut (MPI) 19268. AL-B-E-I-NL. Moderately susceptible to PLRV (6), to PVX (6) and to PVY (6); slightly susceptible to PVA (7) and to spraing.

Jefta. Bred NL 1966 from Karna 54-57 × Profijt. Slightly susceptible to PLRV (6.5), to PVY (7.5); moderately susceptible to PVA (6.5), to spraing (7); insusceptible to PVY^C. Variety not listed.

Jubel. Bred Germany 1908 from Victoria Augusta × Seedling 78/92. SU. Carrier of PVS and PVX; slightly susceptible to PVY; fairly susceptible to spraing.

Juli (synonyms Juliniere, Immune Ashleaf). Bred Germany 1891 from Joseph Rigault × Pflückmaus. Carrier of PVA and PVS.

Katahdin. Bred USA 1932 from Seedling United States Department of Agriculture (USDA) 24642 × 40568. AUS-CDN-DK-E-GR-I-NL-RA-USA. Insusceptible to PVA; moderately susceptible to PVY.

Kennebec. Bred USA 1948 from (Chippewa × Katahdin) × (Earline × variety W). CDN-DK-E-GB(EW)-GB(IRL)-GB(SC)-I-J-NL-P-R-RA-USA-YU-YV. Moderately susceptible to PLRV (5) and to PVX; slightly susceptible to PVA (9) and to PVY (7.5).

King Edward VII (synonym King Edward). Bred GB(EW) 1902 from Magnum Bonum × Beauty of Hebron. B-DK-E-ET-GB(EW)-GB(IRL)-GB(SC)-IL-IRL-N-P-S. Insusceptible to PVA and to PVX; moderately susceptible to PVY.

Koopman's Blauwe. Bred NL 1937 from Zeeuwse Blauwe × Alpha. NL. Fairly susceptible to PVX and to PVY.

Krasava. Bred CS 1940 from Visnovské rohlícky × B 53. CS-F.

Kwinta. Bred NL 1939 from Eigenheimer × Record. Insusceptible to PVA. No longer listed.

Libertas. Bred NL 1946 from Record × 31185 (Souvenir × Bato). IRL-NL. Moderately susceptible to PLRV (5); slightly susceptible to PVA, to PVX, to PVY (7.5) and to spraing (8).

Lichte Industrie. See Industrie. Carrier of PVA.

Majestic. Bred GB(SC) 1911 from unknown variety × British Queen. DK-GB(EW)-GB(IRL)-GB(SC)-I-IRL-N?-NL-P-PL-S-SU-YU. Moderately susceptible to PLRV (6), to PVS and to PVX (5); slightly susceptible to PVA (7) and to PVY (7.5).

Maritta. Bred D(BR) 1947 from Seedling 66/102 × Mittelfrühe. A-D(BR)-DK-F-I-L-NL-RI-S. Moderately susceptible to PLRV (5) and to PVX (6); slightly susceptible to PVA (7) and to PVY (8.5).

Maryke. Bred NL 1968 from Stichting voor Plantenveredeling (SVP) M 194-10 × Max-Planck-Institut (MPI) 19268. AL-B-D(BR)-E-F-MA-NL-TU. Slightly susceptible to PLRV (7); insusceptible to PVA and to PVX; moderately susceptible to PVY (6) and to spraing.

May Queen (synonym Koksiaan). Bred GB(EW) 1900 from unknown parents. IRL-J. Carrier of PAMV; fairly susceptible to PLRV.

Meerlander. Bred NL 1947 from Bevelander × Record. NL. Moderately susceptible to PLRV (6) and to PVY (4.5); insusceptible to PVA; slightly susceptible to PVX (7).

Mentor. Bred NL 1960 from Maritta × Matador. D(BR)-NL-U. Moderately susceptible to PLRV (6), to PVX (4) and to stem mottle; slightly susceptible to PVA, to PVY (7) and to spraing.

Multa. Bred NL from Oberarnbacher Frühe × (Record × Commonwealth Potato Collection (CPC) 1673-1)? D(BR)-E-F-NL-PAK. Slightly susceptible to PLRV, to PVA, to PVX, to PVY (7.5) and to spraing.

Nascor. Bred NL 1967 from Max-Planck-Institut (MPI) 19268 × Libertas. NL. Slightly susceptible to PLRV; moderately susceptible to PVY.

Ninetyfold. Bred GB(EW) 1897 from Elephant × Patersons Victoria. GB(EW)-GB(IRL)-GB(SC)? Fairly susceptible to PLRV and to PVY; carrier of PAMV and PVS; insusceptible to PVA and to PVX.

Noordeling. Bred NL 1928 from Bravo × Jam. NL. Moderately susceptible to PVY; slightly susceptible to spraing and to stem mottle.

Ostara. Bred NL 1962 from Ari × Sientje. A-B-CH-D(BR)-F-I-NL-P-R-RL-TU. Slightly susceptible to PLRV (7), to PVX (7), to PVY (8) and to spraing; insusceptible to PVA.

Patrones. Bred NL 1959 from Ropta Y 226 × Instituut voor Plantenveredeling (IVP) 47-87-7. A-B-BR-CH-CS-CY-DK-ET-F-GB(EW)-GB(IRL)-GB(SC)-GR-IL-L-NL-P-PAK-RA-RI. Slightly susceptible to PLRV (8) and to spraing; moderately susceptible to PVA, to PVX and to PVY (6).

Paul Kruger (synonyms President Krüger, President (IND-S), Krüger, No Blight, Rustproof, Favorit-Östergyllen). Bred NL 1901 from Richters Imperator × Wilhelm Korn. IND-S. Fairly susceptible to PLRV.

Penobscot. Bred USA 1963 from X 927-3 × Katahdin. Slightly susceptible to PLRV; insusceptible to PVA.

Pentland Dell. Bred GB(SC) 1961 from Roslin Chania × Roslin Sasamua. E-GB(EW)-GB(IRL)-GB(SC)-IRL-P. Fairly susceptible to spraing.

Pontiac. Bred USA 1938 from Triumph × Katahdin. CDN.

President. See Paul Kruger. IND-S.

Prevalent. Bred NL 1966 from Ambassadeur × Loman M 54-106-1. F-NL-S. Moderately susceptible to PLRV (6) and to PVY (6); insusceptible to PVA and to PVX; fairly susceptible to spraing.

Primura. Bred NL 1963 from Sirtema × Majestic. B-F-I-L-NL. Moderately susceptible to PLRV (6) and to PVY (4); highly susceptible to PVA (3).

Prinslander. Bred NL 1941 from Record × Alpha. NL. Moderately susceptible to PLRV; insusceptible to PVA; fairly susceptible to other viruses.

Profyt. Bred NL 1940 from Seedling K 264 × Matador. NL. Moderately susceptible to PLRV and to PVA; fairly susceptible to other viruses.

Prominent. Bred NL 1968 from Prummel 54-285 × Prummel 55-259. NL. Moderately susceptible to PLRV and to PVY (6); insusceptible to PVA and to PVX.

Record. Bred 1932 from Trenctria × Energie. B-DK-GB(EW)-GB(IRL)-GB(SC)-IRL-NL-SU. Moderately susceptible to PLRV (5); highly susceptible to PVY (3); insusceptible to PVA; slightly susceptible to PVX (7).

Rector. Bred NL 1968 from Cebeco 53-473-10 × Cebeco 52-30-7. F-NL. Slightly susceptible to PLRV (7); insusceptible to PVA and to PVX; moderately susceptible to PVY (6) and to spraing.

Red Pontiac. Bred USA 1949, mutant from Pontiac. E-NL-PA. Moderately susceptible to PLRV, to PVA and to PVY.

Rode Eersteling. Bred NL 1942, mutant from Eersteling. B-L-NL. Insusceptible to PVA.

Rode Star. Bred NL 1909 from Prof. Wohltmann × Erica. NL. Fairly susceptible to PLRV; moderately susceptible to PVY.

Russet Burbank (synonym Netted Gem). USA, probably mutant from Burbank. CDN-USA.

Saco. Bred USA 1955 from United States Department of Agriculture (USDA) X 96-56 × United States Department of Agriculture (USDA) 41956. Highly susceptible to PVA and to PVX.

Saphir. Bred D(BR) 1960 from 43-141/6 × 44-1016/24 (derivative of *Solanum acaule*). D(BR). Hardly susceptible to PLRV and to PVY; insusceptible to PVA and to PVX.

Saskia. Bred NL 1946 from Rode Eersteling × Herald. A-B-BG-CS-D(BR)-DK-F-I-NL-YU. Slightly susceptible to PLRV (7) and to PVY (8); insusceptible to PVA; moderately susceptible to PVX (4).

Saturna. Bred NL 1964 from Maritta × (Record × Commonwealth Potato Collection (CPC) 1673-1). F-NL. Moderately susceptible to PLRV (5); insusceptible to PVA; slightly susceptible to PVX (7) and to PVY (7.5).

Saucisse (synonym Saucisse Rouge). Bred F 1871 (?) from unknown parents. Carrier of PVS.

Schwalbe. Bred D(DR) 1956 from Aquila × Capella. B-D(DR). Slightly susceptible to PLRV, to PVY and to spraing.

Sebago. Bred USA 1938 from Chippewa × Katahdin. AUS-CDN-ET-GR-NL-USA-YU-YV. Insusceptible to PVA.

Sieglinde. Bred Germany 1935 from a seedling × Juli. A-D(BR)-DK-ET-F-I-PL-TU. Fairly susceptible to PLRV; moderately susceptible to PVY.

Sientje. Bred NL 1951 from Gloria × Matador. A-AL-B-DK-ET-F-GB(EW)-GB(IRL)-GB(SC)-IRL-MA-NL-P-TU. Moderately susceptible to PLRV (5) and to PVX (6); insusceptible to PVA; slightly susceptible to PVY (8).

Sirtema. Bred NL 1951 from 123a (Tinwald's Perfection × Berlikumer Geeltje) × Frühmölle. A-B-CH-D(BR)-DK-F-GB(EW)-GB(IRL)-GB(SC)-I-L-NL-PL-RL-YU.
Moderately susceptible to PLRV, to PVA (6), to PVX (5), to PVY (4) and to spraing.

Spartaan. Bred NL 1963 from Bintje × T III I. B-F-NL. Moderately susceptible to PLRV (6) and to PVX (6); insusceptible to PVA; slightly susceptible to PVY (7).

Surprise. Bred NL 1954 from Noordeling × Libertas. NL. Moderately susceptible to PLRV (6) and to PVA (6); slightly susceptible to PVX (7), to PVY (9) and to spraing (9).

Tanja. Bred NL 1967 from Eersteling × Ropta Y 14 F. NL. Moderately susceptible to PLRV (6), to PVA, to PVX and to PVY (6); slightly susceptible to spraing (8).

Tawa. Bred USA from United States Department of Agriculture (USDA) B 595-76 × United States Department of Agriculture (USDA) B 76-23. Insusceptible to PVA and to PVX.

Thorbecke. Bred NL 1901 from Richter's Imperator × Wilhelm Korn. Carrier of PVY[C].

Triumf. Bred NL 1921 from Eigenheimer × Cimbals Neue Imperator. Carrier of PAMV and PVA; moderately susceptible to PLRV. Withdrawn as commercial variety 1949.

Ulster Chieftain. Bred GB(IRL) 1938 from May Queen × Herald. GB(EW)-GB(IRL)-GB(SC)-IRL-S. Insusceptible to PVA; moderately susceptible to spraing.

Ulster Knight. Bred GB(EW) from Craigs Defiance × (Ballydoon × Katahdin). Insusceptible to PVA and to PVX.

Ulster Prince. Bred GB(IRL) 1947 from Ulster Earl × (Arran Cairn × Herald). GB(EW)-GB(IRL)-GB(SC)-IRL. Moderately susceptible to PLRV and to spraing; insusceptible to PVA.

Ultimus. Bred NL 1935 from Rode Star × Pepo. F-NL-PAK. Moderately susceptible to PLRV and to PVX (6); slightly susceptible to PVA (7) and to PVY (8).

United States Department of Agriculture 41956. Bred USA; spontaneous seedling from Villa roela × (Flourball × White Rose). Fairly susceptible to PLRV and to PVY; insusceptible to PVX. Not grown commercially.

Up to Date. Bred GB(SC) 1894 from Patersons Victoria × Blue Don. DK-E-GB(EW)-GB(IRL)-GB(SC)-GR-IL-IRL-IND-N-RL-S. Fairly susceptible to PLRV and to PVY; insusceptible to PVA.

Voran. Bred Germany 1932 from Kaiserkrone × Herbstgelbe. A-B-D(BR)-F-NL-P-PL(synonym Pionier)-R-RI-SU. Moderately susceptible to PLRV (6) and to PVA (6); slightly susceptible to PVX, to PVY (7.5) and to spraing.

White Rose (synonyms Aroostook Wonder, American Giant, American Wonder, Wisconsin Pride). Bred USA 1871 from unknown parents. RA-USA.

Ysselster. Bred NL 1943 from Record × Populair. B-NL. Moderately susceptible to PLRV (6) and to PVX (6); slightly susceptible to PVA (7), to PVY (6.5) and to spraing.

Zeeuwse Blauwe (synonyms Gelderse Blauwe, Turken). Bred NL 1870 from unknown parents. Carrier of PVY[C]. Withdrawn as commercial variety 1949.

Subject index

The numbers in italics refer to pages with principle references to the subject

α-naphthalene acetic acid 162
α-optimum 97
A6 83, 102–110, 123, 127, 209, 213
aardappelstengelbont 137
abigarramiente del tallo 137
ABC disease 58, 140
abrasive 32, 33, 105, 106
  inoculation 61
absorption 88, *91*
Aceratagallia sanguinolenta 141
Aceratagallia spp. 141
acetone 69, 71
acidification, clarification 68, 71
Ackersegen 34, 152, 216
acquisition of virus 51, 134
Acyrthosiphon pisum 133
Agallia constricta 141
  quadripunctata 141
agar 69, 162, 164
agar double-diffusion test 70, 95
agarose 69
agglutination reaction 91, 93, 94, 100
  on slides 93
  under paraffin oil 93, 94
alatae 36–56, 168–170
Albion 216
Alcmaria 181, 216
alfalfa mosaic virus 72, 81, 104, 114, 120–121, 132, 152
alfalfa virus 1 132
alfalfa virus 2 132
Allerfrüheste Gelbe 216
Alpha 128, 139, 188, 189, 192, 213, 216
aluminium foil 173
Amaryl 181, 216
Ambassadeur 31, 61, 180, 184, 217
American bird cherry 37
ammonium sulphate 68–73
amyl acetate 79

analytical centrifugation 70
anaphylactic shock 89
Andean potato latent virus 81, 136
anemone brown ring virus 103
Anett 181, 217
aniline blue 111
animals as vectors 32, 116
anthocyanin 131
antibody 87, 90, 91, 97
antigen 87, 88, 97
antigen-antibody reaction 87, 98
antigenic determinants 87
antiserum 87
  aquisition of blood 90
  production 87
  storage 91
  titre 88, 90, 91, 96, *97*
aphicidal fungi 55, 56
aphicide; see also insecticide 46, 52, 54, 173
aphids 21, 26, 36
  alate (winged) 36–56, 168–170
  apterous (wingless) 36–56, 167–169
  beat-sampling 43, 44, 47, 168
  control 167–173
  estimation spring population 42
  estimation summer population 44
  life cycle 36
  oviparous 39, 40, 43, 49
  predators 38, 43, 44, 47–49, 53–55, 169
  resistance to insecticides 26
  retention or circulative period 36, 51
  sensitivity to colour 38
  viviparous 37, 39
Aphis fabae 37, *39*, 49, 53, 125
  frangulae 125, 128
  nasturtii 37, *39*, 122, 125, 128, 134
  rhamni 39
Aphrodes bicinctus 142

224

225

May Queen 130, 131, 219
mechanical inoculation 105
medulla 113
Meerlander 128, 219
Melanoplus spp. 121
Mentor 120–121, 186, 189, 219
mercuric chloride 27
meristem 25, 158, 160–166
merthiolate 91
metadioxybenzol 112
Meta-iso-Systox 167
metastolbur virus 142
methyl mercuric benzoate 193
micro-agglutination test 93
micro-precipitin test 92
mineral oil; see oil
Moericke trap 37, *46*, 49, 50, 149
molecular sieves 69
morphology of virus particles 23, 81,
mosaic 102, 120–121, 210, 211
mosaic aucuba de la pomme de terre 129
mosaico 121
   abigarrado 129
   aucuba 129
   latente 116
   leve 116
   necrótico 129
   severo 124
Mowital B 30 H 92
Multa 153, 173, 185, 220
mutagens 23
mutant 159
mutation 207
mycoplasma 24, 32, 115, 140–142
Myzodes persicae 36
Myzus ascalonicus 36, *39*, 43, 47, 134
   certus 45, 47, 49, 53, 125
   ornatus 125
   persicae 21, 36, *37*, 38–45, 47–49, 52–
   55, 104, 122, 124, 128, 129, 133–135,
   168, 169, 176

NAK 100, 201, 206–215
Nascor 185, 220
natural enemies; see predators
necrosi pseudoreticulata 129
necrosis 102
necrotic spots 141
nectarine 37
negative stain 80, 83
nematode vectors 22, 62
Neomyzus cirumflexus 122, 125, 134
Nepoviruses 58, 59, 60
net necrosis 135

Netuviruses 58, 60
New York aster yellows virus 141
Nicandra physaloides 104, 124
Nicotiana clevelandii 139
   debneyi 85, 120, 129, 139
   glutinosa 32, 72, 104, 107, 109, 118,
   120, 124, 129, 132
   rustica 70–72, 141, 165
   tabacum 32, 62, 63, 66, 70–72, 85, 102,
   104, 117, 118, 120, 124, 125, 129, 134,
   138, 139, 140
Nicotiana virus 5 137
nicotine 26, 37, 51, 167
   sulphate 46, 106
Ninetyfold 180, 220
nitrogen 150, 152, 190, 195, 210
nitrous acid, mutagen 23
non-persistent 36, 37, 40, 50–52, 171
non-specific reaction 100
Noordeling 128, 184, 185, 186, 220
normal length of virus particle 82
northern stolbur 142
nucleic acid 22, 23
   double-stranded 23, 121
   single-stranded 23
nucleoprotein 87
nutrient conditions, effect on virus production 66
nutrient medium, meristem culture 160,
   164, 165

oil, effect on aphids 158, 172, 173, 202
Olpidium brassicae 57, 58, 59
onion yellow dwarf virus 36
Ononis yellow mosaic virus 136
Ophiola flavopicta 142
Orosius argentatus 142
osmium tetroxide 80
Ostara 213, 220
Ouchterlony double-diffusion test 95
oviparae 39, 40, 43, 49

palladium 79
palm tree type 125
papaw mild mosaic virus 103
paracrinkle 127, 128
paraffin 30
Parafilm 160, 162
parastolbur 142
particle
   counting 83
   measurement 82
   size 23, 81
Pasteur pipette 80, 83

stability of virus in desiccated tissue (SIDT);
see physical properties
of virus in vitro at 20°C (SIV); see
physical properties
starch 112
statistical analysis 109
steaming of soil 28
Stellaria media 62, 138
stem grafting 28
stem mottle 59, 60, 62, 120–121, 138, 184, 185, 186, 210
stengelbont 60, 137
Stengelbuntkrankheit 137
stipple-streak 125–127, 210
stolon end 147
storage of
antiserum 91
leaves 209
tubers 192, 193, 203–205
virus 70
virus-infected plant material 66, 67
strains of
alfalfa mosaic virus 134
potato aucuba mosaic virus 131
potato leafroll virus 136
potato spindle tuber virus 121
potato virus A 122
potato virus M 128
potato virus S 120
potato virus X 117
potato virus Y 125
tobacco rattle virus 138
stray plants 211
streak 21, 124
Streptomyces scabies 189, 200, 201
Strichelkrankheit 124
stunting 131, 135
stylet-borne viruses 36, 122, 124, 128, 133, 136, 158, 170, 173
stylets 36, 51, 57
subcutaneous injection 88, 89
sucrose 68, 69
suction trap 37, 45
suedonecrosis reticular 129
sugar-cane ratoon stunt 159
summer flight of aphids 49
summer host; see host, secondary
summer population of aphids 44
supermild mosaic 121
superphosphate 195
Surprise 185, 186, 221
susceptibility 21, 31, 174, 181
of test leaves 106, 107, 108
swing-out rotor 69

symptoms of
alfalfa mosaic virus 133
potato aucuba mosaic virus 130
potato leafroll virus 134
potato mop-top virus 139
potato spindle tuber virus 121
potato virus A 122
potato virus M 128
potato virus S 119
potato virus X 116
potato virus Y 125
potato yellow dwarf virus 141
tobacco necrosis virus 140
tobacco rattle virus 137
Synchytrium endobioticum 59, 116
systemic symptoms 22, 102
Systox 167–172

Tabakrippenbräune-Virus 124
tacheture de la tige 137
Tanja 153, 221
Tawa 181, 221
temperature, effect on
aphid population 40, 41
local-lesion production 108, 109
virus production 66
test plants 102–110
therapy of virus diseases 158–166
thermal inactivation point (TIP); see physical properties
thioglycollic acid 67, 72
Thorbecke 125, 221
Thrips spp. 136
tipping cart 203
titre of antiserum 88, 90, 91, 96, 97
tobacco etch virus 104
mosaic virus 22, 23, 25, 27, 28, 81, 82, 99, 104, 107, 109, 121, 165
necrosis virus 32, 57, 58, 71, 81, 140
'partridge' virus 137
rattle virus 32, 58–63, 66, 71–73, 81, 104, 137, 138, 183–186
veinal necrosis 124
virus 11 137
tolerance 22, 174, 175
tomato big bud 24, 142
big bud virus 142
black ring virus 58–60, 71–73, 81, 103, 104, 140
blue top 142
bunchy top 142
rosette 142
spotted wilt virus 72, 136
stolbur 24, 28, 32, 111, 142